Knife Laws of the Fifty States

A Guide for the Law-Abiding Traveler

Researched and written by
David Wong, Esq.

Bloomington, IN  Milton Keynes, UK

authorHOUSE®

AuthorHouse™
1663 Liberty Drive, Suite 200
Bloomington, IN 47403
www.authorhouse.com
Phone: 1-800-839-8640

AuthorHouse™ UK Ltd.
500 Avebury Boulevard
Central Milton Keynes, MK9 2BE
www.authorhouse.co.uk
Phone: 08001974150

First published by AuthorHouse 8/7/2006

ISBN: 1-4259-5092-2 (sc)

Printed in the United States of America
Bloomington, Indiana

This book is printed on acid-free paper.

Library of Congress Control Number: 2006906467

Table of Contents

Important Notice

This book is not "the law", does not purport to offer legal advice, and is not a substitute for such advice. The information in this book is of a general nature and is presented for informational purposes only, and should not be used as a substitute for competent legal advice regarding specific situations from a lawyer licensed to practice in the jurisdiction you are in, or traveling to or through.

The author is a licensed attorney and has researched and consulted with a variety of sources in preparing this book, and the information is believed to be generally accurate as of the date of publication. **However, no guarantee of accuracy is expressed or implied, and the reader should <u>not</u> consider any information in this book (including, but not limited to, any explanatory or summary text) as legal advice, or a restatement of the law.** The author and publisher of this book expressly disclaim any and all liability whatsoever arising out of any reliance on the information contained in this book, or due to any errors or omissions therein.

Laws and regulations concerning weapons, and specifically such items as knives, are constantly changing. What's legal today may not be legal tomorrow. In addition, court decisions (case law) can, and often do, change the law and/or affect the meaning and interpretation of statutory law. Also, a great number of cities, towns, county governments and governmental agencies have enacted their own rules, regulations, and ordinances concerning weapons within their respective jurisdictions. The author and publisher make <u>no representation</u> that the information in this book includes all such laws, rules, regulations, ordinances, or other legal requirements, restrictions or prohibitions.

<u>You</u> are responsible for complying with all of the laws and other legal requirements of any jurisdiction that you are in, or traveling to or through, and are strongly urged to consult with a competent, qualified attorney and/or local authorities in advance to determine the current status and applicability of such laws or other legal requirements to specific situations or circumstances you may face.

1   Introduction

Knives are one of man's oldest and most useful tools. In fact, one would be hard pressed indeed to find an adult man or woman in our society that doesn't use a knife on a regular, even daily, basis for one task or another: preparing and eating food, opening boxes and packages, etc. Today, a growing number of people carry a pocket knife of some sort, whether it be a small Swiss Army knife, a folding knife with a locking blade, or a multi-tool with a knife blade of some sort.

With the increasing numbers of states that issue concealed carry weapon (CCW) permits on a "shall-issue" basis, where the government is required to issue a permit to anyone meeting statutory requirements such as no disqualifying felony convictions, more and more average citizens are (legally) carrying concealed handguns. Many of these citizens also carry knives, typically a folding pocket knife, as part of their everyday kit. Mostly, these pocket knives are carried and used as the useful tools they are, although of course virtually any knife can also be used as a self-defense weapon in a life of death situation.

This book was born of the author's extensive cross-country travels, and the need to determine whether a particular knife, typically a folding pocket knife, was legal to carry in a particular state the author was visiting. If you're going to be traveling to another state, you will be subject to that state's law. The knife that you carry today may be legal to carry in your home state, but that very same knife may not be legal in the state you're visiting. For example, in some states, a folding knife with a five inch blade is legal to carry. In others, it's four inches. Or three and a half. In some, three inches is the maximum legal blade length for carry.

These aren't mere distinctions without a difference. People do get arrested for violating knife carry laws. They get prosecuted, convicted, and they go to jail. After conviction, they will have a criminal record that may adversely affect them for the rest of their lives, whether via adverse employment, hiring or professional licensure decisions, the inability to possess firearms or other weapons, or the denial or revocation of certain types of business licenses. If they're lucky, they avoid a criminal conviction, usually after spending many thousands of dollars of their own money on a good defense attorney.

Unfortunately, finding out what's legal to carry, and where, is often not an easy thing to do, even in the age of the Internet. In fact, Internet message boards are filled with innumerable "Is this legal?" type discussion threads, where someone, usually after searching in vain, is trying to figure out what's legal in a particular state. Sometimes, such online forums provide useful and accurate information. But more often than not, the accurate information is mixed in with inaccurate, incomplete, outdated, or just flat out wrong information.

My goal in writing this book is to provide you, the law-abiding traveler, with a better understanding of the knife laws of each state, particularly the laws related to what's legal to carry, and where, so that you may abide by the laws of the state(s) you visit, and not have any unpleasant encounters with our criminal-justice system. In reading this book, you will discover, as I did, that knife laws vary widely from state to state, and even within a state, from city to city, or town to town! My hope is that you will not only be able to use the information in this book to have a safe and legally uneventful trip or vacation, but will gain a greater appreciation of the diversity and complexity of knife regulation throughout our great Nation.

2   Using this Guide

First, this book assumes that you, the reader, possess a certain key characteristic, namely, that you are a law-abiding adult citizen. State law in virtually every state prohibits convicted felons from possessing and carrying deadly or dangerous weapons. (Of course, if you're a convicted felon, you're probably not reading this book anyway.) In addition, many states prohibit minors from possessing deadly or dangerous weapons, without the permission and/or supervision of their parents or legal guardians.

Second, the book generally assumes that you are carrying a knife primarily for use as a utility tool, e.g., for opening packages, peeling fruit, etc., and *not* specifically as a weapon. While knives make excellent weapons, this is an important distinction. Many states have laws that prohibit persons from possessing or carrying deadly or dangerous weapons with the specific intent to use such weapons unlawfully against others. Prosecution under such statutes generally requires the government to prove (1) the knife was a deadly or dangerous weapon, and (2) that you knowingly carried the weapon with (3) the intent to use unlawfully against another. Therefore, if you carry a knife primarily as a weapon, or a knife designed as, or particularly well-suited for use as, a weapon, you should realize that this fact will be used against you if you're prosecuted under these statutes, regardless of whether, for example, your knife met all the criteria for blade length, type, etc., and may otherwise have been legal to carry if carried as a non-weapon tool.

Additionally, you should get used to thinking of your knife primarily as a tool, even if you also carry the knife as a weapon. You will no doubt use your knife for everyday utility purposes and chores a lot more than you will ever use it as a weapon. Consider this: If you're stopped, and the officer asks whether you have any weapons on you, and you say "yes, officer, I have a pocket knife", you have indicated to that officer that you consider the knife to be a weapon. In some states, carrying such a weapon may be illegal, and you may be cited or arrested. If you instead think of your knife as a tool (and use it as such), and in response to "do you have any weapons on you?" you answer "no officer, but I do have a pocket knife, although I don't consider that a weapon", your legal situation is much enhanced, and it will be much more difficult to use your statement against you should you be charged with unlawful carry of a deadly weapon or similar crime.

Obviously, the decision to carry a knife, whether primarily as a tool, or primarily as a weapon, is ultimately yours alone. My purpose in writing this book is simply to provide information on the laws of the various states that impose legal restrictions, prohibitions or other limitations on such carry. As the saying goes, knowledge is power, and knowing the law will enable you to make an informed decision on whether to carry a particular knife, given your particular situation.

2.1 Selecting a Legally "Friendly" Knife

So, what characteristics should you consider when selecting a knife for everyday carry and use that will minimize the chances of inadvertently running afoul of knife carry laws or ordinances? First off, let me say that I have nothing against buying and collecting any of the many fine, quality knives available today. We are truly blessed in this country to have a vast range of great, high quality knives and knife-makers to choose from, and nothing I say here should stop you or anyone else from purchasing, using, appreciating, or otherwise indulging in your passion for knives. Having said that, there are knives you collect, and then there are knives you carry. Of the knives you carry, some are more legally "friendly" than others, regardless of whether you carry the knife primarily as a utility tool, or as a weapon.

For example, let's assume you're in a state (or traveling to, or through, such a state) where you may not legally carry a knife as a concealed deadly weapon, but an "ordinary pocket knife", as that term is used in many statutes, may be carried as a utility tool. Which knife do you think would look more like a utility tool, versus a weapon, should it come before a jury – a simple pocket knife with a stainless, common spearpoint blade marked "Woodsman Model" or "Camper's Friend", or your Ninja Masters folder with the "tactical" black tanto-style blade, emblazoned with a skull and crossbones and "**S**pecial **T**actical **A**ssault Blade"? If, heaven forbid, you had to use a knife as a weapon to defend your life, think about which bloody knife you'd rather have a police investigator, prosecutor, grand juror, judge, or petit (trial) juror examine. In a clear-cut case of self-defense, it may not matter. But in a close case, or in a jurisdiction or with a prosecutor hostile to citizens defending themselves with deadly force, perception can make all the difference between being prosecuted, or not, or between a conviction, and an acquittal.

Even if you aren't criminally prosecuted, or are prosecuted but acquitted on self-defense grounds, in many jurisdictions (not all) you can still be sued in civil court by your attacker, his family, or his estate, as the case may be. Which bloody knife would you rather those civil trial jurors, none of whom will likely be "knife" enthusiasts, have to examine in the jury room as they decide, by the lower proof standard of a civil trial, whether or not you should be liable to the attacker or his family or estate for money damages? The appearance of your knife can make a lot of difference in a close case.

Indeed, you should realize that jurors are drawn from the general population, and as a practical matter are free to draw upon their own life experiences and subjective cultural preconceptions regarding knives and knife usage in weighing the evidence and arriving at their verdict. If you used an automatic knife (which the prosecutor or plaintiff's attorney will describe as an evil "switchblade", possibly along with a dramatic in-court demonstration by a suitable witness) or boot knife, for example, you run the risk of invoking a negative image in the minds of the average juror due to the portrayal of such knives by Hollywood and the media as weapons often used by violent criminals for criminal purposes. Regardless of whether this portrayal is accurate or not, such will often be the stereotype in the mind of the typical, non-knife carrying juror, especially one from an urban area. Couple that with photos of your attacker's injuries (presented as the "victim's" injuries), inflicted with that knife, and that negative image may work against you. In general, you want the jury to identify with you and what you did, especially in a close case; the more you appear as an honest, upstanding citizen defending himself and his loved ones with an uncontroversial, familiar defensive tool, the better.

Now, some people say "it's better to be judged by twelve, than carried by six," that is to say, it's better to be alive and tried by a jury of twelve, than to be dead, carried by six pallbearers at your funeral. No doubt this is true, and I wholeheartedly agree. Most of the people who say such things, however, have never been through the criminal justice system, with their freedom hanging in the balance, or survived a multi-million dollar civil lawsuit, with every penny they own or will earn in the next twenty years at stake. Obviously, you need to survive and prevail against your attacker(s), but the reality is that you also want every possible advantage to survive and prevail in the legal struggle that will almost inevitably follow. Although only one small factor, in general, the more innocuous and commonplace your knife looks, the better your chances of surviving and prevailing in that legal struggle.

So my recommendation for an everyday carry knife is to get and carry a knife that obviously meets all of the technical legal requirements of the jurisdictions you plan on carrying it in, i.e., one that meets any blade length restrictions, if any, and isn't of a proscribed type, such as a dagger, or bowie knife, and so forth. Avoid knives with names that include words like "combat", "assault", or "fighting", or knives specifically marketed or touted as being designed or suitable for combat or fighting. Does the name of the knife really matter? Having read literally hundreds upon hundreds of cases involving knives in writing this book, I can tell you that there are cases where the name of the knife is specifically mentioned and discussed as providing insight into the knife's designed purpose or the intent of the person carrying the knife, i.e., as a tool or a prohibited weapon. In fact, I have cited some of those cases in the selected case law sections of this book.

Even if you carry your knife as both a utility tool and self-defense tool or weapon, you should actually use your knife for those utility or work tasks, so that you can honestly say, and the knife's physical appearance and forensic evidence will support, that you in fact used and considered your knife a utility tool, rather than a weapon. Obviously, you should keep your knife sharp, as a sharp knife is a safe knife. If you don't know how to sharpen your knives, learn. Knife sharpening is a valuable skill, and worth putting in your toolbox of life skills.

As an aside, if you train, or plan to train with a knife as a self-defense tool, you should consider selecting an instructor who teaches tactics and techniques that work with the types and sizes of knife that you can legally carry, and who has at least researched the laws pertaining to knife carry and the use of deadly force in the state(s) where he or she teaches. For instance, tactics and techniques that may work well with a large bowie knife, may not work well at all with the three inch blade folding knife you actually carry. I am not saying don't learn how to use a large blade; for the serious student of the martial arts and self-defense, such training serves to advance your knowledge and skills by helping you understand the various methods of employment of such large bladed weapons, and helps prepare you to counter an attacker(s) using such weapons. What I am suggesting, however, is that your instructor should be conversant with, and the tactics and techniques he or she teaches should reflect, both the tactical *and* legal realities you will face in a real-life defensive situation.

Finally, you should realize that if you carry more than one or two knives, the chances that at least one of your knives will be considered a weapon increases with each additional knife you carry. If a police officer finds four concealed knives on you, and you're in a state with an unlawful use or carry of weapons statute and you don't otherwise have a permit that would cover such carry, you may be getting a first-hand look at that state's criminal justice system. I'm not saying don't carry more than one knife; I'm saying you should have a reasonable, and believable, explanation for why you carry more than one, especially if you're in a state that prohibits carry of concealed weapons.

2.2 A Note on Blade Length Measurement

Many knife statutes list specific blade length restrictions. But what exactly does a folding knife with, for example, a "four inch" blade mean? More precisely, how is such blade length measured? Does it include the entire blade, or only the sharpened edge? Do you measure in a straight line, or along the edge? What about blades types with different shapes – spear point, drop point, tanto, clip point, etc? Depending on the measurement method used, a blade may measure 3.8 inches, or 4.2 inches. In a state with a four inch blade length restriction, how you measure can mean the difference between a legal and illegal blade length.

Don't think it matters? People have been arrested, prosecuted, and convicted for carrying knives with blades that exceeded the statutory maximum by literally a fraction of an inch. Their convictions have been upheld on appeal. In fact, I have cited a couple of such cases in the various selected case law sections of this book.

Unfortunately, most statutes and municipal ordinances are silent on exactly how blade length is measured. A few statutes and ordinances do explicitly specify how blade length is to be measured, but these are the exception, not the rule. When in doubt, the safe route is to include the entire blade, including any unsharpened portion, in your blade length measurement, as this represents the worst-case measurement scenario. In fact, appellate courts in several states with statutory blade length limits have held that the blade measurement includes both the sharpened and unsharpened portions of the blade, as measured from the tip of the blade to the point where the blade enters the handle.

The American Knife and Tool Institute, a knife-maker's industry association, has proposed a standard protocol for measuring blade length that appears to incorporate the results of such case law, where the blade is measured in a straight line from the tip to the "forward-most aspect of the hilt or handle."[1] Of course, such a protocol has no binding legal effect on any law enforcement entity, but may serve as persuasive authority on such entities in considering whether the blade in question exceeds a particular jurisdiction's specified regulatory maximum.

3   Before You Travel

Before traveling, I suggest you read the specific sections for each state you intend to travel to or through. Just because you may legally carry a particular knife in your home state and in your destination state, does not mean that you may legally do so in the states you may simply be traveling through. As an example, in Oregon, a switchblade with a three inch blade is legal to carry openly under state law. Right next door in our most populous state, California, that same knife is illegal to carry. Or, how about a folding pocket knife with a four inch blade? In Texas, such as knife may legally be carried concealed. A short trip through the Oklahoma panhandle into Colorado, however, and such concealed carry is illegal, as Colorado has a statutory three and a half inch blade length limit for concealed carry. As a general rule, you are responsible for complying with the laws of any state you happen to be in, even if you are merely traveling through that state.

In addition, you should be aware that in most states, individual cities and towns have enacted their own ordinances and regulations concerning knife carry. For example, in Massachusetts, a number of cities, including Boston, prohibit carry of knives with blade lengths exceeding two and a half inches, even though state law does not impose a maximum blade length limit. In a few states, violations of such ordinances are considered infractions, with the penalty "only" a hefty fine, but no criminal record. In most states, however, violations of weapons-related

---

[1] *See*, AMER. KNIFE & TOOL INST., PROTOCOL FOR MEASURING KNIFE BLADE LENGTH, in ATKI NEWS & UPDATE, VOL. 6, ISSUE 1 (2004)

ordinances are criminal offenses, either misdemeanors or felonies, depending on the offense and the particular state and city/town/county.

In the few states where violation of the municipal ordinance is only an infraction, some may argue that failure to observe such city ordinances may often "only" result in a violation punished with a hefty fine and no criminal misdemeanor or felony conviction. Readers should be aware, however, that even in such cases the ordinances often specifically authorize law enforcement to arrest you. So now you have an arrest record. Try explaining why your arrest for unlawful weapon possession, even if it only resulted in a fine and no criminal conviction, is "no big deal" on your next concealed carry permit renewal, if the renewal application requires disclosure of your arrest record.

A word of caution: as stated previously, a lot of information exists online, on websites, message boards, online forums and the like regarding knives and what's legal or not. Some of the information is quite accurate, some is emphatically not. You should be aware that some of the information you will find on these sites will likely be incomplete, partially or wholly inaccurate, or in some cases, outdated. This is especially true when it comes to state laws regarding legal knife carry, as state legislatures repeal or amend existing laws, or pass new laws regulating knife carry. The older the information, the more likely that the law, statutory or judge made, will have changed. For example, I have come across online summaries for particular states' knife laws that may at one point have been accurate, but that today are inaccurate, due to changes in those states' laws.

In addition, courts interpreting statutes for issues of first impression, where the law is ambiguous whether a particular type of knife, not specifically listed in the statute, is legal or not, may declare certain types of knives legal, or illegal to carry. For example, in Alaska, prior to about 1990, the legal status of balisongs or butterfly knives was unclear. In 1990, the Court of Appeals of Alaska ruled that such knives did not fall under the statutory prohibition on switchblades or gravity knives, and thus, the persons arrested and criminally prosecuted for carrying balisongs were not convicted.[2] They now have arrest records, spent at least some time in lockup, and their lawyers are richer for the experience. My point: Don't be the test case.

4   Interacting with Law Enforcement

In the event that you are stopped, say, for speeding, you should be aware of your rights and consider handling the interaction with the officer as follows. First, remain calm. You may wish to place your hands in a relaxed position on the steering wheel as the officer approaches your vehicle to show him or her that you aren't holding any weapons. Avoid making any sudden movements during the stop. The officer has the right to inquire about your operation of the vehicle, and can generally require that you produce your driver's license[3] and registration. In most cases, the officer will issue you a warning or ticket and you will be on your way.

---

[2] *See*, State v. Strange, 785 P.2d 563, 566 (Alaska Ct. App. 1990).

[3] *See*, Hiibel v. Sixth Judicial Dist. Ct. of Nevada, 542 U.S. 177 (2004) (affirming conviction under Nevada's "stop and identify" statute for failure to produce driver's license upon request by law enforcement officer). In *Hiibel*, a divided United States Supreme Court upheld Larry Hiibel's conviction for failure to produce identification upon request by a deputy sheriff investigating a reported assault, and held that such request (and subsequent conviction) did not violate his Fourth or Fifth Amendment Constitutional protections. *See, id*. Note that many states have similar "stop and identify" statutes.

In the event that the officer decides to question you about, e.g., possible contraband in your vehicle, you have the right to refuse to answer questions that would be self-incriminating, and may inform the officer that you would prefer to consult with counsel before answering such questions. Sometimes, the officer will be interested in searching your vehicle. You should be aware that, in order for a search for contraband to be legal, the officer will generally need either probable cause, or your consent. In general, most stops for routine traffic violations do not provide sufficient probable cause for an officer to search your vehicle. As such, the officer will often politely ask for your consent to search, often at the end of the traffic stop, after the officer has handed you back your license and papers and told you that you're free to go. You have the right to say no, and in most cases, probably should. Simply tell the officer that you will not consent to such a search, and that if he wants to search he will have to do so without your consent. Without your consent, most officers will not search unless they believe they have enough probable cause to withstand judicial scrutiny.

Note, however, that the officer generally can require that you exit the vehicle, and if he has concern for his safety, can perform a limited search of your person and the areas of the vehicle that you would have immediate access to, for weapons. The search, however, must be limited to weapons that might pose a danger to the officer's safety, and may not be extended to a general search for contraband without probable cause or your consent.

With regard to carry of your knife in public, particularly open carry of large fixed blades in urban areas, you should understand that even if such carry is technically legal in that particular state and municipality, in many cases you may still potentially be arrested and charged under other statutes or ordinances. For example, the circumstances of such carry ("sir, why are you carrying that machete / dagger / bowie / big evil knife in downtown Sheepsville?") may support a charge under a disturbing the peace, disorderly conduct, or brandishing statute or ordinance, depending on the state or municipality involved. Thus, the savvy traveler would be wise to carefully consider the nature and circumstances of his or her knife carry, in order to minimize the likelihood of presenting a threatening or intimidating appearance to the typical persons the traveler is likely to encounter under those circumstances, and possible unwanted law enforcement attention as a result. For example, if you're carrying a hunting knife while lawfully hunting, you are not likely to raise any eyebrows or cause alarm among the other hunters you meet in the field doing the same, but carrying that same knife in a densely populated urban area will likely generate considerable concern (and a possible 9-1-1 emergency call) from the many city-dwellers who don't carry a knife, have never hunted, and who associate the carrying of any knife with unlawful criminal activity.

Finally, if you use a knife to defend yourself against a violent, unlawful criminal attack, you should realize that the use of your knife will almost certainly be considered deadly force. As such, you had better be sure that the circumstances warrant use of deadly force, typically defined as the level of force likely to result in death or serious bodily injury. In general, you are authorized to use deadly force in defense of your life or the lives of your loved ones if you are not the initial aggressor and are facing grave, immediate, and otherwise unavoidable danger of death or serious bodily injury. All of those factors must be present for your use of deadly force to be legally justified. In some states, if the attack occurs outside your home, state law requires you to retreat from the attack if you can do so safely. In states with so-called "stand your ground" laws, the law does not require you to retreat if you attacked outside your home, so long as you are in a place where you have a legal right to be, and were not the initial aggressor.

In the event that you have to use a knife or other deadly weapon in defense of your life or the lives of your loved ones, you should understand your rights, and should consider using the following protocol in dealing with responding law enforcement officers. Your first priority is obviously your safety and the safety of your loved ones – once the fight is over, and if needed, emergency medical services have been called and first aid efforts are underway, then worry about dealing with the responding officers. You need to convey the following information to the 9-1-1 operator and to responding officers: you were attacked; you feared for your life or the lives of your loved ones; you acted in self-defense. If your attacker(s) have fled the scene, you should be prepared to give a description to responding officers. You may or may not get arrested. Identify any potential witnesses who might be able to corroborate your story that you were the one attacked. Point out any potential evidence that your attacker(s) may have left – spent cartridge casings, the probable locations of bullet holes from the shots the assailant(s) fired at you, the baseball bat your attacker tried to smash your brains out with, etc., etc.

At this point, you should inform the officers that while you fully intend to cooperate with their investigation, having just used deadly force in defense of your life, you understand the gravity of the situation, and need to speak with your attorney before answering any questions concerning the details of the event. At this point, you should also consider explicitly stating that you wish to exercise your constitutional right to remain silent pending consultation with your lawyer. Exercising your right to have your attorney present during questioning will give you time to collect your thoughts, and will help you avoid making unwise statements during the extremely agitated mental and emotional state you will likely be in, having just been in a life or death struggle.

5   Federal Knife Law

While knives and knife carry tend for the most part to be regulated at the state level, an understanding of some federal knife-related carry law is important for the law-abiding traveler.

Federal law prohibits carry of firearms and dangerous weapons in federal buildings and facilities (other than a Federal court facility).[4] The term "dangerous weapon" includes knives, but does not include a pocket knife with a blade less than two and a half inches in length. The law also provides an exemption for lawful carry of such weapons incident to hunting or other lawful purposes.

Federal law prohibits firearms in federal court facilities, and allows federal courts to regulate, restrict or prohibit possession of other weapons in their facilities.[5]

Federal law prohibits the mailing, via the U.S. Postal Service, of automatic knives, including switchblades, gravity knives, and ballistic knives, and prohibits the introduction or manufacture for introduction into interstate commerce, or the transport or distribution in interstate commerce, of switchblades and gravity knives, and possession of ballistic knives.[6] The law prohibits possession of automatic knives (switchblades, gravity knives, ballistic knives) in territories

---

[4] *See*, 18 U.S.C. § 930 (2006).

[5] *See*, *id.*

[6] *See*, 18 U.S.C. § 1716 (mailing certain items prohibited); 15 U.S.C. § 1241-45 (switchblade and ballistic knife restrictions).

or U.S. possessions, and Indian Country, which includes all Indian reservations under the jurisdiction of the federal government.[7] A number of exceptions exist, most of which will not apply to the typical traveler, although federal law allows the possession and carry of a switchblade with a blade three inches or less by a person with only one arm.[8]

Finally, federal law prohibits carry of concealed dangerous weapons on, or attempting to get on, a passenger aircraft.[9] The law authorizes both felony criminal charges and hefty civil fines for violators, and in a post-9/11 world, prosecutions and fines for even inadvertent violations of these statutes are real possibilities. The Transportation Security Administration (TSA) is responsible for security screening at airports, and has published regulations concerning the specific types of items that may be carried on board with you.[10] In December 2005, TSA amended its rules to allow metal scissors with pointed tips and blades less than four inches in length, and tools such as screwdrivers seven inches or less in length. Knives and other edged instruments, other than plastic knives or round-bladed butter knives, remain prohibited as carry-on items. Notably, knitting and crochet needles are permitted as carry-on items.

6   How to Use the State Summaries

Each state's knife law is listed in its own section.[11] Within each section, a summary table listing various knife types and their carry status under that state's knife-related statutory and case law is provided, along with a short discussion of the state's general view of knife carry. In the summary tables and in the text I have used the term "automatic knife" to encompass switchblades, gravity knives, and ballistic knives, since state laws usually treat these sub-types similarly, and in many cases identically, as to prohibited conduct (penalties may differ in some states, with typically harsher treatment for illegal use or possession of ballistic knives). I have grouped daggers, dirks, and stilettos together, as these items are also often treated similarly under most state laws. In the rare case that one is treated substantially differently, I have noted this in the textual discussion that follows the summary table. In cases where a statute may be ambiguous or conflicting, I have generally taken the conservative approach and listed that carry mode as prohibited.

In most cases, I have tried to characterize the overall legal environment for knife carry, based on an assessment of both the statutory law, as well as the case law for that state, and have tried to describe the basic tenor of the state's historical or cultural perspective on knives and knife carry. I have used phrases like "moderately permissive", "fairly restrictive", and so forth to describe my subjective assessment of the state's "knife friendliness." As such, you may see two states with the same or similar summary tables, but different subjective assessments, reflecting differences in, for example, the types of prosecutions for knife offenses as evidenced through case law, the existence of restrictive municipal ordinances, etc.

In some states, a knife may be legally carried if the person possesses a valid CCW permit. In other states, however, CCW permits are really only concealed firearm or concealed handgun

---

[7] *See*, 15 U.S.C. § 1241-45 (2006).

[8] *See*, 15 U.S.C. § 1244.

[9] *See*, 49 U.S.C. § 46505 (2006) (criminal penalties); 49 U.S.C. § 46303 (civil penalties).

[10] *See*, Permitted and Prohibited Items, Trans. Sec. Admin., U.S. Dep't of Homeland Sec., *available at* http://www.tsa.gov/public/interweb/assetlibrary/Permitted_Prohibited_Facts.doc (last modified Mar. 2, 2006)

[11] The violent crime rates and relative ranking for each state have been tabulated from crime rate data from 2004 published by the Bureau of Justice Statistics, U.S. Department of Justice, and is available at http://www.ojp.usdoj.gov/bjs/.

permits, and do not cover other types of deadly weapons. Where applicable, I have typically indicated whether the existence of a valid, recognized CCW permit would allow the otherwise unlawful possession or carry of certain types of knives.

I have endeavored to list prohibited places for carry where specific statutory restrictions under state law exist. Note that locations such as the secure areas of commercial passenger airports, federal buildings, and federal courts already have their own restrictions under federal law (or regulatory authority to enact same) on weapon, including knife, carry within their facilities. Also, locations which may not have specific statutory restrictions on weapon carry, such as state court facilities, state prisons, etc., typically restrict knife carry under their own regulatory powers as provided for in state law.

In addition, since most states do not preempt local municipal governments from enacting their own knife restrictions, most states have cities, towns, or counties with knife ordinances that are more stringent that those restrictions embodied in state law. As such, I have listed a few selected municipalities, typically the state's larger cities, with knife ordinances more restrictive than state law. Obviously, it would be impractical to list every such city, but typically the larger cities listed impose the most restrictive knife possession or carry restrictions. Thus, if your knife meets those restrictions, your knife will likely meet the less restrictive ordinances of most other towns or cities. As always, however, exceptions may exist.

To assist you in safely navigating the legal minefield of state knife carry law, I have also included section references and excerpts of relevant state statutes, so that you can look up the statutes to make sure they are still current if you choose. For the truly motivated, I have also included some selected knife-related case law, to serve as a starting point for further legal research should you be so inclined.

Finally, you may want to check with the relevant state authorities if you have specific questions about the legality of your knife. I have included the contact information and website, if available, for each state's attorney general and primary state-wide law enforcement agency.

Good luck with your travels, stay sharp, and stay safe!

For further information, you may wish to visit www.KnifeLawsOnline.com,
where you can sign up for my FREE email newsletter on knife laws and knife regulation,
read knife and knife law related news, and more.

7   Alabama – The Heart of Dixie

Area: 50,744 sq.mi. (Rank: 28th)   Population: 4,486,508 (Rank: 23rd)
Violent Crime Rate (per 100,000 residents): 426.6 (Rank: 29th Safest)
State Motto: *Audemus Iura Nostra Defendere (We Dare Defend Our Rights)*

7.1   Knife Carry Law Summary

<u>Note:</u> Blade length limits, if any, in parentheses.

Knife Type	Open Carry	Concealed Carry	Notes
Folding Knives	Yes	Yes	
Fixed Bladed Knives	Yes	No	See note[12]
Dirks, Daggers, & Stilettos	Yes	No	See note[12]
Automatic Knives	Yes	Yes	
Balisongs	Yes	Yes	

7.2   Discussion

Visitors to Alabama will find a fairly permissive legal environment for knife carry, with a strong preference for open, versus concealed, carry. Ordinary folding pocket knives should pose no problem, and may be carried openly or concealed. There is no statutorily defined blade length limit. State law strictly prohibits concealed carry of bowies and similar knives. Unfortunately, the legal boundaries of what is considered a "bowie knife or knife or instrument of like kind or description" are fuzzy, and may very well include such knives as daggers, dirks, stilettos, and large fixed blades. Given the inherent difficulty of determining exactly what a court may consider a prohibited knife under the broad wording of the statute, the cautious traveler would do well to avoid concealed carry of fixed bladed knives, particularly large fixed bladed knives, as such knives may fall within the statutory prohibition described.

State law prohibits carry of deadly weapons on school property "with intent to do bodily harm[.]" The definition of "deadly weapon" includes a "switch-blade knife, gravity knife, stiletto, sword, or dagger[.]" Travelers should be aware that cities and towns may also pass their own ordinances restricting knife carry. Alabama does not preempt its cities and towns from regulating knife carry, unlike the case for firearms, where the state has prohibited cities and towns from enacting their own handgun carry restrictions, ensuring uniform state-wide handgun laws. For example, cities may restrict knife carry in bars and restaurants that serve alcohol, on school grounds, city parks, etc.

7.3   Selected Statutes

CODE OF ALA. 1975, AS AMENDED §§ (2001)

---

[12] Alabama law prohibits concealed carry of bowie knives or similar knives. *See*, ALA. CODE § 13A-11-50 (2001). Caution is advised in carrying any fixed bladed knife in a concealed mode, particularly large fixed bladed knives. The limited case law on the subject indicates that at least one Alabama appellate court has described a bowie knife as "a long knife shaped like a dagger but having only one edge," indicating the possibility that daggers and the like may be considered a knife "of like kind or description" under the statute. *See*, Smelley v. State, 472 So.2d 715, 717 (Ala. Crim. App. 1985) (quoting Tennessee Supreme Court's description of bowie knife (citation omitted)).

13A-1-2 Definitions –

...

(5) DANGEROUS INSTRUMENT. Any instrument, article, or substance which, under the circumstances in which it is used, attempted to be used, or threatened to be used, is highly capable of causing death or serious physical injury. The term includes a "vehicle," as that term is defined in subdivision (15).

(6) DEADLY PHYSICAL FORCE. Physical force which, under the circumstances in which it is used, is readily capable of causing death or serious physical injury.

(7) DEADLY WEAPON. A firearm or anything manifestly designed, made, or adapted for the purposes of inflicting death or serious physical injury. The term includes, but is not limited to, a pistol, rifle, or shotgun; or a switch-blade knife, gravity knife, stiletto, sword, or dagger; or any billy, black-jack, bludgeon, or metal knuckles.

...

13A-11-50 Carrying concealed weapons.

...

Except as otherwise provided in this Code, a person who carries concealed about his person a bowie knife or knife or instrument of like kind or description or a pistol or firearm of any other kind or an air gun shall, on conviction, be fined not less than $50.00 nor more than $500.00, and may also be imprisoned in the county jail or sentenced to hard labor for the county for not more than six months.

13A-11-72 Certain persons forbidden to possess pistol.

...

(c) Subject to the exceptions provided by Section 13A-11-74, no person shall knowingly with intent to do bodily harm carry or possess a deadly weapon on the premises of a public school.

(d) Possession of a deadly weapon with the intent to do bodily harm on the premises of a public school in violation of subsection (c) of this section is a Class C felony.

...

(g) The term "deadly weapon" as used in this section means a firearm or anything manifestly designed, made, or adapted for the purposes of inflicting death or serious physical injury, and such term includes, but is not limited to, a bazooka, hand grenade, missile, or explosive or incendiary device; a pistol, rifle, or shotgun; or a switch-blade knife, gravity knife, stiletto, sword, or dagger; or any club, baton, billy, black-jack, bludgeon, or metal knuckles.

7.4   Selected Caselaw

Smelley v. State, 472 So.2d 715 (Ala. Crim. App. 1985) (holding folding pocket-knife six inches long and carried concealed not "bowie knife or knife or instrument of like kind or description").

7.5   Preemption Law

No knife law preemption, firearms (handgun) law preemption only. *See,* Ala. Code § 11-45-1.1 (2001).

7.6   Places Off-Limits While Carrying

No specific prohibitions for knives, most prohibitions relate to firearms.

7.7   School/College Carry

State law prohibits carry or possession of a deadly weapon on school grounds "with intent to do bodily harm".

7.8 Selected City Ordinances

Decatur – Carry of "bowie knife or knife or instrument of like kind or description" prohibited in city parks and places licensed to serve alcohol. *See*, Decatur, Ala., Code § 16-22.1 (2005).

Mobile – Unlawful to sell, or have in possession for sale, any switchblade within the city or its police jurisdiction. *See*, Mobile, Ala., Code of Ordinances § 62-3 (2005).

Muscle Shoals – Concealed carry of bowie knives or "other knife or instrument of like kind or description," or razors, prohibited. *See*, Muscle Shoals, Ala., Code § 70-82 (2005).

7.9 State Resources

Alabama Dept. of Public Safety
500 Dexter Avenue
Montgomery, AL 36130
Phone: (334)242-4392
Fax: (334) 242-4385
Website: http://www.dps.state.al.us/

Attorney General of Alabama
Alabama State House
Montgomery, AL 36130
Phone: (334) 242-7300
Website: http://www.ago.state.al.us/

8   Alaska – The Last Frontier

Area: 571,951 sq.mi. (Rank: 1st)   Population: 643,786 (Rank: 47th)
Violent Crime Rate (per 100,000 residents): 634.5 (Rank: 44th Safest)
State Motto: *North to the Future*

8.1 *Knife Carry Law Summary*

Note: Blade length limits, if any, in parentheses.

Knife Type	Open Carry	Concealed Carry	Notes
Folding Knives	Yes	Yes	See notes[13,14]
Fixed Bladed Knives	Yes	Yes	See note[14]
Dirks, Daggers, & Stilettos	Yes	Yes	See note[15]
Automatic Knives	No	No	
Balisongs	Yes	Yes	See note[14]

8.2 *Discussion*

The Nation's largest state by area, and more than twice as large as Texas, Alaska's over half a million square miles makes even large states like Texas and California look small by comparison. The state's rugged wilderness, vast distances, and few population centers foster a spirit of independence and self-sufficiency in its citizens. This spirit of self-sufficiency is notably reflected in Alaska's liberal firearms laws, Alaska being one of only two states that do not require its law-abiding citizens to obtain permits to carry concealed firearms.

Visitors to Alaska will likewise find a generally permissive legal environment for knife carry. Ordinary folding pocket knives should pose no problem, and may be carried openly or concealed. There is no statutorily defined blade length limit. Carry or possession, however, of automatic knives in the form of switchblades and gravity knives is strictly prohibited. Fixed blades may be carried openly or concealed, but if carried concealed, state law requires the wearer to immediately disclose the presence of the weapon upon contact with any law enforcement officer acting in an official capacity, and to allow the officer to secure the weapon.

Case law indicates that balisongs, or butterfly knives, do not fall within the statutory prohibition on switchblade or gravity knives. While no explicit statutory prohibition on dirks, daggers, or stilettos appears to exist, the wise traveler would be well-advised to avoid carrying these types of knives, as some municipalities, notably Anchorage, specifically prohibit concealed carry of dirks and daggers.

---

[13] The careful traveler would be wise to avoid exceptionally large folders or those that appear particularly "weapon like". Ordinary pocket knives are excluded from the law enforcement notification requirement for concealed deadly weapons. *See*, ALASKA STAT. § 11.61.220 (2004).

[14] If carried concealed, and you are contacted by a law enforcement officer for an official purpose, state law requires you to immediately inform the officer of that fact, and allow the officer to secure the weapon. *See*, ALASKA STAT. § 11.61.220 (2004). In addition, you cannot carry a concealed deadly weapon into another person's residence without first obtaining permission to do so from an adult residing in that residence. *See, id.*

[15] While no explicit state law prohibition appears to exist, some municipalities specifically prohibit concealed carry of these types of knives.

No state-wide statutory prohibitions on off-limits locations for otherwise legal knife carry exist, although travelers should be aware that cities and towns may pass their own ordinances restricting knife carry. Alaska does not preempt its cities and towns from regulating knife carry, unlike the case for firearms, where the state has prohibited cities and towns from enacting their own handgun carry restrictions, ensuring uniform state-wide laws. As such, towns and cities may regulate knife carry in or on such areas as school property.

8.3 Selected Statutes

ALASKA STAT. §§ (2004)

11.61.220. Misconduct Involving Weapons in the Fifth Degree.

(a) A person commits the crime of misconduct involving weapons in the fifth degree if the person

(1) is 21 years of age or older and knowingly possesses a deadly weapon, other than an ordinary pocket knife or a defensive weapon,

(A) that is concealed on the person, and, when contacted by a peace officer, the person fails to

(i) immediately inform the peace officer of that possession; or

(ii) allow the peace officer to secure the deadly weapon, or fails to secure the weapon at the direction of the peace officer, during the duration of the contact;

(B) that is concealed on the person within the residence of another person unless the person has first obtained the express permission of an adult residing there to bring a concealed deadly weapon within the residence;

...

(5) possesses or transports a switchblade or a gravity knife; or

(6) is less than 21 years of age and knowingly possesses a deadly weapon, other than an ordinary pocket knife or a defensive weapon, that is concealed on the person.

11.81.900. Definitions.

(a) For purposes of this title, unless the context requires otherwise,

...

(15) "dangerous instrument" means any deadly weapon or anything that, under the circumstances in which it is used, attempted to be used, or threatened to be used, is capable of causing death or serious physical injury;

(16) "deadly force" means force that the person uses with the intent of causing, or uses under circumstances that the person knows create a substantial risk of causing, death or serious physical injury; "deadly force" includes intentionally discharging or pointing a firearm in the direction of another person or in the direction in which another person is believed to be and intentionally placing another person in fear of imminent serious physical injury by means of a dangerous instrument;

(17) "deadly weapon" means any firearm, or anything designed for and capable of causing death or serious physical injury, including a knife, an axe, a club, metal knuckles, or an explosive;

...

(20) "defensive weapon" means an electric stun gun, or a device to dispense mace or a similar chemical agent, that is not designed to cause death or serious physical injury;

8.4 Selected Caselaw

State v. Strange, 785 P.2d 563 (Alaska Ct. App. 1990) (holding balisong knife not prohibited switchblade or gravity knife).

8.5 Preemption Law

No knife law preemption, firearms law preemption only. *See*, ALASKA STAT. § 18.65.778 (2004).

8.6 Places Off-Limits While Carrying

No state law limitation. Towns and cities, however, may pass their own local ordinances prohibiting carry.

8.7 School/College Carry

No state law limitation. Towns and cities, however, may pass their own local ordinances prohibiting carry on school grounds.

8.8 Selected City Ordinances

Anchorage – Concealed carry of knives other than ordinary pocket knives prohibited. *See*, ANCHORAGE, ALASKA, MUNICIPAL CODE § 8.25.020 (1996).

Fairbanks – Possession of "dangerous weapons" on school grounds prohibited. The definition of "dangerous weapons" specifically includes knives other than ordinary pocket knives of blade length not more than 3½ inches. *See*, FAIRBANKS, ALASKA, CODE OF ORDINANCES § 46-294 (2006)

8.9 State Resources

Alaska Department of Public Safety
450 Whittier Street
PO Box 111200
Juneau, AK 99811-1200
Phone: (907) 465-4322
Fax: (907) 465-4362
Website: http://www.dps.state.ak.us/

Attorney General of Alaska
P.O. Box 110300
Juneau, AK 99811-0300
Phone: (907) 465-2133
Website: http://www.law.state.ak.us/

9   Arizona – The Grand Canyon State

Area: 113,635 sq.mi. (Rank: 6th)   Population: 5,456,453 (Rank: 19th)
Violent Crime Rate (per 100,000 residents): 504.1 (Rank: 38th Safest)
State Motto: *Ditat Deus (God Enriches)*

9.1 Knife Carry Law Summary

Note: Blade length limits, if any, in parentheses.

Knife Type	Open Carry	Concealed Carry	Notes
Folding Knives	Yes	Yes	See notes[16,18]
Fixed Bladed Knives	Yes	No	See note[17]
Dirks, Daggers, & Stilettos	Yes	No	See note[17]
Automatic Knives	Yes	No	See note[17]
Balisongs	Yes	No	See note[17]

9.2 Discussion

The law-abiding traveler to the Grand Canyon State will find a generally favorable environment for knife carry, especially outside the state's major cities.

With respect to knives, ordinary folding pocket knives should pose no problem, and may be carried either openly visible or concealed, although pocket knives with large blades should be carried openly, unless the wearer possesses a recognized concealed weapons permit.[18] There is no statutorily defined blade length limit. Note, however, that some cities may have ordinances requiring a shorter blade length.

There also appears to be no explicit statutory prohibition on dirks, daggers, stilettos, and automatic knives, although such knives may fall under the statutory definition of "deadly weapons", and therefore concealed carry would require a valid concealed carry weapons permit. In addition, since Arizona's preemption law only relates to firearms, cities and towns are free to regulate carry of other weapons such as knives, and several do just that. For knives other than ordinary pocket knives, open carry is legal, provided that such knives are carried in a visible scabbard.

Balisongs should be carried openly, or concealed with a recognized permit, as such knives are likely to be deemed weapons, due to their association with the martial arts, and public perception as martial arts weapons.

---

[16] State law permit concealed carry of pocket knives without a permit. *See,* ARIZ. REV. STAT. § 13-3102 (2006). Note, however, that the term "pocket knife" is not defined in the statute. Travelers should avoid carry of folding knives with large blades without a recognized concealed weapons permit.

[17] May be carried concealed with a valid, recognized concealed weapons permit.

[18] Some (erroneous) information available online has indicated that, ostensibly pursuant to an opinion of the state's Attorney General, a pocket knife with a blade less than four inches may be carried concealed without a recognized concealed weapons permit. A search of the state's Attorney General formal opinions from 1999 through March 2006, however, has revealed no such public opinion. Furthermore, in response to an inquiry from the author, the Arizona Attorney General's office has indicated that they "did not find any opinions specifically discussing pocket knives with blades under four inches." *See,* Email from Ariz. Att'y Gen. Office (Jun. 5, 2006) (on file with author).

State law prohibits carry of deadly weapons on school grounds. Apart from schools, however, no state-wide statutory prohibitions on off-limits locations for otherwise legal knife carry exist, although travelers should be aware that cities and towns may pass their own ordinances restricting knife carry. Court buildings and other secured government buildings may also restrict or prohibit knife carry of any kind within their facilities.

9.3 Selected Statutes

Ariz. Rev. Stat. §§ (2006)

13-3101. Definitions

A. In this chapter, unless the context otherwise requires:

1. "Deadly weapon" means anything that is designed for lethal use. The term includes a firearm.

13-3102. Misconduct involving weapons; defenses; classification; definitions

A. A person commits misconduct involving weapons by knowingly:

1. Carrying a deadly weapon without a permit pursuant to section 13-3112 except a pocket knife concealed on his person; or

2. Carrying a deadly weapon without a permit pursuant to section 13-3112 concealed within immediate control of any person in or on a means of transportation; or

...

12. Possessing a deadly weapon on school grounds; or

...

F. Subsection A, paragraph 1 of this section shall not apply to a weapon or weapons carried in a belt holster which holster is wholly or partially visible, or carried in a scabbard or case designed for carrying weapons which scabbard or case is wholly or partially visible or carried in luggage. Subsection A, paragraph 2 of this section shall not apply to a weapon or weapons carried in a case, holster, scabbard, pack or luggage that is carried within a means of transportation or within a storage compartment, trunk or glove compartment of a means of transportation.

...

I. Subsection A, paragraph 12 of this section shall not apply to the possession of a:

1. Firearm that is not loaded and that is carried within a means of transportation under the control of an adult provided that if the adult leaves the means of transportation the firearm shall not be visible from the outside of the means of transportation and the means of transportation shall be locked.

2. Firearm for use on the school grounds in a program approved by a school.

9.4 Selected Caselaw

Dano v. Collins, 166 Ariz. 322, 802 P.2d 1021 (Ariz. Ct. App. 1990) (upholding power of state to regulate concealed carry of weapons).

State v. Carreon, 210 Ariz. 54, 107 P.3d 900 (Ariz. 2005) (affirming conviction under weapon misconduct statute for prohibited possessor).

9.5 Preemption Law

No knife law preemption, firearms law preemption only. *See*, Ariz. Rev. Stat. § 13-3108 (2006).

9.6 Places Off-Limits While Carrying

No state law limitation. Towns and cities, however, may pass their own local ordinances prohibiting carry in specified areas. In addition, courts and other secured state buildings may restrict and/or prohibit a broad range of weapons, including knives, on their premises. *See, e.g.,* Policies and Procedures Manual § 4.11, Ariz. Admin. Ofc. of Courts (1991).

9.7 School/College Carry

No state law limitation. Towns and cities, however, may pass their own local ordinances prohibiting carry on school grounds.

9.8 Selected City Ordinances

Phoenix – Concealed carry of dirks, daggers, bowie knives, or knives other than ordinary pocket knives prohibited. *See,* Phoenix, Ariz., City Code § 23-40 (2006).

Tucson – Carry of "weapons of any kind or description" prohibited on any part of Tucson-Pima library grounds posted as prohibiting weapons or firearms. *See,* Tucson, Ariz., Code of Ord. § 11-160 (2006).

Chandler – Carry of "deadly weapons" in city parks prohibited. Excludes pocket knives with blade lengths no longer than 3½ inches. *See,* Chandler, Ariz., City Code § 31-2.3 (2005).

9.9 State Resources

Arizona Department of Public Safety
P.O. Box 6488
Phoenix, AZ 85005
Phone: (602) 256-6280 or (800) 256-6280
Fax: (602) 223-2928
Website: http://www.dps.state.az.us/ccw/default.asp

Arizona Attorney General
1275 W. Washington Street
Phoenix, AZ 85007
Phone: (602) 542-4266 or (888) 377-6108
Website: http://www.attorney_general.state.az.us/

10 Arkansas – The Natural State

Area: 52,068 sq.mi. (Rank: 27th)   Population: 2,710,079 (Rank: 33rd)
Violent Crime Rate (per 100,000 residents): 499.1 (Rank: 36th Safest)
State Motto: *Regnat Populus (The People Rule)*

10.1 Knife Carry Law Summary

Note: Blade length limits, if any, in parentheses.

Knife Type	Open Carry	Concealed Carry	Notes
Folding Knives	Yes (< 3½ ")	Yes (< 3½ ")	
Fixed Bladed Knives	Yes (< 3½ ")	Yes (< 3½ ")	
Dirks, Daggers, & Stilettos	Yes (< 3½ ")	Yes (< 3½ ")	
Automatic Knives	Yes (< 3½ ")	Yes (< 3½ ")	
Balisongs	Yes (< 3½ ")	Yes (< 3½ ")	

10.2 Discussion

Travelers to Arkansas will find the state's laws fairly permissive with regards to knife carry in general, but otherwise fairly restrictive when it comes to blade length. Arkansas law provides that any knife with a blade three and a half inches in length or greater is presumptively a weapon, and a corollary statute makes carry of any knife with the intent to use as a weapon a crime. The statute does not differentiate between open and concealed carry. Thus, the law abiding traveler would be well served to avoid carrying any knife with a blade three and a half inches or longer, as such "long" bladed knives will be presumed to be weapons under state law. In fact, in one case the Arkansas Supreme Court upheld a conviction under the statute for carrying a knife that was *exactly* three and a half inches long.

While state law provides an affirmative defense for persons carrying a weapon on a "journey", the exact parameters of what constitutes a journey remain unclear. In addition, once the journey ends, the affirmative defense would no longer be available. Typically, an interstate traveler on a continuous, uninterrupted trip through the state would likely be able to avail him or herself of this defense.

Travelers should note that cities and towns are not preempted from regulating knife carry, unlike the case with firearms, which is exclusively regulated by state and federal law. While state law does not specifically prohibit dirks, daggers, stilettos, balisongs and automatic knives, travelers should be aware that some cities and towns do prohibit such knives, *regardless of blade length*.

Under state law, it is illegal to carry a weapon into an establishment that serves alcohol.

10.3 Selected Statutes

Ark. Code §§ (2005)

5-1-102. Definitions.

As used in this code:

(4) "Deadly weapon" means:

(A) A firearm or anything manifestly designed, made, or adapted for the purpose of inflicting death or serious physical injury; or

(B) Anything that in the manner of its use or intended use is capable of causing death or serious physical injury;

5-73-120. Carrying a weapon.

(a) A person commits the offense of carrying a weapon if he or she possesses a handgun, knife, or club on or about his or her person, in a vehicle occupied by him or her, or otherwise readily available for use with a purpose to employ the handgun, knife, or club as a weapon against a person.

(b) As used in this section:

(3)(A) "Knife" means any bladed hand instrument that is capable of inflicting serious physical injury or death by cutting or stabbing.

(B) "Knife" includes a dirk, sword or spear in a cane, razor, ice pick, throwing star, switchblade, and butterfly knife.

(c) It is a defense to a prosecution under this section that at the time of the act of carrying a weapon:

(1) The person is in his or her own dwelling, place of business, or on property in which he or she has a possessory or proprietary interest;

...

(4) The person is carrying a weapon when upon a journey, unless the journey is through a commercial airport when presenting at the security checkpoint in the airport or is in the person's checked baggage and is not a lawfully declared weapon;

...

(8) The person is in a motor vehicle and the person has a license to carry a concealed weapon pursuant to § 5-73-301 et seq.

(d)(1) Any person who carries a weapon into an establishment that sells alcoholic beverages is guilty of a misdemeanor and subject to a fine of not more than two thousand five hundred dollars ($2,500) or imprisonment for not more than one (1) year, or both.

(2) Otherwise, carrying a weapon is a Class A misdemeanor.

5-73-121. Carrying a knife as a weapon.

(a) A person who carries a knife as a weapon, except when upon a journey or upon his or her own premises, shall be punished as provided by § 5-73-123(b) [repealed].

(b) If a person carries a knife with a blade three and one-half inches (3½") long or longer, this fact is prima facie proof that the knife is carried as a weapon.

(c) This section does not apply to:

(1) An officer whose duties include making an arrest or keeping and guarding a prisoner; or

(2) A person summoned by the officer to aid in the discharge of the officer's duties while actually engaged in the discharge of the officer's duties.

10.4 Selected Caselaw

Garcia v. State, 969 S.W.2d 591 (Ark. 1998) (affirming conviction for possession of knife with three and one half inch blade).

10.5 Preemption Law

No knife law preemption, firearms law preemption only. *See,* Ark. Code § 14-16-504 (2005).

10.6 Places Off-Limits While Carrying

State law prohibits carrying of weapons in establishments that serve alcohol. The definition of weapon specifically includes knives carried with intent to use as a weapon. Knives with blade length of three and a half inches or greater are presumptively considered weapons. In addition, towns and cities may pass their own local ordinances prohibiting carry.

10.7 School/College Carry

No state law limitation. Towns and cities, however, may pass their own local ordinances prohibiting carry on public school grounds.

10.8 Selected City Ordinances

Eureka Springs – Carry of "crabapple switch, dirk, dagger, pick" or similar knives within city limits prohibited. *See,* Eureka Springs, Ark., Municipal Code § 74-4 (2002).

10.9 State Resources

Arkansas State Police
One State Police Plaza Drive
Little Rock, AR 72209-2971
Phone: (501) 618-8000
Fax: (501) 618-8647
Website: http://www.state.ar.us/asp/asp.html

Office of the Attorney General
200 Catlett-Prien Tower
323 Center Street
Little Rock, AR 72201
Phone: (501) 682-1323 or (800) 448-3014
Website: http://www.ag.state.ar.us/

11 California – The Golden State

Area: 155,959 sq.mi. (Rank: 3rd)   Population: 35,116,033 (Rank: 1st)
Violent Crime Rate (per 100,000 residents): 551.8 (Rank: 41st Safest)
State Motto: *Eureka! (I Have Found It!)*

11.1 Knife Carry Law Summary

<u>Note:</u> Blade length limits, if any, in parentheses.

Knife Type	Open Carry	Concealed Carry	Notes
Folding Knives	Yes	Yes	Assisted opening ok.
Fixed Bladed Knives	Yes	No	
Dirks, Daggers, & Stilettos	Yes	No	
Automatic Knives	Yes (< 2")	Yes (< 2")	
Balisongs	Yes (< 2")	Yes (< 2")	
Sword Canes	No	No	

11.2 Discussion

Visitors to the Golden State will find state law relatively permissive when it comes to knife carry. This relative permissiveness stands in contrast to lawful firearms carry, which is heavily regulated and restricted, especially in the large urban population centers.

Ordinary folding pocket knives, including knives with assisted opening mechanisms, are legal to carry in the closed (folded) position either openly or concealed. Such folding knives must be designed to have a bias towards closure, that is, the design must be such that the mechanism "provides resistance that must be overcome in opening the blade, or that biases the blade back toward its closed position."[19]

Apart from switchblades, no statutorily defined blade length limit exists. Appellate case law has held that blade length refers to the sharpened portion only. Dirks, daggers, stilettos, and other fixed bladed knives must be carried openly, and cannot be carried concealed. Automatic knives ("switchblades") with blades less than two inches long are legal, and may be carried openly or concealed. Balisongs are considered switchblades under California law, and thus are prohibited unless the blade is less than two inches long. Disguised edged weapons, such as sword canes, belt-buckle knives, lipstick case knives, etc. are strictly prohibited.

Carry of most knives on school grounds is prohibited. The statute permits carry of folding knives with *non-locking* blades up to (and including) 2 ½ inches in length. The law does, however, permit carry of folding knives with blades longer than 2 ½ inches, including those with locking blades, on college or university grounds.

California does not preempt its cities and towns from regulating knife carry, unlike the case for firearms, where the state has prohibited cities and towns from enacting their own firearms regulations. As such, carry in towns or cities may be subject to additional restrictions. For

---

[19] See, CAL. PENAL CODE § 653k (2006).

example, the city of Los Angeles prohibits open carry of any knife with a blade longer than three inches.[20]

11.3 Selected Statutes

CAL. PENAL CODE §§ (2005)

653k. Every person who possesses in the passenger's or driver's area of any motor vehicle in any public place or place open to the public, carries upon his or her person, and every person who sells, offers for sale, exposes for sale, loans, transfers, or gives to any other person a switchblade knife having a blade two or more inches in length is guilty of a misdemeanor. For the purposes of this section, "switchblade knife" means a knife having the appearance of a pocketknife and includes a spring-blade knife, snap-blade knife, gravity knife or any other similar type knife, the blade or blades of which are two or more inches in length and which can be released automatically by a flick of a button, pressure on the handle, flip of the wrist or other mechanical device, or is released by the weight of the blade or by any type of mechanism whatsoever. "Switchblade knife" does not include a knife that opens with one hand utilizing thumb pressure applied solely to the blade of the knife or a thumb stud attached to the blade, provided that the knife has a detent or other mechanism that provides resistance that must be overcome in opening the blade, or that biases the blade back toward its closed position. For purposes of this section, "passenger's or driver's area" means that part of a motor vehicle which is designed to carry the driver and passengers, including any interior compartment or space therein.

12020. (a) Any person in this state who does any of the following is punishable by imprisonment in a county jail not exceeding one year or in the state prison:

(1) Manufactures or causes to be manufactured, imports into the state, keeps for sale, or offers or exposes for sale, or who gives, lends, or possesses any cane gun or wallet gun, any undetectable firearm, any firearm which is not immediately recognizable as a firearm, any camouflaging firearm container, any ammunition which contains or consists of any flechette dart, any bullet containing or carrying an explosive agent, any ballistic knife, any multiburst trigger activator, any nunchaku, any short-barreled shotgun, any short-barreled rifle, any metal knuckles, any belt buckle knife, any leaded cane, any zip gun, any shuriken, any unconventional pistol, any lipstick case knife, any cane sword, any shobi-zue, any air gauge knife, any writing pen knife, any metal military practice handgrenade or metal replica handgrenade, or any instrument or weapon of the kind commonly known as a blackjack, slungshot, billy, sandclub, sap, or sandbag.

...

(4) Carries concealed upon his or her person any dirk or dagger. ...

...

(b) ...

(24) As used in this section, a "dirk" or "dagger" means a knife or other instrument with or without a handguard that is capable of ready use as a stabbing weapon that may inflict great bodily injury or death. A nonlocking folding knife, a folding knife that is not prohibited by Section 653k, or a pocketknife is capable of ready use as a stabbing weapon that may inflict great bodily injury or death only if the blade of the knife is exposed and locked into position.

...

171b. (a) Any person who brings or possesses within any state or local public building or at any meeting required to be open to the public pursuant to Chapter 9 (commencing with Section 54950) of Part 1 of Division 2 of Title 5 of, or Article 9 (commencing with Section 11120) of Chapter 1 of Part 1 of Division 3 of Title 2 of, the Government Code, any of the following is guilty of a public offense punishable by imprisonment in a county jail for not more than one year, or in the state prison:

(1) Any firearm.

(2) Any deadly weapon described in Section 653k or 12020.

---

[20] See, LOS ANGELES, CAL., MUNICIPAL CODE § 55.10 (2006)

(3) Any knife with a blade length in excess of four inches, the blade of which is fixed or is capable of being fixed in an unguarded position by the use of one or two hands.

...

626.10. (a) Any person, except a duly appointed peace officer as defined in Chapter 4.5 (commencing with Section 830) of Title 3 of Part 2, a full-time paid peace officer of another state or the federal government who is carrying out official duties while in this state, a person summoned by any officer to assist in making arrests or preserving the peace while the person is actually engaged in assisting any officer, or a member of the military forces of this state or the United States who is engaged in the performance of his or her duties, who brings or possesses any dirk, dagger, ice pick, knife having a blade longer than 21/2 inches, folding knife with a blade that locks into place, a razor with an unguarded blade, a taser, or a stun gun, as defined in subdivision (a) of Section 244.5, any instrument that expels a metallic projectile such as a BB or a pellet, through the force of air pressure, CO2 pressure, or spring action, or any spot marker gun, upon the grounds of, or within, any public or private school providing instruction in kindergarten or any of grades 1 to 12, inclusive, is guilty of a public offense, punishable by imprisonment in a county jail not exceeding one year, or by imprisonment in the state prison.

(b) Any person, except a duly appointed peace officer as defined in Chapter 4.5 (commencing with Section 830) of Title 3 of Part 2, a full-time paid peace officer of another state or the federal government who is carrying out official duties while in this state, a person summoned by any officer to assist in making arrests or preserving the peace while the person is actually engaged in assisting any officer, or a member of the military forces of this state or the United States who is engaged in the performance of his or her duties, who brings or possesses any dirk, dagger, ice pick, or knife having a fixed blade longer than 21/2 inches upon the grounds of, or within, any private university, the University of California, the California State University, or the California Community Colleges is guilty of a public offense, punishable by imprisonment in a county jail not exceeding one year, or by imprisonment in the state prison.

...

11.4 Selected Caselaw

People Ex Rel. Mautner v. Quattrone (1989) 211 Cal. App. 3d 1389 (1989) (holding butterfly knife falls under switchblade prohibition).

In Re Rosalio S. 35 Cal. App. 4th 775, 41 Cal. Rptr. 2d 534 (1995) (reversing conviction for unlawful knife possession and holding "blade" refers to sharpened portion only).

People v. Rubalcava 23 Cal. 4th 322 , 96 Cal.Rptr.2d 735; 1 P.3d 52 (2000) (holding no showing of intent to use as weapon required for conviction for carrying concealed dirk or dagger).

11.5 Preemption Law

No knife law preemption, firearms law preemption only. *See*, CAL. GOV'T CODE § 53071 (2005). Towns and cities can have their own regulations regarding knife carry.

11.6 Places Off-Limits While Carrying

California prohibits the carry of firearms and other deadly weapons, including knives falling under the switchblade prohibition, or knives or any kind with a blade length over four inches in state or local public buildings, or public meetings. *See*, CAL. PENAL CODE § 171b (2005).

11.7 School/College Carry

State law prohibits carry of most knives on school grounds. The statute permits carry of folding knives with *non-locking* blades up to (and including) 2 ½ inches in length. The law does, however, permit carry of folding knives with blades longer than 2 ½ inches, including those with locking blades, on college or university grounds.

11.8 Selected City Ordinances

Los Angeles – Open carry of knives with blades three inches or longer prohibited. *See*, LOS ANGELES, CAL., MUNICIPAL CODE § 55.10 (2006).

Oakland – Carry of dirks, daggers, and spring-blade knives with blades of any length prohibited. Carry of knives with blades three inches or longer prohibited. *See*, OAKLAND, CAL., MUNICIPAL CODE § 9.36.020 (2005).

San Francisco – Unlawful to loiter with concealed knife with blade three inches or longer, or with any switchblade knife. Unlawful to possess switchblade knife of any length. *See*, SAN FRANCISCO, CAL., MUNICIPAL CODE §§ 1291-92 (2005).

11.9 State Resources

California Highway Patrol
P.O. Box 942898
Sacramento, CA 94298-0001
Phone: (916) 657-7261
Website: http://www.chp.ca.gov/

Attorney General of California
4949 Broadway
Sacramento, CA 95820
Phone: (916) 445-9555 or (916) 322-3360
Website: http://caag.state.ca.us/

12 Colorado – The Centennial State

Area: 103,718 sq.mi. (Rank: 8th)   Population: 4,506,542 (Rank: 22nd)
Violent Crime Rate (per 100,000 residents): 373.5 (Rank: 26th Safest)
State Motto: *Nil Sine Numine (Nothing Without Providence)*

12.1 Knife Carry Law Summary

<u>Note</u>: Blade length limits, if any, in parentheses.

Knife Type	Open Carry	Concealed Carry	Notes
Folding Knives	Yes	Yes (<= 3.5")	
Fixed Bladed Knives	Yes	Yes (<= 3.5")	
Dirks, Daggers, & Stilettos	Yes	Yes (<= 3.5")	
Automatic Knives	No	No	
Balisongs	No	No	

12.2 Discussion

Nestled amidst the majestic Rockies, visitors to Colorado will appreciate its scenic grandeur and Western heritage, reflected in the state's firearms-friendly laws. Those carrying knives, however, will find the state somewhat less friendly.

With respect to knives, concealed carry of fixed and folding knives should pose no problem, provided that the blades of such knives do not exceed three and a half inches in length. This limit is set by statute. Automatic knives such as ballistic knives, gravity knives, and switchblades are prohibited. Note that concealed carry of any knife, regardless of blade length, with the specific intent to use such knife as a weapon, is a violation of the statutory concealed carry prohibition as well.[21]

Open carry of knives with blades longer than three and a half inches is legal under state law, although travelers should note that some cities and towns restrict such carry. State law permits carry of weapons in private vehicles for lawful hunting or self-defense, and prohibits cities and towns from imposing additional restrictions on private vehicle carry.[22]

Colorado does not preempt its cities and towns from regulating knife carry. As such, cities and towns may impose their own additional restrictions concerning knife carry. In particular, travelers to the state's urban centers will generally find knife carry regulation more restrictive. For example, Denver prohibits both concealed and open carry of knives with blades greater than three and a half inches.[23]

---

[21] *See*, A.P.E. v. People, 20 P.3d. 1179 (Colo. 2001) (holding state must prove defendant's intent to use as weapon knife with blade less than 3 ½ inches for violation of concealed carry statute to occur).

[22] *See*, COLO. REV. STAT. ANN. § 18-12-105.6 (2005). While the state's general preemption statute, §§ 29-11.7-101 *et. seq.*, deals exclusively with firearms, the vehicle carry preemption statute appears to apply more broadly. *See, id.*

[23] *See*, DENVER REV. MUNICIPAL CODE § 38-117(a) & (b) (2006). Subsection (a) prohibits concealed carry, and subsection (b) prohibits open carry or knives with blades greater than 3 ½ inches. *Id.*

State law prohibits carry of "deadly weapon[s]," whose definition specifically includes knives, on school, college, or university grounds. Violation of this law is a felony. A separate section of the law defines a knife as "any dagger, dirk, knife, or stiletto with a blade over three and one-half inches in length...,"[24] so it would appear that knives with blades three and a half inches or less may be allowable.

12.3 Selected Statutes

COLO. REV. STAT. ANN. §§ (2005)

18-1-901. Definitions.

(3) ...

(e) "Deadly weapon" means any of the following which in the manner it is used or intended to be used is capable of producing death or serious bodily injury:

(I) A firearm, whether loaded or unloaded;

(II) A knife;

(III) A bludgeon; or

(IV) Any other weapon, device, instrument, material, or substance, whether animate or inanimate.

18-12-101. Definitions.

(1) As used in this article, unless the context otherwise requires:

(a.3) "Ballistic knife" means any knife that has a blade which is forcefully projected from the handle by means of a spring-loaded device or explosive charge.
...
(e) "Gravity knife" means any knife that has a blade released from the handle or sheath thereof by the force of gravity or the application of centrifugal force, that when released is locked in place by means of a button, spring, lever, or other device.
...
(f) "Knife" means any dagger, dirk, knife, or stiletto with a blade over three and one-half inches in length, or any other dangerous instrument capable of inflicting cutting, stabbing, or tearing wounds, but does not include a hunting or fishing knife carried for sports use. The issue that a knife is a hunting or fishing knife must be raised as an affirmative defense.
...
(j) "Switchblade knife" means any knife, the blade of which opens automatically by hand pressure applied to a button, spring, or other device in its handle.

18-12-105. Unlawfully carrying a concealed weapon - unlawful possession of weapons.

(1) A person commits a class 2 misdemeanor if such person knowingly and unlawfully:

(a) Carries a knife concealed on or about his or her person; or
...
(2) It shall not be an offense if the defendant was:

(a) A person in his or her own dwelling or place of business or on property owned or under his or her control at the time of the act of carrying; or

---

[24] *See,* COLO. REV. STAT. ANN. § 18-12-101 (1)(f) (2005)

(b) A person in a private automobile or other private means of conveyance who carries a weapon for lawful protection of such person's or another's person or property while traveling; or

(c) A person who, at the time of carrying a concealed weapon, held a valid written permit to carry a concealed weapon issued pursuant to section 18-12-105.1, as it existed prior to its repeal, or, if the weapon involved was a handgun, held a valid permit to carry a concealed handgun or a temporary emergency permit issued pursuant to part 2 of this article; except that it shall be an offense under this section if the person was carrying a concealed handgun in violation of the provisions of section 18-12-214; or

...

18-12-105.5. Unlawfully carrying a weapon - unlawful possession of weapons - school, college, or university grounds.

(1) A person commits a class 6 felony if such person knowingly and unlawfully and without legal authority carries, brings, or has in such person's possession a deadly weapon as defined in section 18-1-901 (3) (e) in or on the real estate and all improvements erected thereon of any public or private elementary, middle, junior high, high, or vocational school or any public or private college, university, or seminary, except for the purpose of presenting an authorized public demonstration or exhibition pursuant to instruction in conjunction with an organized school or class, for the purpose of carrying out the necessary duties and functions of an employee of an educational institution that require the use of a deadly weapon, or for the purpose of participation in an authorized extracurricular activity or on an athletic team.

...

12.4 Selected Caselaw
A.P.E. v. People, 20 P.3d 1179, 1186 (Colo. 2001) (holding intent to use knife with blade 3 ½ inches or less as weapon an element of offense of carrying concealed weapon).

12.5 Preemption Law
No knife law preemption, firearms law preemption only. *See*, COLO. REV. STAT. ANN. § 29-11.7-101 *et. seq.* (2005).

12.6 Places Off-Limits While Carrying
Colorado prohibits the carry of knives with blades over 3 ½ inches long on school or college grounds. In addition, cities and towns may further limit where such knives are carried on public property, and the manner of carry.

12.7 School/College Carry
Colorado prohibits the carry of knives with blades over 3 ½ inches long on school or college grounds.

12.8 Selected City Ordinances
Denver – Concealed or open carry of knives with blades greater than three and a half inches prohibited. *See*, DENVER, COLO., REV. MUNICIPAL CODE § 38-117 (2006). Exceptions for carry in private vehicle, home, bona fide hunting purpose, etc. exist. *See, id.* at § 38-118 (listing affirmative defenses to prosecution for violations of carry prohibitions).

Steamboat Springs – Concealed carry of knives with blades greater than three and a half inches prohibited. *See*, STEAMBOAT SPRINGS, COLO., REV. MUNICIPAL CODE § 10-169 (2005).

Open carry of knives with blades greater than three and a half inches prohibited, with certain exceptions such as bona fide hunting trip. *See, id.*

Englewood – Concealed carry of knives with blades greater than three and a half inches prohibited. *See*, ENGLEWOOD, COLO., MUNICIPAL CODE § 7-6C-1 (2005).

Boulder – Concealed carry of knives with blades greater than three and a half inches prohibited. *See*, BOULDER, COLO., REV. CODE § 5-8-9. Carry of deadly weapon prohibited in city council chambers while council in session, or in any public building posted as prohibiting carry. *See, id.* at § 5-8-15 (2003).

12.9 State Resources

Colorado State Patrol Headquarters
700 Kipling Street
Lakewood, CO 80215
Phone: (303) 239-4500
Website: http://www.csp.state.co.us/

Attorney General of Colorado
Department of Law
1525 Sherman 5th Floor
Denver, CO 80203
Phone: (303) 866-4500
Fax: (303) 866-5691
Website: http://www.ago.state.co.us/

13 Connecticut – The Constitution State

Area: 4,845 sq.mi. (Rank: 48th)   Population: 3,460,503 (Rank: 29th)
Violent Crime Rate (per 100,000 residents): 286.3 (Rank: 17th Safest)
State Motto: *Qui Transtulit Sustinet (He Who Transplanted Still Sustains)*

13.1 Knife Carry Law Summary

<u>Note:</u> Blade length limits, if any, in parentheses.

Knife Type	Open Carry	Concealed Carry	Notes
Folding Knives	Yes (< 4")	Yes (< 4")	
Fixed Bladed Knives	Yes (< 4")	Yes (< 4")	
Dirks, Daggers, & Stilettos	Yes (<= 1.5")	Yes (<= 1.5")	Stilettos are banned.
Automatic Knives	Yes (<= 1.5")	Yes (<= 1.5")	
Balisongs	Yes (<= 1.5")	Yes (<= 1.5")	

13.2 Discussion

Visitors to the Constitution State will find a somewhat restrictive legal environment for knife carry, particularly with regards to blade length.

With respect to knives, travelers to the Constitution State will find that carry of ordinary fixed and folding knives with blades less than the statutorily defined four inches should pose no problem. Dirks, daggers, and automatic knives, however, are restricted to blade lengths of one and a half inches or less. Carry of stilettos is banned. Knives such as balisongs, while not specifically prohibited, may fall under the switchblade restriction, as balisongs do in some states, and so be limited to blades of one and a half inches or less.

State law prohibits carry of deadly weapons on elementary and secondary school grounds. Violation of this statute is a felony. The definition of "deadly weapon" pertinent to this prohibition includes switchblades and gravity knives of any length.

Connecticut does not preempt its cities and towns from regulating knife carry. As such, cities and towns are free to impose additional restrictions on knife carry, although few municipalities appear to have done so.

13.3 Selected Statutes

Conn. Gen. Stat. §§ (2005)

Sec. 53a-3. Definitions. Except where different meanings are expressly specified, the following terms have the following meanings when used in this title:

...

(5) "Deadly physical force" means physical force which can be reasonably expected to cause death or serious physical injury;

(6) "Deadly weapon" means any weapon, whether loaded or unloaded, from which a shot may be discharged, or a switchblade knife, gravity knife, billy, blackjack, bludgeon, or metal knuckles. The definition of "deadly weapon" in this subdivision shall be deemed not to apply to section 29-38 or 53-206;

(7) "Dangerous instrument" means any instrument, article or substance which, under the circumstances in which it is used or attempted or threatened to be used, is capable of causing death or serious physical injury, and includes a "vehicle" as that term is defined in this section and includes a dog that has been commanded to attack, except a dog owned by a law enforcement agency of the state or any political subdivision thereof or of the federal government when such dog is in the performance of its duties under the direct supervision, care and control of an assigned law enforcement officer;

Sec. 53a-217b. Possession of a weapon on school grounds: Class D felony. (a) A person is guilty of possession of a weapon on school grounds when, knowing that such person is not licensed or privileged to do so, such person possesses a firearm or deadly weapon, as defined in section 53a-3, (1) in or on the real property comprising a public or private elementary or secondary school, or (2) at a school-sponsored activity as defined in subsection (h) of section 10-233a.

(b) The provisions of subsection (a) of this section shall not apply to the otherwise lawful possession of a firearm (1) by a person for use in a program approved by school officials in or on such school property or at such school-sponsored activity, (2) by a person in accordance with an agreement entered into between school officials and such person or such person's employer, (3) by a peace officer, as defined in subdivision (9) of section 53a-3, while engaged in the performance of such peace officer's official duties, or (4) by a person while traversing such school property for the purpose of gaining access to public or private lands open to hunting or for other lawful purposes, provided such firearm is not loaded and the entry on such school property is permitted by the local or regional board of education.

(c) Possession of a weapon on school grounds is a class D felony.

Sec. 53-206. Carrying of dangerous weapons prohibited. (a) Any person who carries upon his or her person any BB. gun, blackjack, metal or brass knuckles, or any dirk knife, or any switch knife, or any knife having an automatic spring release device by which a blade is released from the handle, having a blade of over one and one-half inches in length, or stiletto, or any knife the edged portion of the blade of which is four inches or over in length, any police baton or nightstick, or any martial arts weapon or electronic defense weapon, as defined in section 53a-3, or any other dangerous or deadly weapon or instrument, shall be fined not more than five hundred dollars or imprisoned not more than three years or both. Whenever any person is found guilty of a violation of this section, any weapon or other instrument within the provisions of this section, found upon the body of such person, shall be forfeited to the municipality wherein such person was apprehended, notwithstanding any failure of the judgment of conviction to expressly impose such forfeiture.

(b) The provisions of this section shall not apply to (1) any officer charged with the preservation of the public peace while engaged in the pursuit of such officer's official duties; (2) the carrying of a baton or nightstick by a security guard while engaged in the pursuit of such guard's official duties; (3) the carrying of a knife, the edged portion of the blade of which is four inches or over in length, by (A) any member of the armed forces of the United States, as defined in section 27-103, or any reserve component thereof, or of the armed forces of this state, as defined in section 27-2, when on duty or going to or from duty, (B) any member of any military organization when on parade or when going to or from any place of assembly, (C) any person while transporting such knife as merchandise or for display at an authorized gun or knife show, (D) any person who is found with any such knife concealed upon one's person while lawfully removing such person's household goods or effects from one place to another, or from one residence to another, (E) any person while actually and peaceably engaged in carrying any such knife from such person's place of abode or business to a place or person where or by whom such knife is to be repaired, or while actually and peaceably returning to such person's place of abode or business with such knife after the same has been repaired, (F) any person holding a valid hunting, fishing or trapping license issued pursuant to chapter 490 or any salt water fisherman carrying such knife for lawful hunting, fishing or trapping activities, or (G) any person while participating in an authorized historic reenactment; (4) the carrying by any person enrolled in or currently attending, or an instructor at, a martial arts school of a martial arts weapon while in a class or at an authorized event or competition or while transporting such weapon to or from such class, event or competition; (5) the carrying of a BB. gun by any person taking part in a supervised event or competition of the Boy Scouts of America or the Girl Scouts of America or in any other authorized event or competition while taking part in such event or competition or while transporting such weapon to or from such event or competition; and (6) the carrying of a BB. gun by any person upon such person's own property or the property of another person provided such other person has authorized the carrying of such weapon on such property, and the transporting of such weapon to or from such property.

Sec. 29-38. Weapons in vehicles. (a) Any person who knowingly has, in any vehicle owned, operated or occupied by such person, any weapon, any pistol or revolver for which a proper permit has not been issued as provided in section 29-28 or any machine gun which has not been registered as required by section 53-202, shall be fined not more than one thousand dollars or imprisoned not more than five years or both, and the presence of any such weapon, pistol or revolver, or machine gun in any vehicle shall be prima facie evidence of a violation of this section by the owner, operator and each occupant thereof. The word "weapon", as used in this section, means any BB. gun, any blackjack, any metal or brass knuckles, any police baton or nightstick, any dirk knife or switch knife, any knife having an automatic spring release device by which a blade is released from the handle, having a blade of over one and one-half inches in length, any stiletto, any knife the edged portion of the blade of which is four inches or over in length, any martial arts weapon or electronic defense weapon, as defined in section 53a-3, or any other dangerous or deadly weapon or instrument.

(b) The provisions of this section shall not apply to: (1) Any officer charged with the preservation of the public peace while engaged in the pursuit of such officer's official duties; (2) any security guard having a baton or nightstick in a vehicle while engaged in the pursuit of such guard's official duties; (3) any person enrolled in and currently attending a martial arts school, with official verification of such enrollment and attendance, or any certified martial arts instructor, having any such martial arts weapon in a vehicle while traveling to or from such school or to or from an authorized event or competition; (4) any person having a BB. gun in a vehicle provided such weapon is unloaded and stored in the trunk of such vehicle or in a locked container other than the glove compartment or console; and (5) any person having a knife, the edged portion of the blade of which is four inches or over in length, in a vehicle if such person is (A) any member of the armed forces of the United States, as defined in section 27-103, or any reserve component thereof, or of the armed forces of this state, as defined in section 27-2, when on duty or going to or from duty, (B) any member of any military organization when on parade or when going to or from any place of assembly, (C) any person while transporting such knife as merchandise or for display at an authorized gun or knife show, (D) any person while lawfully removing such person's household goods or effects from one place to another, or from one residence to another, (E) any person while actually and peaceably engaged in carrying any such knife from such person's place of abode or business to a place or person where or by whom such knife is to be repaired, or while actually and peaceably returning to such person's place of abode or business with such knife after the same has been repaired, (F) any person holding a valid hunting, fishing or trapping license issued pursuant to chapter 490 or any salt water fisherman while having such knife in a vehicle for lawful hunting, fishing or trapping activities, or (G) any person participating in an authorized historic reenactment.

13.4 Selected Caselaw

State v. Ramos, 271 Conn. 785, 798 (2004) (holding state need not prove prior intent to use item as dangerous instrument for conviction of weapon in vehicle statute).

State v. Holloway, 11 Conn. App. 665, 669 (1987) (upholding trial court's determination that 3 ½ inch knife can support prosecution for carrying dangerous weapon).

13.5 Preemption Law

No knife law preemption.

13.6 Places Off-Limits While Carrying

State law prohibits carry of deadly weapons on elementary and secondary school grounds. Violation of this statute is a felony. The definition of "deadly weapon" includes switchblades and gravity knives of any length. Cities and towns may impose their own restrictions.

13.7 School/College Carry

State law prohibits carry of deadly weapons on elementary and secondary school grounds. Violation of this statute is a felony. The definition of "deadly weapon" relevant to this prohibition includes switchblades and gravity knives of any length.

13.8 Selected City Ordinances

Cheshire – Carry of any weapon, including deadly weapon or dangerous instruments prohibited in public parks or recreational facilities, regardless of whether carrier has a permit. *See*, CHESHIRE, CONN., CODE OF ORD. § 11-20 (2004).

13.9 State Resources

Department of Public Safety
Division of State Police
1111 Country Club Road
Middletown, CT 06457-9294
Phone: (860) 685-8000
Fax: (860) 685-8354
Website: http://www.state.ct.us/dps/CSP.htm

Attorney General of Connecticut
55 Elm Street
Hartford, CT 06106
Phone: (860) 808-5318
Fax: (860) 808-5387
Website: http://www.cslib.org/attygenl/

14   Delaware – The First State

Area: 1,954 sq.mi. (Rank: 49th)   Population: 807,385 (Rank: 45th)
Violent Crime Rate (per 100,000 residents): 568.4 (Rank: 42nd Safest)
State Motto: *Liberty and Independence*

14.1 Knife Carry Law Summary

<u>Note</u>: Blade length limits, if any, in parentheses.

Knife Type	Open Carry	Concealed Carry	Notes
Folding Knives	Yes	Yes (<= 3")	> 3" concealed with permit.
Fixed Bladed Knives	Yes	No	Concealed with permit ok.
Dirks, Daggers, & Stilettos	Yes	No	Concealed with permit ok.
Automatic Knives	No	No	See note[25]
Balisongs	No	No	

14.2 Discussion

Visitors to Delaware, the first state to sign the Declaration of Independence, will find the state typical of its Eastern brethren when it comes to laws governing knife carry.

State law allows ordinary fixed and folding knives to be carried openly, although carry of large fixed bladed knives should be avoided in urban areas, due to the likelihood of unwanted law enforcement attention. Ordinary folding pocket knives with blades three inches or less may be carried concealed without a permit. Note that the Delaware Supreme Court has held that blade length measurement includes the *entire* length of the blade from the tip to the handle, and includes any unsharpened portion.[26]

Concealed carry of knives with longer blades requires a concealed weapon permit issued or otherwise recognized by the state. Delaware provides for reciprocity for other states' permits that meet certain statutory requirements. Travelers wishing to determine whether Delaware recognizes a particular state's permit may contact the Delaware Attorney General.

State law bans automatic knives, the definition of which includes gravity knives. Knives such as balisongs, while not specifically prohibited, may fall under the switchblade ban (as balisongs do in some states), so the careful traveler would do well to avoid carry of such knives in the state.

State law prohibits carry on educational institution property and school or municipal recreational facilities, such as sports stadiums, athletic fields, etc. An exception exists, however, for legitimate educational instruction, sporting or recreational use.

---

[25] Even though Delaware law provides for the issuance of a concealed weapons permit, which by the statute's wording authorizes the holder to carry deadly weapons concealed, the statute appears to envision, and deals primarily with, firearms. *See*, DEL. CODE tit. 11 § 1441 (2006). Furthermore, Title 11, § 1446 appears to completely ban even mere possession of switchblades, the definition of which includes gravity knives. *See*, DEL CODE tit. 11 § 1446 (2006). The cautious traveler would thus be well advised to avoid carry or possession of switchblades or gravity knives in the state.

[26] *See*, State v. Harmon, No. 606-2001 (Del. Supr. 2002) (reinstating conviction for weapons offense for possession of knife with blade greater than three inches long).

14.3 Selected Statutes

DEL. CODE. TIT. 11 §§ (2006)

§ 222. General definitions.

When used in this Criminal Code:

...

(4) "Dangerous instrument" means any instrument, article or substance which, under the circumstances in which it is used, attempted to be used or threatened to be used, is readily capable of causing death or serious physical injury, or any disabling chemical spray, as defined in subdivision (6) of this section.

(5) "Deadly weapon" includes a firearm, as defined in subdivision (11) of this section, a bomb, a knife of any sort (other than an ordinary pocketknife carried in a closed position), switchblade knife, billy, blackjack, bludgeon, metal knuckles, slingshot, razor, bicycle chain or ice pick or any dangerous instrument, as defined in subdivision (4) of this section, which is used, or attempted to be used, to cause death or serious physical injury. For the purpose of this definition, an ordinary pocketknife shall be a folding knife having a blade not more than 3 inches in length.

§ 1442. Carrying a concealed deadly weapon; class G felony; class E felony.

A person is guilty of carrying a concealed deadly weapon when the person carries concealed a deadly weapon upon or about the person without a license to do so as provided by § 1441 of this title.

Carrying a concealed deadly weapon is a class G felony, unless the accused has been convicted within the previous 5 years of the same offense, in which case it is a class E felony. (11 Del. C. 1953, § 1442; 58 Del. Laws, c. 497, § 1; 59 Del. Laws, c. 547, § 13; 67 Del. Laws, c. 130, § 8; 70 Del. Laws, c. 186, § 1.)

§ 1443. Carrying a concealed dangerous instrument; class A misdemeanor.

(a) A person is guilty of carrying a concealed dangerous instrument when the person carries concealed a dangerous instrument upon or about the person.

(b) It shall be a defense that the defendant was carrying the concealed dangerous instrument for a specific lawful purpose and that the defendant had no intention of causing any physical injury or threatening the same.

(c) For the purposes of this section, disabling chemical spray, as defined in § 222 of this title, shall not be considered to be a dangerous instrument.

(d) Carrying a concealed dangerous instrument is a class A misdemeanor. (11 Del. C. 1953, § 1443; 58 Del. Laws, c. 497, § 1; 59 Del. Laws, c. 547, § 14; 67 Del. Laws, c. 130, § 8; 70 Del. Laws, c. 186, § 1; 71 Del. Laws, c. 374, § 6.)

§ 1446. Unlawfully dealing with a switchblade knife; unclassified misdemeanor.

A person is guilty of unlawfully dealing with a switchblade knife when the person sells, offers for sale or has in possession a knife, the blade of which is released by a spring mechanism or by gravity.

Unlawfully dealing with a switchblade knife is an unclassified misdemeanor. (11 Del. C. 1953, § 1446; 58 Del. Laws, c. 497, § 1; 67 Del. Laws, c. 130, § 8; 70 Del. Laws, c. 186, § 1.)

§ 1452. Unlawfully dealing with knuckles-combination knife; class B misdemeanor.

A person is guilty of unlawfully dealing with a knuckles-combination knife when the person sells, offers for sale or has in possession a knife, the blade of which is supported by a knuckle ring grip handle.

Unlawfully dealing with a knuckles-combination knife is a class B misdemeanor. (65 Del. Laws, c. 465, § 1; 67 Del. Laws, c. 130, § 8; 70 Del. Laws, c. 186, § 1.)

§ 1457. Possession of a weapon in a Safe School and Recreation Zone; class D, E, or F: class A or B misdemeanor.

(a) Any person who commits any of the offenses described in subsection (b) of this section, or any juvenile who possesses a firearm or other deadly weapon, and does so while in or on a "Safe School and Recreation Zone" shall be guilty of the crime of possession of a weapon in a Safe School and Recreation Zone.

(b) The underlying offenses in Title 11 shall be:

(1) Section 1442. Carrying a concealed deadly weapon; class G felony; class E felony.

(2) Section 1444. Possessing a destructive weapon; class E felony.

(3) Section 1446. Unlawfully dealing with a switchblade knife; unclassified misdemeanor.

(4) Section 1448. Possession and purchase of deadly weapons by persons prohibited; class F felony.

(5) Section 1452. Unlawfully dealing with knuckles-combination knife; class B misdemeanor.

(6) Section 1453. Unlawfully dealing with martial arts throwing star; class B misdemeanor.

(c) For the purpose of this section, "Safe School and Recreation Zone" shall mean:

(1) Any building, structure, athletic field, sports stadium or real property owned, operated, leased or rented by any public or private school including, but not limited to, any kindergarten, elementary, secondary or vocational-technical school or any college or university, within 1,000 feet thereof; or

(2) Any motor vehicle owned, operated, leased or rented by any public or private school including, but not limited to, any kindergarten, elementary, secondary, or vocational-technical school or any college or university; or

(3) Any building or structure owned, operated, leased or rented by any county or municipality, or by the State, or by any board, agency, commission, department, corporation or other entity thereof, or by any private organization, which is utilized as a recreation center, athletic field or sports stadium.

(d) Nothing in this section shall be construed to preclude or otherwise limit a prosecution of or conviction for a violation of this chapter or any other provision of law. A person may be convicted both of the crime of possession of a weapon in a Safe School and Recreation Zone and of the underlying offense as defined elsewhere by the laws of the State.

(e) It shall not be a defense to a prosecution for a violation of this section that the person was unaware that the prohibited conduct took place on or in a Safe School and Recreation Zone.

(f) It shall be an affirmative defense to a prosecution for a violation of this section that the weapon was possessed pursuant to an authorized course of school instruction, or for the purpose of engaging in any legitimate sporting or recreational activity. The affirmative defense established in this section shall be proved by a preponderance of the evidence. Nothing herein shall be construed to establish an affirmative defense with respect to a prosecution for any offense defined in any other section of this chapter.

(g) It is an affirmative defense to prosecution for a violation of this section that the prohibited conduct took place entirely within a private residence, and that no person under the age of 18 was present in such private residence at any time during the commission of the offense. The affirmative defense established in this section shall be proved by the defendant by a preponderance of the evidence. Nothing herein shall be construed to establish an affirmative defense with respect to a prosecution for an offense defined in any other section of this chapter.

(h) This section shall not apply to any law enforcement or police officer, or to any security officer as defined in Chapter 13 of Title 24.

(i) For purposes of this section only, "deadly weapon" shall include any object described in § 222(6) or § 222(11) of this title or BB guns.

(j) The penalty for possession of a weapon in a Safe School and Recreation Zone shall be:

(1) If the underlying offense is a class B misdemeanor, the crime shall be a class A misdemeanor;

(2) If the underlying offense is an unclassified misdemeanor, the crime shall be a class B misdemeanor;

(3) If the underlying offense is a class E, F, or G felony, the crime shall be one grade higher than the underlying offense.

(4) In the event that an elementary or secondary school student possesses a firearm or other deadly weapon in a Safe School and Recreation Zone in addition to any other penalties contained in this section, the student shall be expelled by the local School Board or charter school board of directors for a period of not less than 180 days unless otherwise provided for in federal or state law. (70 Del. Laws, c. 213, § 1; 74 Del. Laws, c. 131, §§ 1-4.)

14.4 Selected Caselaw

State v. Harmon, Case No. 606-2001 (Del. 2002) (reinstating conviction for weapons offense for pocket knife with blade greater than three inches, and finding blade length includes entire length of blade, including unsharpened portion).

14.5 Preemption Law

No knife law preemption, firearms law preemption only. *See*, Del. Code tit. 22 § 835 (2006).

14.6 Places Off-Limits While Carrying

Delaware prohibits the carry of firearms and other deadly weapons, the definition of which includes knives other than ordinary pocket knives with blades three inches or less in length, on school grounds or school or municipal recreational facilities. *See*, Del Code tit. 11 § 1457 (2006).

14.7 School/College Carry

Delaware prohibits the carry of firearms and other deadly weapons, the definition of which includes knives other than ordinary pocket knives with blades three inches or less in length, on school grounds or school or municipal recreational facilities. *See*, Del Code tit. 11 § 1457 (2006).

14.8 Selected City Ordinances

Dover – Carry of knives of any type or length without permit prohibited. *See*, Dover , Del., Code of Ordinances § 70-2 (2006).

14.9 State Resources

Delaware State Police
P.O. Box 430
Dover, DE 9903-0430
Phone: (302) 739-5901
Website: http://www.state.de.us/dsp/

Attorney General of Delaware
Carvel State Office Building
820 N. French Street
Wilmington, DE 19801
Phone: (302) 577-8400
Website: http://www.state.de.us/attgen/index.htm

15 District of Columbia – D.C.

Area: 68.25 sq.mi. (Rank: N/A)   Population: 572,059 (Rank: N/A)
Violent Crime Rate (per 100,000 residents): 1,371.2 (Rank: N/A)
State Motto: *Justia Omnibus (Justice for All)*

15.1 Knife Carry Law Summary

Note: Blade length limits, if any, in parentheses.

Knife Type	Open Carry	Concealed Carry	Notes
Folding Knives	Yes (<= 3")	Yes (<= 3")	
Fixed Bladed Knives	No	No	
Dirks, Daggers, & Stilettos	No	No	
Automatic Knives	No	No	
Balisongs	No	No	

15.2 Discussion

Visitors to our nation's capital will encounter a decidedly hostile legal environment for knife carry. The District of Columbia, which has the dubious distinction of being one of the most violent cities in the country (if D.C. was a state, it would be the most violent state by a wide margin), has enacted a fairly draconian series of laws ostensibly designed to curb violent crime. For example, D.C. law prohibits carry on or about the person, whether open or concealed, of any deadly or dangerous weapon.[27] Period. Even in your own home.[28] Carry in public of any such weapon is a felony, punishable by up to five years in prison.[29]

Another statute prohibits possession, with intent to use unlawfully against another, of any dagger, dirk, stiletto, razor, or knife with a blade greater than three inches long, or other dangerous weapon.[30] While technically the Code permits possession (but not carry) of such knives so long as the possessor has no intent to use them unlawfully against another, as a practical matter, and as is the case in some states with similar statutes, unlawful intent will often be presumed, especially for larger or aggressive looking knives.

Switchblades are prohibited. Balisongs, while not specifically listed as a prohibited knife, may fall under the switchblade prohibition, as balisongs do in some states. In addition, balisongs are often associated with, and perceived as, martial arts weapons. As such, visitors should avoid carry of balisongs in the District.

In addition to the broad carry prohibitions already codified in the D.C. Code, many buildings in the District are home to government agencies and institutions, many of which prohibit weapons under their own regulatory authority, or which are federal buildings and thus are

---

[27] *See,* D.C. CODE ANN. § 22-4504 (2006).

[28] *See, id.* The current statute, strictly interpreted, reads that carry in your home is a misdemeanor (less than one year in prison), while carry outside your home (or fixed place of business, etc.) is a felony punishable by up to five years in prison. *See, id.* Interestingly, a predecessor statute did have an exception for carry at home, fixed place of business, etc. *See, e.g,* Monroe v. U.S., 598 A.2d 439, note 1 (D.C. 1991) (citing predecessor statute).

[29] *See,* D.C. CODE ANN. § 22-4504 (2006).

[30] *See, id.* at § 22-4514.

subject to the weapon-related statutes pertaining to such buildings and facilities.[31] Weapons are also prohibited in such places as, e.g., Capitol grounds. D.C. law incorporates enhanced penalties for firearms possession on school property, although apparently not for other dangerous weapons such as knives. Of course, such possession is prohibited, and is already subject to harsh penalties.

15.3 Selected Statutes

D.C. CODE ANN. §§ (2006)

§ 22-4502. Additional penalty for committing crime when armed.

(a) Any person who commits a crime of violence, or a dangerous crime in the District of Columbia when armed with or having readily available any pistol or other firearm (or imitation thereof) or other dangerous or deadly weapon (including a sawed-off shotgun, shotgun, machine gun, rifle, dirk, bowie knife, butcher knife, switchblade knife, razor, blackjack, billy, or metallic or other false knuckles):

(1) May, if such person is convicted for the first time of having so committed a crime of violence, or a dangerous crime in the District of Columbia, be sentenced, in addition to the penalty provided for such crime, to a period of imprisonment which may be up to, and including, 30 years for all offenses except first degree murder while armed, second degree murder while armed, first degree sexual abuse while armed, and first degree child sexual abuse while armed, and shall, if convicted of such offenses while armed with any pistol or firearm, be imprisoned for a mandatory-minimum term of not less than 5 years; and

...

§ 22-4504. Carrying concealed weapons; possession of weapons during commission of crime of violence; penalty.

(a) No person shall carry within the District of Columbia either openly or concealed on or about their person, a pistol, without a license issued pursuant to District of Columbia law, or any deadly or dangerous weapon capable of being so concealed. Whoever violates this section shall be punished as provided in § 22-4515, except that:

(1) A person who violates this section by carrying a pistol, without a license issued pursuant to District of Columbia law, or any deadly or dangerous weapon, in a place other than the person's dwelling place, place of business, or on other land possessed by the person, shall be fined not more than $5,000 or imprisoned for not more than 5 years, or both; or

...

§ 22-4514. Possession of certain dangerous weapons prohibited; exceptions.

(a) No person shall within the District of Columbia possess any machine gun, sawed-off shotgun, or any instrument or weapon of the kind commonly known as a blackjack, slungshot, sand club, sandbag, switchblade knife, or metal knuckles, nor any instrument, attachment, or appliance for causing the firing of any firearm to be silent or intended to lessen or muffle the noise of the firing of any firearms; provided, however, that machine guns, or sawed-off shotguns, and blackjacks may be possessed by the members of the Army, Navy, Air Force, or Marine Corps of the United States, the National Guard, or Organized Reserves when on duty, the Post Office Department or its employees when on duty, marshals, sheriffs, prison or jail wardens, or their deputies, policemen, or other duly-appointed law enforcement officers, including any designated civilian employee of the Metropolitan Police Department, or officers or employees of the United States duly authorized to carry such weapons, banking institutions, public carriers who are engaged in the business of transporting mail, money, securities, or other valuables, wholesale dealers and retail dealers licensed under § 22-4510.

(b) No person shall within the District of Columbia possess, with intent to use unlawfully against another, an imitation pistol, or a dagger, dirk, razor, stiletto, or knife with a blade longer than 3 inches, or other dangerous weapon.

---

[31] *See supra* Section 5 for a discussion of federal knife-related law.

(c) Whoever violates this section shall be punished as provided in § 22-4515 unless the violation occurs after such person has been convicted in the District of Columbia of a violation of this section, or of a felony, either in the District of Columbia or in another jurisdiction, in which case such person shall be imprisoned for not more than 10 years.

15.4 Selected Caselaw

Coleman v. U.S., 619 A.2d 40 (D.C. 1993) (affirming conviction for carrying dangerous weapon, buck knife with three and a half inch blade, and explaining that "time and place of possession and absence of conceivable legitimate reason for carrying a weapon pertinent to inquiry of weapon's dangerousness" (quoting *In re S.P.*, 465 A.2d. 823, 826 (D.C. 1983))).

Mihas v. U.S., 618 A.2d 197 (D.C. 1992) (affirming convictions for, *inter alia*, possession of prohibited weapon and carrying deadly or dangerous weapon, paring knife with two and three-quarters inch blade).

McIntyre v. U.S., 283 A.2d 814 (D.C. 1971) (affirming conviction for possession of prohibited weapon, knife with blade length exceeding statutory three inch limit "by a fraction of an inch", and with cutting edge less than three inches).

Monroe v. U.S., 598 A.2d 439 (D.C. 1991) (affirming conviction under predecessor statute for carrying deadly or dangerous weapon in public place, Ka-Bar knife with blade over six inches long, and indicating that reasonable juror could have found design of knife, time, place, conduct of defendant, and defendant's expressed purpose for carrying knife, *inter alia*, justify conclusion that intent was to use as dangerous weapon).

15.5 Preemption Law
Not applicable.

15.6 Places Off-Limits While Carrying
In addition to the broad carry prohibitions already codified in the D.C. Code, many buildings in the District are home to government agencies and institutions, many of which prohibit weapons under their own regulatory authority, or which are federal buildings and thus are subject to the weapon-related statutes pertaining to such buildings and facilities. Weapons are also prohibited in such places as, e.g., Capitol grounds. D.C. law incorporates enhanced penalties for firearms possession on school property, although apparently not for other dangerous weapons such as knives. Of course, such possession is prohibited, and is already subject to harsh penalties.

15.7 School/College Carry
D.C. law incorporates enhanced penalties for firearms possession on school property, although apparently not for other dangerous weapons such as knives. Of course, such possession is prohibited, and is already subject to harsh penalties.

15.8 Selected City Ordinances
Not applicable.

15.9 State Resources

Metropolitan Police Department
300 Indiana Avenue, NW
Washington, DC 20001
Phone: (202) 727-4218
Fax: (202) 727-9524
Website: http://mpdc.dc.gov/main.shtm

Office of Corporation Counsel
441 4th Street, NW, Suite 1060N
Washington, DC 20001
Phone: (202) 727-3400
Website: http://occ.dc.gov/occ/site/default.asp

16   Florida – The Sunshine State

Area: 53,927 sq.mi. (Rank: 26th)   Population: 16,713,149 (Rank: 4th)
Violent Crime Rate (per 100,000 residents): 711.3 (Rank: 49th Safest)
State Motto: *In God We Trust*

16.1 Knife Carry Law Summary

Note: Blade length limits, if any, in parentheses.

Knife Type	Open Carry	Concealed Carry	Notes
Folding Knives	Yes	Yes	See note[32]
Fixed Bladed Knives	Yes	No	Concealed with permit ok.
Dirks, Daggers, & Stilettos	Yes	No	Concealed with permit ok.
Automatic Knives	Yes	No	Concealed with permit ok.
Balisongs	Yes	No	Concealed with permit ok.

16.2 Discussion

Visitors to the Sunshine State will find a generally hospitable legal environment for knife carry so long as the visitor possesses a recognized permit. The law provides an exception for "common pocketknives" to the prohibition against concealed carry of weapons without a permit. Unfortunately, Florida courts have struggled to define what exactly constitutes a "common pocketknife," and so the cautious traveler would be wise to avoid overly "large" or "aggressive" looking folders.

Folding pocket knives that do not meet the definition of "common pocketknife" may still be carried concealed if the carrier possesses a valid concealed weapon permit. Fortunately, Florida recognizes a large number of out-of-state permits. Concealed carry of fixed blades, dirks, daggers, stilettos, and automatic knives is prohibited without a permit, although open carry is legal.

State law bans carry on school property. Florida does not preempt its cities and towns from regulating knife carry, unlike the case for firearms, where the state has prohibited cities and towns from enacting their own firearms carry restrictions, ensuring uniform state-wide firearms laws. As such, municipalities may pass their own additional knife carry restrictions, although not many appear to have done so.

16.3 Selected Statutes

FLA. STAT. CHS. (2005)

790.001   Definitions.--As used in this chapter, except where the context otherwise requires:

...

(3)(a) "Concealed weapon" means any dirk, metallic knuckles, slungshot, billie, tear gas gun, chemical weapon or device, or other deadly weapon carried on or about a person in such a manner as to conceal the weapon from the ordinary sight of another person.

---

[32] Concealed carry of a "common pocketknife" is legal, although case law relating to what exactly that term means is not definitive, and in some cases, conflicting. Concealed carry of folding knives that do not meet the definition of "common pocketknife" is, however, legal with a concealed weapon permit.

...

(13) "Weapon" means any dirk, metallic knuckles, slungshot, billie, tear gas gun, chemical weapon or device, or other deadly weapon except a firearm or a common pocketknife.

790.01 Carrying concealed weapons.--

(1) Except as provided in subsection (4), a person who carries a concealed weapon or electric weapon or device on or about his or her person commits a misdemeanor of the first degree, punishable as provided in s. 775.082 or s. 775.083.

(2) A person who carries a concealed firearm on or about his or her person commits a felony of the third degree, punishable as provided in s. 775.082, s. 775.083, or s. 775.084.

(3) This section does not apply to a person licensed to carry a concealed weapon or a concealed firearm pursuant to the provisions of s. 790.06.

790.06 License to carry concealed weapon or firearm.--

(1) The Department of Agriculture and Consumer Services is authorized to issue licenses to carry concealed weapons or concealed firearms to persons qualified as provided in this section. Each such license must bear a color photograph of the licensee. For the purposes of this section, concealed weapons or concealed firearms are defined as a handgun, electronic weapon or device, tear gas gun, knife, or billie, but the term does not include a machine gun as defined in s. 790.001(9). Such licenses shall be valid throughout the state for a period of 5 years from the date of issuance. Any person in compliance with the terms of such license may carry a concealed weapon or concealed firearm notwithstanding the provisions of s. 790.01. The licensee must carry the license, together with valid identification, at all times in which the licensee is in actual possession of a concealed weapon or firearm and must display both the license and proper identification upon demand by a law enforcement officer. Violations of the provisions of this subsection shall constitute a noncriminal violation with a penalty of $25, payable to the clerk of the court.

16.4 Selected Caselaw

L.B. v. State, 700 So. 2d 370 (Fla. 1997) (holding term "common pocketknife" not unconstitutionally vague and pocket knife with three and a half inch blade met statutory exception to weapon definition).

Bunkley v. State, 882 So. 2d 890 (Fla. 2004) (affirming conviction based on jury's finding that folding pocket knife with 2 ½ to 3 inch blade was dangerous weapon, despite statutory "common pocketknife" exception to weapon definition).

16.5 Preemption Law

No knife law preemption, firearms law preemption only. *See*, FLA. STAT. CH. 790.33 (2005).

16.6 Places Off-Limits While Carrying

Florida law prohibits carry on school grounds. *See*, FLA. STAT. CH. 790.115 (2005). In addition, towns and cities may pass their own local ordinances prohibiting or otherwise restricting knife carry in other areas within their jurisdictions.

16.7 School/College Carry

Florida law prohibits carry on school grounds. *See*, FLA. STAT. CH. 790.115 (2005).

16.8 Selected City Ordinances

Metropolitan Miami-Dade County – Carry of dirks, daggers, bowie knives, switchblades, or other "dangerous or deadly weapon[s]" prohibited. *See,* METRO. MIAMI-DADE COUNTY, FLA., CODE § 21-14 (2005).

Sarasota – Carry of any "dirk ... or other weapon," other than "common pocket knife," prohibited within city limits. *See,* SARASOTA, FLA., CODE OF ORDINANCES § 21-143 (2005).

16.9 State Resources

Florida Department of Law Enforcement
P.O. Box 1489
Tallahassee, FL 32302-1489
Phone: (850) 410-7000
E-Mail: info@fdle.state.fl.us
Website: http://www.fdle.state.fl.us/

Attorney General of Florida
Office of Attorney General
Tallahasse, FL 32399-1050
Phone: (850) 487-1963
Fax: (850) 487-2564
Website: http://myfloridalegal.com/

17 Georgia – The Peach State

Area: 57,906 sq.mi. (Rank: 21st)   Population: 8,560,310 (Rank: 10th)
Violent Crime Rate (per 100,000 residents): 455.5 (Rank: 32nd Safest)
State Motto: *Wisdom, Justice, and Moderation*

17.1 Knife Carry Law Summary

Note: Blade length limits, if any, in parentheses.

Knife Type	Open Carry	Concealed Carry	Notes
Folding Knives	Yes	Yes	See note[33]
Fixed Bladed Knives	Yes	No	Local restrictions may apply
Dirks, Daggers, & Stilettos	Yes	No	Local restrictions may apply
Automatic Knives	Yes	No	Local restrictions may apply
Balisongs	Yes	No	Local restrictions may apply

17.2 Discussion

Visitors to the Peach State will find that state law prohibits concealed carry of knives "designed for the purpose of offense and defense." Thus, cautious travelers would be well advised to avoid concealed carry of so-called "tactical" knives that appear overly aggressive or weapon-like. Open carry, however, is legal. Note, however, that Georgia does not preempt its cities and towns from regulating knife carry, and so municipalities may impose additional, more restrictive requirements on knife carry within their jurisdictions. For example, Atlanta prohibits carry of automatic knives with blades more than two inches, or any other knife with a blade more than three inches.

State law prohibits carry of dirks, bowie knives, switchblades, ballistic knives, straight razors, and razor blades of any blade length, or any other knife with a blade of two or more inches on school grounds.

17.3 Selected Statutes

Ga. Code §§ (2005)

16-11-126.

(a) A person commits the offense of carrying a concealed weapon when such person knowingly has or carries about his or her person, unless in an open manner and fully exposed to view, any bludgeon, metal knuckles, firearm, knife designed for the purpose of offense and defense, or any other dangerous or deadly weapon or instrument of like character outside of his or her home or place of business, except as permitted under this Code section.

(b) Upon conviction of the offense of carrying a concealed weapon, a person shall be punished as follows:

(1) For the first offense, he or she shall be guilty of a misdemeanor; and

(2) For the second offense, and for any subsequent offense, he or she shall be guilty of a felony and, upon conviction thereof, shall be imprisoned for not less than two years and not more than five years.

---

[33] State law prohibits concealed carry of any knife "designed for the purpose of offense and defense." *See*, Ga. Code § 16-11-126 (2005). Travelers should thus exercise caution when describing the reasons for concealed carry of a particular knife, and should avoid concealed carry of "tactical" type folders.

16-11-127.

(a) Except as provided in Code Section 16-11-127.1, a person is guilty of a misdemeanor when he or she carries to or while at a public gathering any explosive compound, firearm, or knife designed for the purpose of offense and defense.

(b) For the purpose of this Code section, 'public gathering' shall include, but shall not be limited to, athletic or sporting events, churches or church functions, political rallies or functions, publicly owned or operated buildings, or establishments at which alcoholic beverages are sold for consumption on the premises. Nothing in this Code section shall otherwise prohibit the carrying of a firearm in any other public place by a person licensed or permitted to carry such firearm by this part.

(c) This Code section shall not apply to competitors participating in organized sport shooting events. Law enforcement officers, peace officers retired from state or federal law enforcement agencies, judges, magistrates, solicitors-general, and district attorneys may carry pistols in publicly owned or operated buildings.

(d) It is an affirmative defense to a violation of this Code section if a person notifies a law enforcement officer or other person employed to provide security for a public gathering of the presence of such item as soon as possible after learning of its presence and surrenders or secures such item as directed by the law enforcement officer or other person employed to provide security for a public gathering.

16-11-127.1.

(a) As used in this Code section, the term:

(1) 'School safety zone' means in, on, or within 1,000 feet of any real property owned by or leased to any public or private elementary school, secondary school, or school board and used for elementary or secondary education and in, on, or within 1,000 feet of the campus of any public or private technical school, vocational school, college, university, or institution of postsecondary education.

(2) 'Weapon' means and includes any pistol, revolver, or any weapon designed or intended to propel a missile of any kind, or any dirk, bowie knife, switchblade knife, ballistic knife, any other knife having a blade of two or more inches, straight-edge razor, razor blade, spring stick, metal knucks, blackjack, any bat, club, or other bludgeon-type weapon, or any flailing instrument consisting of two or more rigid parts connected in such a manner as to allow them to swing freely, which may be known as a nun chahka, nun chuck, nunchaku, shuriken, or fighting chain, or any disc, of whatever configuration, having at least two points or pointed blades which is designed to be thrown or propelled and which may be known as a throwing star or oriental dart, or any weapon of like kind, and any stun gun or taser as defined in subsection (a) of Code Section 16-11-106. This paragraph excludes any of these instruments used for classroom work authorized by the teacher.

(b) Except as otherwise provided in subsection (c) of this Code section, it shall be unlawful for any person to carry to or to possess or have under such person's control while within a school safety zone or at a school building, school function, or school property or on a bus or other transportation furnished by the school any weapon or explosive compound, other than fireworks the possession of which is regulated by Chapter 10 of Title 25. Any person who violates this subsection shall be guilty of a felony and, upon conviction thereof, be punished by a fine of not more than $10,000.00, by imprisonment for not less than two nor more than ten years, or both; provided, however, that upon conviction of a violation of this subsection involving a firearm as defined in paragraph (2) of subsection (a) of Code Section 16-11-131, or a dangerous weapon or machine gun as defined in Code Section 16-11-121, such person shall be punished by a fine of not more than $10,000.00 or by imprisonment for a period of not less than five nor more than ten years, or both. A child who violates this subsection shall be subject to the provisions of Code Section 15-11-63.

...

17.4 Selected Caselaw

Sinclair v. State, 248 Ga. App. 132, 546 SE2d 7 (2001) (affirming concealed weapon conviction for possession of "razor carpet knife").

17.5 Preemption Law

No knife law preemption, firearms law preemption only. *See*, GA. CODE § 16-11-173 (2005).

17.6 Places Off-Limits While Carrying

State law prohibits carry of dirks, bowie knives, switchblades, ballistic knives, straight razors, and razor blades of any blade length, or any other knife with a blade of two or more inches on school grounds. Violation of this law is a felony, with a two year mandatory minimum sentence. *See*, GA. CODE § 16-11-127.1 (2005). In addition, towns and cities may pass their own more restrictive local ordinances prohibiting carry.

17.7 School/College Carry

State law prohibits carry of dirks, bowie knives, switchblades, ballistic knives, straight razors, and razor blades of any blade length, or any other knife with a blade of two or more inches. Violation of this law is a felony, with a two year mandatory minimum sentence. *See*, GA. CODE § 16-11-127.1 (2005). In addition, towns and cities may pass their own more restrictive local ordinances prohibiting carry.

17.8 Selected City Ordinances

Atlanta – Sale of dirks, bowie knives, and switchblades prohibited. *See*, ATLANTA, GA., CODE OF ORDINANCES § 106-305 (2006). Carry, whether open or concealed, of automatic knives with blades more than two inches, or any other knife with a blade more than three inches prohibited. *See, id.* at § 106-306. Carry of any knife, regardless of blade length, prohibited at parades or public assemblies. *See, id.* at § 138-236.

Macon – Carry of automatic knives with blade over two inches, any other knife with a blade more than three inches, razors and ice picks prohibited. *See*, MACON, GA., CODE OF ORDINANCES § 13-26 (2005).

17.9 State Resources

Georgia Bureau of Investigation
3121 Panthersville Road
Decatur, GA 30037-0808
Phone: (404) 244-2639
Website: http://www.state.ga.us/gbi/

Georgia Attorney General
40 Capitol Square, SW
Atlanta, GA 30334-1300
Phone: (404) 656-3300
Fax: (404) 657-8733
Website: http://www.ganet.org/ago/

18 Hawaii – The Aloha State

Area: 6,423 sq.mi. (Rank: 47th)   Population: 1,244,898 (Rank: 42nd)
Violent Crime Rate (per 100,000 residents): 254.4 (Rank: 12th Safest)
State Motto: *Ua mau ke ea o ka aina I ka pono (The life of the Land is Perpetuated in Righteousness)*

18.1 Knife Carry Law Summary

Note: Blade length limits, if any, in parentheses.

Knife Type	Open Carry	Concealed Carry	Notes
Folding Knives	Yes	Yes	See note[34]
Fixed Bladed Knives	Yes	Yes	See note[34]
Dirks, Daggers, & Stilettos	No	No	
Automatic Knives	No	No	
Balisongs	No	No	

18.2 Discussion

America's 50th state, Hawaii beckons travelers with its beautiful beaches and tropical climate. Visitors to the Aloha State will find that with respect to knives, ordinary fixed and folding knives should pose no problem, and may be carried openly or concealed. As in many states, the open carry of large fixed blades may result in unwanted law enforcement attention, especially in urban areas. There is no statutorily defined blade length limit. State law prohibits carry of dirks, daggers, and stilettos. In addition, state law prohibits mere possession of automatic knives such as switchblades and gravity knives, as well as balisongs (butterfly knives).

No state-wide statutory prohibitions on off-limit locations for legal knife carry appear to exist. Cities and towns, however, may pass their own ordinances restricting knife carry, although few appear to have done so.

18.3 Selected Statutes

Haw. Rev. Stat. §§ (2005)

§134-51 Deadly weapons; prohibitions; penalty. (a) Any person, not authorized by law, who carries concealed upon the person's self or within any vehicle used or occupied by the person or who is found armed with any dirk, dagger, blackjack, slug shot, billy, metal knuckles, pistol, or other deadly or dangerous weapon shall be guilty of a misdemeanor and may be immediately arrested without warrant by any sheriff, police officer, or other officer or person. Any weapon, above enumerated, upon conviction of the one carrying or possessing it under this section, shall be summarily destroyed by the chief of police or sheriff.

(b) Whoever knowingly possesses or intentionally uses or threatens to use a deadly or dangerous weapon while engaged in the commission of a crime shall be guilty of a class C felony. [L 1937, c 123, §1; RL 1945, §11114; RL 1955, §267-25; HRS §727-25; ren L 1972, c 9, pt of §1; am L 1977, c 191, §2; am L 1983, c 267, §1; gen ch 1985;

---

[34] State law prohibits carry of dirks, daggers, or deadly or dangerous weapons. *See*, Haw. Rev. Stat. § 134-51 (2005). The statute prohibits concealed carry on the person, in a vehicle, or being otherwise "armed with" such weapons, which may be interpreted to include open carry. *See, id.* The cautious traveler should avoid carry of knives that appear overly "tactical", aggressive, or weapon like.

am L 1989, c 211, §10; am L 1990, c 195, §3 and c 281, §11; am L 1992, c 87, §4; am L 1993, c 226, §1; am L 1999, c 285, §2]

§134-52 Switchblade knives; prohibitions; penalty. (a) Whoever knowingly manufactures, sells, transfers, possesses, or transports in the State any switchblade knife, being any knife having a blade which opens automatically (1) by hand pressure applied to a button or other device in the handle of the knife, or (2) by operation of inertia, gravity, or both, shall be guilty of a misdemeanor.

(b) Whoever knowingly possesses or intentionally uses or threatens to use a switchblade knife while engaged in the commission of a crime shall be guilty of a class C felony. [L 1959, c 225, §1; Supp, §264-9; HRS §769-1; ren L 1972, c 9, pt of §1; am L 1990, c 195, §4]

§134-53 Butterfly knives; prohibitions; penalty. (a) Whoever knowingly manufactures, sells, transfers, possesses, or transports in the State any butterfly knife, being a knife having a blade encased in a split handle that manually unfolds with hand or wrist action with the assistance of inertia, gravity or both, shall be guilty of a misdemeanor.

(b) Whoever knowingly possesses or intentionally uses or threatens to use a butterfly knife while engaged in the commission of a crime shall be guilty of a class C felony. [L 1999, c 285, §1]

18.4 Selected Caselaw

State v. Phillips, 67 Haw. 535, 540, 696 P.2d 346, 350 (1985) (citing *State v. Giltner*, 56 Haw. 374, 537 P.2d 14 (1975) and stating mere possession of diver's knife not a crime).

18.5 Preemption Law

No knife law preemption. *See*, HAW. REV. STAT. § 46-1.5 (2005).

18.6 Places Off-Limits While Carrying

No state law limitations. Towns and cities, however, may pass their own local ordinances restricting carry, although not many appear to have done so.

18.7 School/College Carry

No state law limitations. Towns and cities, however, may pass their own local ordinances restricting carry, although not many appear to have done so.

18.8 Selected City Ordinances

(No relevant city ordinances.)

18.9 State Resources

Honolulu Police Department
801 S. Beretania
Honolulu, HI 96818
Phone: (808) 529-3371
Fax: (808) 529-3525
Website: http://www.honolulupd.org/

Attorney General of Hawaii
Department of the Attorney General
425 Queen Street
Honolulu, HI 96813
Phone: (808) 586-1500
Website: http://www.hawaii.gov/ag/index.html

19 Idaho – The Gem State

Area: 82,747 sq.mi. (Rank: 11th)   Population: 1,341,131 (Rank: 39th)
Violent Crime Rate (per 100,000 residents): 244.9 (Rank: 9th Safest)
State Motto: *Esto Perpetua (May It Endure Forever)*

19.1 Knife Carry Law Summary

<u>Note</u>: Blade length limits, if any, in parentheses.

Knife Type	Open Carry	Concealed Carry	Notes
Folding Knives	Yes	Yes	
Fixed Bladed Knives	Yes	No	Concealed with permit ok.
Dirks, Daggers, & Stilettos	No	No	
Automatic Knives	Yes	No	Concealed with permit ok.
Balisongs	Yes	No	Concealed with permit ok.

19.2 Discussion

Idaho's scenic beauty, from the mountains, rivers and lakes of the Idaho Panhandle to the plains of Southern Idado, embrace a frontier heritage that persists to this day outside the major population centers, and the few trendier vacation spots such as Sun Valley. Not surprisingly, the state has firearms-friendly laws and a low violent crime rate, which make for pleasant family vacationing for the outdoors inclined.

With respect to knives, ordinary fixed and folding knives carried openly should pose no problem. There is no statutorily defined blade length limit. Dirks, daggers, and stilettos, however, are prohibited.

State law prohibits carry, open or otherwise, of firearms or other deadly or dangerous weapons, in courthouses, jails, juvenile detention facilities, and schools, regardless of whether the person possesses a concealed weapon permit or not.[35] Pocket knives with blades less than 2 ½ inches in length are exempted from the definition of "deadly or dangerous weapon."[36]

Idaho does not preempt its cities and towns from regulating knife carry, unlike the case for firearms, where the state has prohibited cities and towns from enacting their own firearms carry restrictions, ensuring uniform state-wide firearms laws. As such, towns and cities may enact their own restrictions on knife carry, although few appear to have done so.

19.3 Selected Statutes

IDAHO CODE §§ (2005)

18-3302. ISSUANCE OF LICENSES TO CARRY CONCEALED WEAPONS.

...

(7) Except in the person's place of abode or fixed place of business, a person shall not carry a concealed weapon without a license to carry a concealed weapon. For the purposes of this section, a concealed weapon means any

---

[35] *See,* IDAHO CODE § 18-3302D (2005). The statute refers to the definition of "deadly or dangerous weapon" used in 18 U.S.C. 930. *Id.*
[36] *See,* 18 U.S.C. 930 (2004).

dirk, dirk knife, bowie knife, dagger, pistol, revolver, or any other deadly or dangerous weapon. The provisions of this section shall not apply to any lawfully possessed shotgun or rifle.

...

(9) While in any motor vehicle, inside the limits or confines of any city or inside any mining, lumbering, logging or railroad camp a person shall not carry a concealed weapon on or about his person without a license to carry a concealed weapon. This shall not apply to any pistol or revolver located in plain view whether it is loaded or unloaded. A firearm may be concealed legally in a motor vehicle so long as the weapon is disassembled or unloaded.

...

(12) The requirement to secure a license to carry a concealed weapon under this section shall not apply to the following persons:

...

(d) Any person outside the limits of or confines of any city, or outside any mining, lumbering, logging or railroad camp, located outside any city, while engaged in lawful hunting, fishing, trapping or other lawful outdoor activity;

...

(14) A person carrying a concealed weapon in violation of the provisions of this section shall be guilty of a misdemeanor.

18-3302C. PROHIBITED CONDUCT. Any person obtaining a license under the provisions of section 18-3302, Idaho Code, shall not:

(1) Carry a concealed weapon in a courthouse, juvenile detention facility or jail, public or private school, except as provided in subsection (4)(f) of section 18-3302D, Idaho Code; or

...

18-3302D. POSSESSING WEAPONS OR FIREARMS ON SCHOOL PROPERTY.

(1) (a) It shall be unlawful and is a misdemeanor for any person to possess a firearm or other deadly or dangerous weapon while on the property of a school or in those portions of any building, stadium or   other structure on school grounds which, at the time of the violation, were being used for an activity sponsored by or through a school in this state or while riding school provided transportation.

(b) The provisions of this section regarding the possession of a firearm or other deadly or dangerous weapon on school property shall also apply to students of schools while attending or participating in any school sponsored activity, program or event regardless of location.

(2) Definitions. As used in this section:

(a) "Deadly or dangerous weapon" means any weapon as defined in 18 U.S.C. section 930;

(b) "Firearm" means any firearm as defined in 18 U.S.C. section 921;

(c) "Minor" means a person under the age of eighteen (18) years;

(d) "Possess" means to bring an object, or to cause it to be brought, onto the property of a public or private elementary or secondary school, or onto a vehicle being used for school provided transportation, or to exercise dominion and control over an object located anywhere on such property or vehicle. For purposes of subsection (1)(b) of this section, "possess" shall also mean to bring an object onto the site of a school sponsored activity, program or event, regardless of location, or to exercise dominion and control over an object located anywhere on such a site;

(e) "School" means a private or public elementary or secondary school.

...

19.4 Selected Caselaw

State v. Sheldon, 139 Idaho 980, 88 P.3d 1220 (Idaho Ct. App. 2003) (reversing dismissal of, *inter alia*, concealed weapon charge for possession in vehicle of brass knuckles, nylon and fiberglass knife, and expandable baton).

State v. Veneroso, 138 Idaho 925, 71 P.3d 1072 (Idaho Ct. App. 2003) (affirming conviction for drug possession found during arrest for carrying concealed weapon, a four or five inch double-edged knife).

State v. Gomez, 136 Idaho 480, 36 P.3d 832 (Idaho Ct. App. 2001) (reversing and vacating conviction for carrying concealed five-inch butterfly knife due to illegal search).

19.5 Preemption Law

No knife law preemption, firearms law preemption only. *See,* IDAHO CODE §§ 18-3302(6), 31-872, 50-343 (2005). Towns and cities may regulate knife carry.

19.6 Places Off-Limits While Carrying

State law prohibits the carry of firearms and other deadly weapons, the definition of which includes knives, in courthouses, jails or juvenile detention facilities, or public or private schools. *See,* IDAHO CODE § 18-3302C (2005).

19.7 School/College Carry

State law prohibits the carry of firearms and other deadly weapons, the definition of which includes knives, in public or private schools. *See,* IDAHO CODE § 18-3302C (2005).

19.8 Selected City Ordinances

Boise – Concealed carry of knives, dirks, daggers, and other deadly or dangerous weapons prohibited. *See,* BOISE, IDAHO, CITY CODE § 6-04-02 (2006). This prohibition may not apply to holders of concealed weapon permits.

19.9 State Resources

Idaho Department Of Law Enforcement
700 S. Stratford Drive
Meridian, ID 83680-0700
Phone: (208) 884-7000
Fax: (208) 884-7090
Website: http://www.isp.state.id.us/

Idaho Attorney General
700 W. Jefferson Street
Boise, ID 83720-0010
Phone: (208) 334-2400
Fax: (208) 334-2530
Website: http://www.state.id.us/ag/

20 Illinois – Land of Lincoln

Area: 55,584 sq.mi. (Rank: 24th)   Population: 12,600,620 (Rank: 5th)
Violent Crime Rate (per 100,000 residents): 542.9 (Rank: 40th Safest)
State Motto: *State Sovereignty, National Union*

20.1 Knife Carry Law Summary

Note: Blade length limits, if any, in parentheses.

Knife Type	Open Carry	Concealed Carry	Notes
Folding Knives	Yes	Yes	See note[37]
Fixed Bladed Knives	Yes	Yes	See note[37]
Dirks, Daggers, & Stilettos	Yes	Yes	See note[37]
Automatic Knives	No	No	
Balisongs	Yes	Yes	Some localities prohibit carry

20.2 Discussion

As it the case with firearms, travelers to Illinois will find state law generally unfriendly to knife carry. While folding knives, fixed bladed knives, daggers, dirks, stilettos, and balisongs may technically be legal to carry under state law absent an intent to use such knife unlawfully against another, as a practical matter carry of anything but a small folder is likely asking for trouble should you be stopped, especially in any of the larger cities. Indeed, Chicago prohibits concealed carry of a bewildering variety of knives, including dirks, daggers, stilettos, bowie knives, "commando knives", switchblades, and any other knife with a blade longer than two and a half inches.[38] Oh, did I forget razors and "other dangerous weapons"? Chicago didn't, and bans concealed carry of those too.[39]

State law considers daggers, dirks, stilettos, and any knife with a blade three inches or longer to be *per se* dangerous weapons. Switchblades and ballistic knives are completely banned and are illegal to even possess. Balisongs, while not specifically prohibited, may fall under the switchblade prohibition, as balisongs do in some states. Note that some cities, such as Aurora, specifically prohibit carry of balisongs. The cautious traveler would be well advised to avoid larger knives, daggers, dirks, stilettos, and the like on your visit to the land of Lincoln, especially in the larger cities.

State law prohibits carry of deadly weapons in establishments that serve alcohol, or at "public gatherings" such as concerts. In addition, carry of knives with intent to use unlawfully is a felony if carried in or on school property, public housing, public parks, courthouses, or on a public way within 1,000 feet of such locations.

20.3 Selected Statutes

720 ILL. COMP. STAT. §§ (2005)

---

[37] State law considers daggers, dirks, stilettos, and any knife with a blade three inches or longer to be *per se* dangerous weapons. *See,* 720 ILL. COMP. STAT. § 5/33A-1 (2005). Carry as weapon with intent to use unlawfully against another is prohibited. *See, id.* at § 5/24-1.

[38] *See,* CHICAGO, ILL., MUNICIPAL CODE § 8-24-020 (2005).

[39] *See, id.*

Sec. 5/24-1. Unlawful Use of Weapons.

(a) A person commits the offense of unlawful use of weapons when he knowingly:

(1) Sells, manufactures, purchases, possesses or carries any bludgeon, black-jack, slung-shot, sand-club, sand-bag, metal knuckles, throwing star, or any knife, commonly referred to as a switchblade knife, which has a blade that opens automatically by hand pressure applied to a button, spring or other device in the handle of the knife, or a ballistic knife, which is a device that propels a knifelike blade as a projectile by means of a coil spring, elastic material or compressed gas; or

(2) Carries or possesses with intent to use the same unlawfully against another, a dagger, dirk, billy, dangerous knife, razor, stiletto, broken bottle or other piece of glass, stun gun or taser or any other dangerous or deadly weapon or instrument of like character; or

...

(c) Violations in specific places.

...

(2) A person who violates subsection 24-1(a)(1), 24-1(a)(2), or 24-1(a)(3) in any school, regardless of the time of day or the time of year, in residential property owned, operated or managed by a public housing agency or leased by a public housing agency as part of a scattered site or mixed-income development, in a public park, in a courthouse, on the real property comprising any school, regardless of the time of day or the time of year, on residential property owned, operated or managed by a public housing agency or leased by a public housing agency as part of a scattered site or mixed-income development, on the real property comprising any public park, on the real property comprising any courthouse, in any conveyance owned, leased or contracted by a school to transport students to or from school or a school related activity, or on any public way within 1,000 feet of the real property comprising any school, public park, courthouse, or residential property owned, operated, or managed by a public housing agency or leased by a public housing agency as part of a scattered site or mixed-income development commits a Class 4 felony. "Courthouse" means any building that is used by the Circuit, Appellate, or Supreme Court of this State for the conduct of official business.

...

Sec. 5/33A-1. Legislative intent and definitions.

...

(c) Definitions.

(1) "Armed with a dangerous weapon". A person is considered armed with a dangerous weapon for purposes of this Article, when he or she carries on or about his or her person or is otherwise armed with a Category I, Category II, or Category III weapon.

(2) A Category I weapon is a handgun, sawed-off shotgun, sawed-off rifle, any other firearm small enough to be concealed upon the person, semiautomatic firearm, or machine gun. A Category II weapon is any other rifle, shotgun, spring gun, other firearm, stun gun or taser as defined in paragraph (a) of Section 24-1 of this Code, knife with a blade of at least 3 inches in length, dagger, dirk, switchblade knife, stiletto, axe, hatchet, or other deadly or dangerous weapon or instrument of like character. As used in this subsection (b) "semiautomatic firearm" means a repeating firearm that utilizes a portion of the energy of a firing cartridge to extract the fired cartridge case and chamber the next round and that requires a separate pull of the trigger to fire each cartridge.

(3) A Category III weapon is a bludgeon, black-jack, slungshot, sand-bag, sand-club, metal knuckles, billy, or other dangerous weapon of like character.

...

20.4 Selected Caselaw

People v. Espinoza, Ill. Supr. Ct., No. 85050, (1998) (holding, *inter alia*, that defendant's use of beer bottle during assault could support prosecution under armed violence statute as Category II knife-like weapon).

20.5 Preemption Law

No knife law preemption. Towns and cities may impose their own knife carry restrictions.

20.6 Places Off-Limits While Carrying

Carry of deadly weapons prohibited in any place "licensed to sell intoxicating beverages, or at any public gathering held pursuant to a license issued by any governmental body or any public gathering at which an admission is charged." *See*, 720 ILL. COMP. STAT. § 5/24-1 (2005). Carry of a knife with intent to use unlawfully prohibited on school property, public housing, public parks, courthouses, or on any public way within 1,000 feet of same. Violation of this prohibition is a felony. *See, id.* In addition, towns and cities may pass their own local ordinances prohibiting or restricting knife carry.

20.7 School/College Carry

Carry of knife with intent to use unlawfully prohibited on school property or on public way within 1,000 feet of a school. In addition, towns and cities may pass their own local ordinances prohibiting or restricting knife carry.

20.8 Selected City Ordinances

Aurora – Carry of butterfly knives (balisongs) prohibited. *See*, AURORA, ILL., CODE OF ORDINANCES § 29-43 (2005).

Chicago – Unlawful to possess switchblades. *See*, CHICAGO, ILL., MUNICIPAL CODE § 8-24-020 (2005). Concealed carry of dirks, daggers, stilettos, bowie knives, "commando knives", any knife with blade greater than two and a half inches, ordinary razors, and "other dangerous weapon[s]" prohibited. *See, id.* Unlawful for person under 18 years of age to carry or possess knife with blade two inches in length or longer. *See, id.* Carry on person or in vehicle passenger compartment of "utility knife" (e.g., box cutter) by person under 18 years of age prohibited. Certain exceptions apply. *See, id.* at § 8-24-021.

20.9 State Resources

Illinois state Police
P.O. Box 19461
Springfield, IL 62794-9461
Phone: (217) 782-7263
Fax: (217) 785-2821
Website: http://www.isp.state.il.us/

Attorney General of Illinois
500 South Second St.
Springfield, IL 62706
Phone: (217) 782-1090
Website: http://www.ag.state.il.us/

21 Indiana – The Hoosier State

Area: 35,867 sq.mi. (Rank: 38th)   Population: 6,159,068 (Rank: 14th)
Violent Crime Rate (per 100,000 residents): 325.4 (Rank: 22nd Safest)
State Motto: *The Crossroads of America*

21.1 Knife Carry Law Summary

<u>Note:</u> Blade length limits, if any, in parentheses.

Knife Type	Open Carry	Concealed Carry	Notes
Folding Knives	Yes	Yes	
Fixed Bladed Knives	Yes	Yes	Municipalities may regulate
Dirks, Daggers, & Stilettos	Yes	Yes	Municipalities may regulate
Automatic Knives	No	No	
Balisongs	Yes	Yes	

21.2 Discussion

Visitors to the Hoosier State will find a generally favorable environment for lawful knife carry, in addition to excellent reciprocity and/or recognition of other states' concealed carry handgun permits. With respect to knives, ordinary fixed and folding knives should pose no problem, and may be carried openly or concealed. There is no statutorily defined blade length limit. Automatic knives, such as switchblades and ballistic knives, however, are prohibited. Note that balisongs may fall under the switchblade prohibition, as balisongs do in some states.

No specific state-wide statutory prohibitions on off-limits areas for knife carry exist, although cities and towns may pass their own ordinances restricting knife carry. Indiana does not preempt its cities and towns from regulating knife carry, unlike the case for firearms, where the state has prohibited cities and towns from enacting their own firearms carry restrictions, ensuring uniform state-wide firearms laws. As such, towns and cities may regulate knife carry within their jurisdictions, such as in schools or public parks.

21.3 Selected Statutes

Ind. Code §§ (2005)

IC 35-47-5-2

Knife with blade that opens automatically or may be propelled

Sec. 2. It is a Class B misdemeanor for a person to manufacture, possess, display, offer, sell, lend, give away, or purchase any knife with a blade that:

(1) opens automatically; or

(2) may be propelled; by hand pressure applied to a button, device containing gas, spring, or other device in the handle of the knife.

As added by P.L.311-1983, SEC.32. Amended by P.L.70-2000, SEC.2.

21.4 Selected Caselaw

Willams v. State, 196 Ind. 84, 147 N.E. 153 (1925) (affirming homicide conviction and holding question whether knife used was deadly weapon was one for jury).

Wilcher v. State, 771 N.E.2d 113 (Ind. Ct. App. 2002) (affirming conviction for aggravated assault via use of knife with four to six inch blade).

21.5 Preemption Law

No knife law preemption, firearms law preemption only. *See*, IND. CODE § 35-47-11 (2005).

21.6 Places Off-Limits While Carrying

No state law limitation. Towns and cities, however, may pass their own local ordinances prohibiting carry.

21.7 School/College Carry

No state law limitation. Towns and cities, however, may pass their own local ordinances prohibiting carry on school grounds.

21.8 Selected City Ordinances

Indianapolis – Marion County – Carry of ice picks and similar instruments prohibited. *See*, INDIANAPOLIS – MARION COUNTY, IND., CODE OF ORDINANCES § 451-1 (2005). Selling, or otherwise supplying dagger, dirk, bowie knife, stiletto or other dangerous weapon of similar character to suspected criminal or person with criminal purpose prohibited. *See, id.* at § 451-5.

South Bend – Carry of switchblades, daggers, and hunting knives prohibited in city parks. *See*, SOUTH BEND, IND., CODE OF ORDINANCES § 19-44 (2005).

21.9 State Resources

Indiana State Police
100 North Senate Avenue
Indiana Government Center North, 3rd Floor
Indianapolis, IN 46204-2259
Phone: (317) 232-8200
Website: http://www.state.in.us/isp/

Indiana Attorney General
State House, Room 219
Indianapolis, IN 46204
Phone: (317) 232 - 6201
Website: http://www.state.in.us/hoosieradvocate/

22 Iowa – The Hawkeye State

Area: 55,869 sq.mi. (Rank: 23rd)   Population: 2,936760 (Rank: 30th)
Violent Crime Rate (per 100,000 residents): 270.9 (Rank: 14th Safest)
State Motto: *Our Liberties We Prize and Our Rights We Will Maintain*

22.1 Knife Carry Law Summary

<u>Note:</u> Blade length limits, if any, in parentheses.

Knife Type	Open Carry	Concealed Carry	Notes
Folding Knives	Yes	Yes (<= 5")	
Fixed Bladed Knives	Yes	Yes (<= 5")	Some municipalities regulate.
Dirks, Daggers, & Stilettos	Yes	No	
Automatic Knives	Yes	No	Ballistic knives are prohibited.
Balisongs	Yes	No	

22.2 Discussion

Located in the heart of the Midwest, travelers to Iowa will find only moderate restrictions on knife carry outside of the state's cities. As is perhaps typical of most states, larger cities such as Des Moines impose their own, more restrictive regulations on what legal to carry, and where.

In general, ordinary fixed and folding knives with blades no longer than five inches should pose no problem, and may be carried openly or concealed. Larger folders or fixed blades must be carried openly, although an exception exists for hunting or fishing knives carried concealed while actually engaged in lawful hunting or fishing.[40] State law prohibits concealed carry of dangerous weapons, the definition of which includes daggers, razors, stilettos, switchblades (of any blade length) or any knife with a blade exceeding five inches in length.[41] Note that case law indicates that balisongs, of any blade length, are considered dangerous weapons, and thus may not be carried concealed.[42] The Iowa Supreme Court has ruled that sword canes fall under the prohibition on carrying concealed weapons.[43] Thus, you may not carry a sword cane.

While no specific state-wide statutory prohibitions on off-limits areas for knife carry exist, cities and towns may pass their own ordinances, as the state does not preempt its cities and towns from regulating knife carry, unlike the case for firearms. As such, some municipalities, such as Des Moines, have enacted their own carry restrictions.

22.3 Selected Statutes

IOWA CODE §§ (2005)

702.7 Dangerous weapon.

---

[40] *See*, IOWA CODE § 724.4(4)(h) (2005).
[41] *See*, IOWA CODE §§ 702.7, 724.4 (2005).
[42] *See*, In the Interest of F.A.B., No. 4-086/03-1638 (Iowa Ct. App. 2004).
[43] *See*, State v. McCoy, 618 N.W.2d 324 (Iowa 2000).

A "dangerous weapon" is any instrument or device designed primarily for use in inflicting death or injury upon a human being or animal, and which is capable of inflicting death upon a human being when used in the manner for which it was designed. Additionally, any instrument or device of any sort whatsoever which is actually used in such a manner as to indicate that the defendant intends to inflict death or serious injury upon the other, and which, when so used, is capable of inflicting death upon a human being, is a dangerous weapon. Dangerous weapons include, but are not limited to, any offensive weapon, pistol, revolver, or other firearm, dagger, razor, stiletto, switchblade knife, or knife having a blade exceeding five inches in length.

[S13, §4775-1a; C24, 27, 31, §12936; C35, §12935-g1, 12936; C39, § 12935.1, 12936; C46, 50, 54, 58, 62, 66, 71, 73, 75, 77, §695.1, 695.2; C79, 81, §702.7]

88 Acts, ch 1164, §1

724.1 Offensive weapons.

An offensive weapon is any device or instrumentality of the following types:

...

5. A ballistic knife. A ballistic knife is a knife with a detachable blade which is propelled by a spring-operated mechanism, elastic material, or compressed gas.

6. Any part or combination of parts either designed or intended to be used to convert any device into an offensive weapon as described in subsections 1 to 5 of this section, or to assemble into such an offensive weapon, except magazines or other parts, ammunition, or ammunition components used in common with lawful sporting firearms or parts including but not limited to barrels suitable for refitting to sporting firearms.

...

[C27, 31, 35, §12960-b1; C39, § 12960.01; C46, 50, 54, 58, 62, 66, §696.1; C71, 73, 75, 77, §696.1, 697.10, 697.11; C79, 81, §724.1]

83 Acts, ch 7, §1; 88 Acts, ch 1164, §2, 3; 92 Acts, ch 1004, §1, 2; 2000 Acts, ch 1116, §7

724.3 Unauthorized possession of offensive weapons.

Any person, other than a person authorized herein, who knowingly possesses an offensive weapon commits a class "D" felony.

[C27, 31, 35, §12960-b3; C39, § 12960.03; C46, 50, 54, 58, 62, 66, §696.3; C71, 73, 75, 77, §696.3, 697.11; C79, 81, §724.3]

724.4 Carrying weapons.

1. Except as otherwise provided in this section, a person who goes armed with a dangerous weapon concealed on or about the person, or who, within the limits of any city, goes armed with a pistol or revolver, or any loaded firearm of any kind, whether concealed or not, or who knowingly carries or transports in a vehicle a pistol or revolver, commits an aggravated misdemeanor.

2. A person who goes armed with a knife concealed on or about the person, if the person uses the knife in the commission of a crime, commits an aggravated misdemeanor.

3. A person who goes armed with a knife concealed on or about the person, if the person does not use the knife in the commission of a crime:

a. If the knife has a blade exceeding eight inches in length, commits an aggravated misdemeanor.

b. If the knife has a blade exceeding five inches but not exceeding eight inches in length, commits a serious misdemeanor.

4. Subsections 1 through 3 do not apply to any of the following:

a. A person who goes armed with a dangerous weapon in the person's own dwelling or place of business, or on land owned or possessed by the person.

...

e. A person who for any lawful purpose carries an unloaded pistol, revolver, or other dangerous weapon inside a closed and fastened container or securely wrapped package which is too large to be concealed on the person.

...

h. A person who carries a knife used in hunting or fishing, while actually engaged in lawful hunting or fishing.

i. A person who has in the person's possession and who displays to a peace officer on demand a valid permit to carry weapons which has been issued to the person, and whose conduct is within the limits of that permit. A person shall not be convicted of a violation of this section if the person produces at the person's trial a permit to carry weapons which was valid at the time of the alleged offense and which would have brought the person's conduct within this exception if the permit had been produced at the time of the alleged offense.

...

[S13, §4775-1a, -3a, -4a, -7a, -11a; C24, 27, 31, 35, 39, § 12936 - 12939; C46, 50, 54, 58, 62, 66, 71, 73, 75, 77, §695.2 - 695.5; C79, 81, §724.4]

83 Acts, ch 7, §2; 83 Acts, ch 96, §123, 159; 87 Acts, ch 13, §5; 88 Acts, ch 1164, §4; 98 Acts, ch 1131, §3

724.4A Weapons free zones - enhanced penalties.

1. As used in this section, "weapons free zone" means the area in or on, or within one thousand feet of, the real property comprising a public or private elementary or secondary school, or in or on the real property comprising a public park. A weapons free zone shall not include that portion of a public park designated as a hunting area under section 461A.42 .

2. Notwithstanding sections 902.9 and 903.1 , a person who commits a public offense involving a firearm or offensive weapon, within a weapons free zone, in violation of this or any other chapter shall be subject to a fine of twice the maximum amount which may otherwise be imposed for the public offense.

94 Acts, ch 1172, §53

724.4B Carrying weapons on school grounds - penalty - exceptions.

1. A person who goes armed with, carries, or transports a firearm of any kind, whether concealed or not, on the grounds of a school commits a class "D" felony. For the purposes of this section, "school" means a public or nonpublic school as defined in section 280.2 .

2. Subsection 1 does not apply to the following:

a. A person listed under section 724.4 , subsection 4, paragraphs "b" through "f" or "j" .

b. A person who has been specifically authorized by the school to go armed, carry, or transport a firearm on the school grounds, including for purposes of conducting an instructional program regarding firearms.

95 Acts, ch 191, §53

22.4 Selected Caselaw

State v. McCoy, 618 N.W.2d 324 (Iowa 2000) (holding sword cane falls under prohibition on concealed carry of dangerous weapons).

In the Interest of F.A.B., No. 4-086/03-1638 (Iowa Ct. App. 2004) (affirming delinquency adjudication for carrying dangerous weapon, balisong knife with four and a half inch total blade length, and three and a half inch sharpened edge).

State v. Watts, 223 N.W.2d 234 (Iowa 1974) (holding that state must prove that defendant carried large kitchen knife with ten and a half inch blade with intent to use as weapon).

22.5 Preemption Law

No knife law preemption, firearms law preemption only. *See,* IOWA CODE § 724.28 (2005).

22.6 Places Off-Limits While Carrying

No specific state law prohibition on carry. State law provides for enhanced penalties, however, for public offenses in so-called "weapons-free zones", defined as the area in, on, or within one thousand feet of a school. *See,* IOWA CODE § 724.4A (2005).

22.7 School/College Carry

No state law limitation. Towns and cities, however, may pass their own local ordinances regulating, restricting, or prohibiting carry.

22.8 Selected City Ordinances

Des Moines – Carry of knives of any type, openly or concealed, on school property prohibited. *See,* DES MOINES, IOWA, MUNICIPAL CODE § 70-78 (2006). Concealed carry within the city of daggers, bowie knives, butterfly knives, stilettos, or switchblades prohibited. *See, id.* at § 70-85.

22.9 State Resources

Iowa Department of Public Safety
Wallace State Office Building
Des Moines, IA 50319
Phone: (515) 281-3211
Website: http://www.state.ia.us/government/dps/index.html

Attorney General of Iowa
Department Of Justice
1305 E. Walnut Street
Des Moines, IA 50319
Phone: (515) 281-5164
Fax: (515) 281-4209
Website: http://www.state.ia.us/government/ag/index.html

23 Kansas – The Sunflower State

Area: 81,815 sq.mi. (Rank: 13th) Population: 2,715,884 (Rank: 32nd)
Violent Crime Rate (per 100,000 residents): 374.5 (Rank: 27th Safest)
State Motto: *Ad Astra Per Aspera (To the Stars Through Difficulties)*

23.1 Knife Carry Law Summary

Note: Blade length limits, if any, in parentheses.

Knife Type	Open Carry	Concealed Carry	Notes
Folding Knives	Yes	Yes (<= 4")	
Fixed Bladed Knives	Yes	No	See note[44]
Dirks, Daggers, & Stilettos	Yes	No	
Automatic Knives	No	No	
Balisongs	No	No	See note[44]

23.2 Discussion

Visitors to Kansas, with its vast expanses of rolling plains, will find state law regarding knife carry to be somewhat restrictive as to concealed carry. Ordinary folding pocket knives with blades four inches or less may be carried concealed. Automatic knives, such as switchblades, gravity knives, and ballistic knives, are strictly prohibited.

State law prohibits concealed carry of dirks, daggers, and stilettos. In addition, state law also prohibits possession or carry of any kind with "intent to use ... unlawfully against another."[44] As is the case with many such vaguely worded carry statutes, law enforcement will have broad discretion in interpreting "intent." You may very well prevail in the end, but you'll have an arrest record to show for it. The cautious traveler would do well to avoid dirks, daggers, stilettos, or any knife with an overly aggressive or weapon-like "tactical" appearance.

Note that knives such as balisongs, while not specifically prohibited, may fall under the switchblade prohibition, as balisongs do in some states.

While no specific state-wide statutory prohibitions on off-limits areas for knife carry exist, cities and towns may pass their own ordinances, as the state does not preempt its cities and towns from regulating knife carry.

23.3 Selected Statutes

Kan. Stat. §§ (2005)

21-4201. Criminal use of weapons. (a) Criminal use of weapons is knowingly:

(1) Selling, manufacturing, purchasing, possessing or carrying any bludgeon, sandclub, metal knuckles or throwing star, or any knife, commonly referred to as a switch-blade, which has a blade that opens automatically by hand pressure applied to a button, spring or other device in the handle of the knife, or any knife having a blade that opens or falls or is ejected into position by the force of gravity or by an outward, downward or centrifugal thrust or movement;

---

[44] *See*, Kan. Stat. § 21-4201 (2005).

(2) carrying concealed on one's person, or possessing with intent to use the same unlawfully against another, a dagger, dirk, billy, blackjack, slungshot, dangerous knife, straight-edged razor, stiletto or any other dangerous or deadly weapon or instrument of like character, except that an ordinary pocket knife with no blade more than four inches in length shall not be construed to be a dangerous knife, or a dangerous or deadly weapon or instrument;

...

(i) Violation of subsections (a)(1) through (a)(5) is a class A nonperson misdemeanor. Violation of subsection (a)(6), (a)(7) or (a)(8) is a severity level 9, nonperson felony.

23.4 Selected Caselaw

State v. Dumars, 108 P.3d 448 (Kan. Ct. App. 2005) (upholding conviction for possession of switchblade knife).

23.5 Preemption Law

No knife law preemption.

23.6 Places Off-Limits While Carrying

No state law limitation. Towns and cities, however, may pass their own local ordinances regulating or restricting carry.

23.7 School/College Carry

No state law limitation. Towns and cities, however, may pass their own local ordinances prohibiting carry on school grounds.

23.8 Selected City Ordinances

Atchison – Carry in public park of dangerous or deadly weapons prohibited. *See*, ATCHISON, KAN., CODE OF ORDINANCES § 22-5 (2005).

Manhattan – Concealed carry of bowie knives, switchblades, dirks and other deadly weapons prohibited. *See*, MANHATTAN, KAN., CODE OF ORDINANCES § 22-66 (2006).

Sedgwick County – Carry, concealed or otherwise, of dirks, straight-edge razors, stilettos, switchblades, gravity knives, ballistic knives, or other dangerous knives in clubs or establishments licensed to serve alcohol prohibited. Ordinary pocket knives with blades of four inches or less are excluded from the definition of "dangerous knife" for purposes of these ordinances. *See*, SEDGWICK COUNTY, KAN., CODE OF ORDINANCES §§ 4-36, 4-81 (2005).

23.9 State Resources

Kansas Highway Patrol
General Headquarters
Topeka, KS 66603-3847
Phone: (785) 296-6800
Fax: (785) 296-3049
Website: http://www.ink.org/public/khp/

Attorney General of Kansas
301 S.W. 10th Avenue
Topeka, KS 66612-1597
Phone: (785) 296-2215
Fax: (785) 296-6296
Website: http://www.ink.org/public/ksag/

24 Kentucky – The Bluegrass State

Area: 39,728 sq.mi. (Rank: 36th)   Population: 4,092,891 (Rank: 26th)
Violent Crime Rate (per 100,000 residents): 244.9 (Rank: 9th Safest)
State Motto: *United We Stand, Divided We Fall*

24.1 Knife Carry Law Summary

Note: Blade length limits, if any, in parentheses.

Knife Type	Open Carry	Concealed Carry	Notes
Folding Knives	Yes	Yes	See note[45]
Fixed Bladed Knives	Yes	Yes	See note[45]
Dirks, Daggers, & Stilettos	Yes	No	Concealed with permit ok
Automatic Knives	Yes	No	Concealed with permit ok
Balisongs	Yes	No	Concealed with permit ok

24.2 Discussion

Visitors to the Bluegrass State will find generally favorable state laws concerning knife carry, in addition to favorable firearms carry laws.

Knives may be carried openly, and no statutorily defined blade length limit exists. Ordinary hunting knives and pocket knives are excluded from the statutory definition of deadly weapon, and may thus be carried concealed. As is the case with most states, caution is advised when carrying any large fixed blade, especially in urban areas. This is particularly true given that an older decision from the state's highest court has upheld a deadly weapon concealed carry conviction for carrying a fixed bladed knife with a six inch blade.[46]

Dirks, daggers, and stilettos are considered deadly weapons and may not be carried concealed without a recognized permit. While not specifically prohibited, automatic knives and balisongs may fall outside the "ordinary pocket knife" exception to the concealed carry prohibition. Thus, cautious travelers would be wise to avoid carrying such knives concealed without a valid permit. Fortunately, Kentucky will recognize any valid concealed weapons permit, so out-of-state travelers with such permits may legally carry concealed weapons, subject to Kentucky law, while visiting the state.

Note, however, that municipalities may pass their own ordinances regarding knife carry in their jurisdictions. The state has prohibited municipalities from regulating firearms carry, however.

With respect to knives, no state-wide statutory prohibitions on off-limits areas for otherwise legal knife carry exist, although as mentioned before, cities and towns may pass their own ordinances restricting knife carry. Fortunately, few cities or towns appear to have done so.

---

[45] State law excludes "ordinary pocket knife and hunting knife" from the statutory definition of "deadly weapon", and so the statutory prohibition on carrying concealed deadly weapons does not apply, because such knives are not *per se* deadly weapons under the statute. Of course, ordinary pocket knives and hunting knives may indeed be considered deadly weapons if used as such. *See*, Ky. Rev. Stat. § 500.080 (2005).

[46] *See*, Asher v. Commonwealth, 473 S.W.2d 145 (Ky. 1971).

Note that state law does restrict firearms carry in a number of places, including police stations, courthouses, and schools, even with a valid concealed weapons permit.

24.3 Selected Statutes

Ky. Rev. Stat. §§ (2005)

237.110 License to carry concealed deadly weapon -- Criteria -- Suspension or revocation -- Renewal -- Prohibitions -- Reciprocity -- Reports – Requirements for training classes.

(1) The Department of State Police is authorized to issue licenses to carry concealed firearms or other deadly weapons to persons qualified as provided in this section. The Department of State Police or the Administrative Office of the Courts shall conduct a record check, covering all offenses and conditions which are required under 18 U.S.C. sec. 922(g) and this section, in the manner provided by 18 U.S.C. sec. 922(s). Licenses shall be valid throughout the state for a period of five (5) years from the date of issuance, but their validity may be extended beyond the five (5) year period as provided in subsection (12) of this section. Any person in compliance with the terms of the license may carry a concealed firearm or other deadly weapon or combination of firearms and other deadly weapons on or about his person. The licensee shall carry the license at all times the licensee is carrying a concealed firearm or other deadly weapon and shall display the license upon request of a law enforcement officer. Violation of the provisions of this subsection shall constitute a noncriminal violation with a penalty of twenty-five dollars ($25), payable to the clerk of the District Court.

...

(13) Except as provided in KRS 527.020, no license issued pursuant to this section shall authorize any person to carry a concealed firearm into:

(a) Any police station or sheriff's office;

(b) Any detention facility, prison, or jail;

(c) Any courthouse, solely occupied by the Court of Justice courtroom, or court proceeding;

(d) Any meeting of the governing body of a county, municipality, or special district; or any meeting of the General Assembly or a committee of the General Assembly, except that nothing in this section shall preclude a member of the body, holding a concealed deadly weapon license, from carrying a concealed deadly weapon at a meeting of the body of which he is a member;

(e) Any portion of an establishment licensed to dispense beer or alcoholic beverages for consumption on the premises, which portion of the establishment is primarily devoted to that purpose;

(f) Any elementary or secondary school facility without the consent of school authorities as provided in KRS 527.070, any child-caring facility as defined in KRS 199.011, any day-care center as defined in KRS 199.894, or any certified family child-care home as defined in KRS 199.8982, except however, any owner of a certified child-care home may carry a concealed firearm into the owner's residence used as a certified child-care home;

(g) An area of an airport to which access is controlled by the inspection of persons and property; or

(h) Any place where the carrying of firearms is prohibited by federal law.

(14) The owner, business or commercial lessee, or manager of a private business enterprise, day-care center as defined in KRS 199.894 or certified or licensed family child-care home as defined in KRS 199.8982, or a health-care facility licensed under KRS Chapter 216B, except facilities renting or leasing housing, may prohibit persons holding concealed deadly weapon licenses from carrying concealed deadly weapons on the premises and may prohibit employees, not authorized by the employer, holding concealed deadly weapons licenses from carrying concealed deadly weapons on the property of the employer. If the building or the premises are open to the public, the employer or business enterprise shall post signs on or about the premises if carrying concealed weapons is prohibited. Possession of weapons, or ammunition, or both in a vehicle on the premises shall not be a criminal

offense so long as the weapons, or ammunition, or both are not removed from the vehicle or brandished while the vehicle is on the premises. A private but not a public employer may prohibit employees or other persons holding a concealed deadly weapons license from carrying concealed deadly weapons, or ammunition, or both in vehicles owned by the employer, but may not prohibit employees or other persons holding a concealed deadly weapons license from carrying concealed deadly weapons, or ammunition, or both in vehicles owned by the employee, except that the Justice Cabinet may prohibit an employee from carrying any weapons, or ammunition, or both other than the weapons, or ammunition, or both issued or authorized to be used by the employee of the cabinet, in a vehicle while transporting persons under the employee's supervision or jurisdiction. Carrying of a concealed weapon, or ammunition, or both in a location specified in this subsection by a license holder shall not be a criminal act but may subject the person to denial from the premises or removal from the premises, and, if an employee of an employer, disciplinary measures by the employer.

...

500.080 Definitions for Kentucky Penal Code.

As used in the Kentucky Penal Code, unless the context otherwise requires:

...

(3) "Dangerous instrument" means any instrument, including parts of the human body when a serious physical injury is a direct result of the use of that part of the human body, article, or substance which, under the circumstances in which it is used, attempted to be used, or threatened to be used, is readily capable of causing death or serious physical injury;

(4) "Deadly weapon" means any of the following:

(a) A weapon of mass destruction;

(b) Any weapon from which a shot, readily capable of producing death or other serious physical injury, may be discharged;

(c) Any knife other than an ordinary pocket knife or hunting knife;

(d) Billy, nightstick, or club;

(e) Blackjack or slapjack;

(f) Nunchaku karate sticks;

(g) Shuriken or death star; or

(h) Artificial knuckles made from metal, plastic, or other similar hard material;

527.020 Carrying concealed deadly weapon.

(1) A person is guilty of carrying a concealed weapon when he carries concealed a firearm or other deadly weapon on or about his person.

...

(4) Persons, except those specified in subsection (5) of this section, licensed to carry a concealed deadly weapon pursuant to KRS 237.110 may carry a firearm or other concealed deadly weapon on or about their persons at all times within the Commonwealth of Kentucky, if the firearm or concealed deadly weapon is carried in conformity with the requirements of that section. Unless otherwise specifically provided by the Kentucky Revised Statutes or applicable federal law, no criminal penalty shall attach to carrying a concealed firearm or other deadly weapon with a permit at any location at which an unconcealed firearm or other deadly weapon may be constitutionally carried. No person or organization, public or private, shall prohibit a person licensed to carry a concealed deadly weapon from possessing a firearm, ammunition, or both, or other deadly weapon in his or her vehicle in compliance with the provisions of KRS 237.110 and 237.115. Any attempt by a person or organization, public or private, to violate the provisions of this subsection may be the subject of an action for appropriate relief or for damages in a Circuit Court or District Court of competent jurisdiction.

24.4 Selected Caselaw

Stout v. Commonwealth, 33 S.W.3d 531 (Ky. Ct. App. 2000) (holding "razor box type knife" with three inch locking blade was deadly weapon and not ordinary pocket knife).

Mason v. Commonwealth, 396 S.W.2d 797 (Ky. 1965) (affirming conviction for armed robbery using pocket knife with three inch blade).

Asher v. Commonwealth, 473 S.W.2d 145 (Ky. 1971) (affirming conviction for carrying concealed deadly weapon, holding knife with six inch fixed blade was deadly weapon).

24.5 Preemption Law

No knife law preemption, firearms law preemption only. *See*, KY. REV. STAT. § 65.870 (2005).

24.6 Places Off-Limits While Carrying

State law prohibits carry of concealed firearms, but not specifically other deadly weapons such as knives, in a variety of places, such as police stations, jails, courthouses, schools, and bars. *See*, KY. REV. STAT. § 237.110(13) (2005). Note that such locations may prohibit knife carry by ordinance or other regulatory authority provided under state law.

24.7 School/College Carry

Concealed carry of firearms in schools, even with a permit, is prohibited by statute. State law, however, does not prohibit concealed knife carry with a concealed carry deadly weapon permit in schools. Towns and cities, however, may pass their own local ordinances prohibiting or otherwise restricting knife carry.

24.8 Selected City Ordinances

Owensboro – Knife throwing in city parks prohibited. *See*, OWENSBORO, KY. MUNICIPAL CODE § 19-6 (2005).

24.9 State Resources

Kentucky State Police
919 Versailles Road
Frankfort, KY 40601
Phone: (270) 856-3721
Website: http://www.kentuckystatepolice.org/

Office of the Attorney General
The Capitol, Suite 118
Frankfort, KY 40601-3449
Phone: (502) 696-5300
Fax: (502) 564-2894.
Website: http://ag.ky.gov/

25 Louisiana – The Pelican State

Area: 43,562 sq.mi. (Rank: 33rd)   Population: 4,482,646 (Rank: 24th)
Violent Crime Rate (per 100,000 residents): 638.7 (Rank: 45th Safest)
State Motto: *Union, Justice, and Confidence*

25.1 Knife Carry Law Summary

Note: Blade length limits, if any, in parentheses.

Knife Type	Open Carry	Concealed Carry	Notes
Folding Knives	Yes	Yes	See notes[47,48]
Fixed Bladed Knives	Yes	No	
Dirks, Daggers, & Stilettos	Yes	No	
Automatic Knives	No	No	
Balisongs	No	No	See note[48]

25.2 Discussion

Travelers to Louisiana will find a legal environment that strongly favors open carry, versus concealed carry of knives. State law prohibits concealed carry of any item customarily used or intended for use as a dangerous weapon. Thus, travelers should be wary of carrying even pocket knives with aggressive, weapon-like features or appearance, as such features or appearance simply increase the likelihood that such a knife will be judged a dangerous weapon.

There is no statutorily defined blade length limit. Dirks, daggers, and stilettos, may be carried openly, but not concealed. Automatic knives, however, are prohibited. Note that folding knives with assisted opening devices and balisongs may run afoul of the prohibition on switchblade knives, based on the wording of the statute.

State law prohibits carry of dangerous weapons, concealed or otherwise, on school grounds or school buses. Towns and cities may enact their own additional restrictions or regulations affecting knife carry in their jurisdictions.

25.3 Selected Statutes

La. Rev. Stat. §§ (2006)

§14:2. Definitions

In this Code the terms enumerated shall have the designated meanings:

...

---

[47] State law criminalizes concealed carry of any "instrumentality customarily used or intended for probable use as a dangerous weapon." *See*, La. Rev. Stat. § 14:95 (2006). Knives marketed for "tactical" use as weapons will likely fall under this prohibition. The cautious traveler would do well to avoid concealed carry of such knives.

[48] The state law switchblade definition, which includes any "knife or similar instrument having a blade which may be automatically unfolded or extended from a handle by the manipulation of a button, switch, latch or similar contrivance", may be read to encompass balisongs and assisted opening knives. *See*, La. Rev. Stat. § 14:95 (2006).

(3) "Dangerous weapon" includes any gas, liquid or other substance or instrumentality, which, in the manner used, is calculated or likely to produce death or great bodily harm.

...

§14:95. Illegal carrying of weapons

A. Illegal carrying of weapons is:

(1) The intentional concealment of any firearm, or other instrumentality customarily used or intended for probable use as a dangerous weapon, on one's person; or

(2) The ownership, possession, custody or use of any firearm, or other instrumentality customarily used as a dangerous weapon, at any time by an enemy alien; or

(3) The ownership, possession, custody or use of any tools, or dynamite, or nitroglycerine, or explosives, or other instrumentality customarily used by thieves or burglars at any time by any person with the intent to commit a crime; or

(4) The manufacture, ownership, possession, custody or use of any switchblade knife, spring knife or other knife or similar instrument having a blade which may be automatically unfolded or extended from a handle by the manipulation of a button, switch, latch or similar contrivance.

(5)(a) The intentional possession or use by any person of a dangerous weapon on a school campus during regular school hours or on a school bus. "School" means any elementary, secondary, high school, or vo-tech school in this state and "campus" means all facilities and property within the boundary of the school property. "School bus" means any motor bus being used to transport children to and from school or in connection with school activities.

...

25.4 Selected Caselaw

State v. Pleasant, 508 So.2d 113 (La. Ct. App. 1987) (describing arrest for concealed carry of knife with three inch blade and revocation of probation, reversed on other grounds).

State v. Ordon, 697 So. 2d 1074 (La. Ct. App. 1997) (affirming conviction for carrying concealed weapon by prior felon, pocket knife with four inch locking blade).

State v. Maxwell, 554 So.2d 769 (La. Ct. App. 1989) (affirming conviction for carrying concealed switchblade).

25.5 Preemption Law

No knife law preemption, firearms law preemption only. *See*, La..Rev. Stat. § 40:1796 (2006).

25.6 Places Off-Limits While Carrying

State law prohibits carry of dangerous weapons on school grounds or school buses. Towns and cities may pass their own local ordinances prohibiting or restricting carry.

25.7 School/College Carry

State law prohibits carry of dangerous weapons on school grounds or school buses. Towns and cities may pass their own local ordinances prohibiting or restricting carry.

25.8 Selected City Ordinances

New Orleans – Unlawful to carry any weapon while participating in or attending a demonstration held in a public place. The definition of "weapon" specifically includes knives. *See,* New Orleans, La., Code of Ordinances § 54-342 (2006). Carry of knives in Louisiana Nature and Science Center prohibited. *See, id.* at § 106-296. Possession of knives prohibited in public buildings with posted signs prohibiting weapons, "regardless of whether person may otherwise be in lawful possession of such weapon." *See, id.* at § 54-410.

Baton Rouge, and East Baton Rouge Parish – Carry of dangerous weapons prohibited in places that serve alcohol. *See,* Baton Rouge, and East Baton Rouge Parish, La., Code of Ordinances § 13:95.3 (2005).

Shreveport – Carry of dangerous weapons in courthouses, city hall or other public city buildings and facilities prohibited. *See,* Shreveport, La., Code of Ordinances § 50-135.2 (2006).

25.9 State Resources

Louisiana State Police
P.O. Box 66614
Baton Rouge, LA 70896-6614
Phone: (225) 925-4239
Fax: (225) 925-3717
Website: http://www.lsp.org/welcome.html

Louisiana Attorney General
State Capitol, 24th Floor
Baton Rouge, LA 70802
Phone: (225) 342-7876
Fax: (225) 342-3790
Website: http://www.ag.state.la.us/

26 Maine – The Pine Tree State

Area: 30,862 sq.mi. (Rank: 39th)   Population: 1,294,464 (Rank: 40th)
Violent Crime Rate (per 100,000 residents): 103.5 (Rank: 2nd Safest)
State Motto: *Dirigo (I Direct)*

26.1 Knife Carry Law Summary

<u>Note:</u> Blade length limits, if any, in parentheses.

Knife Type	Open Carry	Concealed Carry	Notes
Folding Knives	Yes	Yes	See note[49]
Fixed Bladed Knives	Yes	No	See note[50]
Dirks, Daggers, & Stilettos	Yes	No	See note[50]
Automatic Knives	No	No	
Balisongs	No	No	See note[51]

26.2 Discussion

Visitors to Maine looking to enjoy its rustic New England charm will also find a fairly favorable environment for legal knife carry, unlike the case with Massachusetts, its neighbor to the South. Ordinary pocket knives may be carried openly or concealed. Ordinary fixed knives should pose no problem, and may be carried openly. Dirks, daggers, and stilettos may similarly be carried openly. No statutorily defined blade length limit exists. Automatic knives, however, are prohibited. In addition, recent case law from the state's highest court has held that butterfly knives (balisongs) fall under the statutory switchblade definition, and are thus prohibited.[51]

Knives used for hunting or fishing may be carried concealed, although prudence suggests that such knives should only be so carried when actually engaged in hunting or fishing. State law prohibits concealed carry of bowie knives, dirks, stilettos and other dangerous or deadly weapons commonly used as weapons for either offense or personal defense.

State courts prohibit carry of weapons in court facilities. In addition, state law prohibits persons involved in a labor dispute or strike to carry weapons at the site of such dispute or strike. Towns and cities may enact their own prohibitions or restrictions affecting knife (but not firearm) carry, although few appear to have done so.

---

[49] State law prohibits concealed carry of dangerous weapons (other than firearms with a valid permit). *See*, ME. REV. STAT. tit. 25, § 2001-A (2005). Travelers should exercise caution when carrying any concealed folding pocket knife with an aggressive weapon-like appearance.

[50] Concealed carry of knives such as bowies, dirks, and stilettos is specifically prohibited. The statute also bans any other dangerous weapon "usually employed in the attack on or defense of a person." *See, id.* Travelers would be wise to avoid concealed carry of any fixed bladed knife, except for a typical hunting or fishing knife carried while actually pursuing such activities.

[51] *See*, State v. Michael M., 772 A.2d 1179, 1179 (Me. 2001) (describing butterfly knife as falling under switchblade prohibition and thus illegal).

26.3 Selected Statutes

Me. Rev. Stat. §§ (2005)

Tit. 17-A, §2. Definitions

As used in this code, unless a different meaning is plainly required, the following words and variants thereof have the following meanings.

...

9. Dangerous weapon.

A. "Use of a dangerous weapon" means the use of a firearm or other weapon, device, instrument, material or substance, whether animate or inanimate, which, in the manner it is used or threatened to be used is capable of producing death or serious bodily injury.

B. "Armed with a dangerous weapon" means in actual possession, regardless of whether the possession is visible or concealed, of:

(1) A firearm;

(2) Any device designed as a weapon and capable of producing death or serious bodily injury; or

(3) Any other device, instrument, material or substance, whether animate or inanimate, which, in the manner it is intended to be used by the actor, is capable of producing or threatening death or serious bodily injury. For purposes of this definition, the intent may be conditional.

C. When used in any other context, "dangerous weapon" means a firearm or any device designed as a weapon and capable of producing death or serious bodily injury.

D. For purposes of this subsection, proof that a thing is presented in a covered or open manner as a dangerous weapon gives rise to a permissible inference under the Maine Rules of Evidence, Rule 303 that it, in fact, is a dangerous weapon.

...

Tit. 17-A, §1055. Trafficking in dangerous knives

1. A person is guilty of trafficking in dangerous knives, if providing he has no right to do so, he knowingly manufactures or causes to be manufactured, or knowingly possesses, displays, offers, sells, lends, gives away or purchases any knife which has a blade which opens automatically by hand pressure applied to a button, spring or other device in the handle of the knife, or any knife having a blade which opens or falls or is ejected into position by the force of gravity, or by an outward, downward or centrifugal thrust or movement.

2. Trafficking in dangerous knives is a Class D crime.

Tit. 25, §2001-A. Threatening display of or carrying concealed weapon

1. Display or carrying prohibited. A person may not, unless excepted by a provision of law:

1. Display or carrying prohibited.

A. Display in a threatening manner a firearm, slungshot, knuckles, bowie knife, dirk, stiletto or other dangerous or deadly weapon usually employed in the attack on or defense of a person; or

B. Wear under the person's clothes or conceal about the person's person a firearm, slungshot, knuckles, bowie knife, dirk, stiletto or other dangerous or deadly weapon usually employed in the attack on or defense of a person.

2. Exceptions. The provisions of this section concerning the carrying of concealed weapons do not apply to:

2. Exceptions.

A. Firearms carried by a person to whom a valid permit to carry a concealed firearm has been issued as provided in this chapter;

B. Disabling chemicals as described in Title 17-A, section 1002;

C. Knives used to hunt, fish or trap as defined in Title 12, section 10001;

...

26.4 Selected Caselaw

State v. Michael M., 2001 Me. 92, 772 A.2d 1179 (2001) (affirming conviction and describing butterfly knife as illegal knife falling under switchblade prohibition).

26.5 Preemption Law

No knife law preemption, firearms law preemption only. *See*, ME. REV. STAT. tit. 25, § 2011 (2005).

26.6 Places Off-Limits While Carrying

State courts, through administrative rule, prohibit the carry of firearms, other dangerous weapons, and disabling chemicals, into courthouses. *See*, ME. SUPR. JUDICIAL CT. ADMIN. ORD. JB05-9 (2005). State law prohibits carry of firearms and other dangerous weapons by any person involved in a labor dispute or strike at the site of such dispute or strike. *See*, ME. REV. STAT. tit. 32, § 9412(5) (2005). State law also prohibits carry of firearms in establishments licensed to serve alcohol that have posted signs to that effect. *See, id.* at tit. 17-A, § 1057.

26.7 School/College Carry

No state law limitation for non-students. State law prohibits students from possessing dangerous weapons on school property. Towns and cities, however, may pass their own local ordinances prohibiting knife carry on school grounds, although few appear to have done so.

26.8 Selected City Ordinances

No relevant ordinances. An examination of ordinances for a number of municipalities shows no knife-related ordinances with restrictions greater than those embodied in state law.

26.9 State Resources

Maine Department of Public Safety
18 Meadow Road
Augusta, ME 04333-0104
Phone: (207) 287-3619
TTY: (207) 287-3659
Fax: (207) 287-3042
Website: http://www.state.me.us/dps/index.html

Attorney General of Maine
6 State House Station
Augusta, ME 04333
Phone: (207) 626-8800
Website: http://www.state.me.us/ag/

27 Maryland – The Old Line State

Area: 9,774 sq.mi. (Rank: 42nd)   Population: 5,458,137 (Rank: 18th)
Violent Crime Rate (per 100,000 residents): 700.5 (Rank: 48th Safest)
State Motto: *Fatti Maschii, Parole Femine (Manly Deeds, Womanly Words)*

27.1 Knife Carry Law Summary

Note: Blade length limits, if any, in parentheses.

Knife Type	Open Carry	Concealed Carry	Notes
Folding Knives	Yes	Yes	
Fixed Bladed Knives	Yes	No	See note[52]
Dirks, Daggers, & Stilettos	Yes	No	See note[52]
Automatic Knives	Yes	No	See note[52]
Balisongs	Yes	No	See note[52]

27.2 Discussion

Travelers to Maryland will find, as a practical matter, some fairly restrictive carry laws pertaining to either firearms or knives.

With respect to knives, concealed or open carry of ordinary folding pocket knives, referred to as "penknives" by statute and in case law, should pose no problem. There is no statutorily defined blade length limit. Bowie knives, dirks, daggers, stilettos, and automatic knives may not be carried concealed. Visitors should note that knives such as balisongs, while not specifically prohibited, may fall under the switchblade restriction, as balisongs do in some states.

While state law technically allows open (but not concealed) carry of a wide variety of knives such as bowie knives, dirks, daggers, stilettos, automatics, and balisongs, so long as the knife is not carried "with the intent or purpose of injuring an individual in an unlawful manner", travelers should be aware that this somewhat nebulous standard will often provide slim protection from arrest, especially in the more urban areas of the state. Regardless of whether such charge actually results in conviction, and bearing in mind that the statute provides for up to three years incarceration under certain circumstances, such an arrest will, at the very least, likely ruin your visit to, and impression of, the state.

State law prohibits the carry of any knife on school grounds. In addition, towns and cities may enact their own prohibitions or restrictions on knife carry.

27.3 Selected Statutes

Md. Code §§ (2005)

§ 4-101. Dangerous weapons.

---

[52] State law prohibits concealed carry of dirks, bowie knives, and switchblades. *See,* Md. Code § 4-101 (2005). Travelers should exercise care in the concealed carry of any fixed bladed knife, lest such knife be judged a bowie knife, dagger or dirk. In addition, state law prohibits open carry of any dangerous weapon with the "intent or purpose of injuring an individual in an unlawful manner." *Id.*

(a) Definitions.-

(1) In this section the following words have the meanings indicated.

(2) "Nunchaku" means a device constructed of two pieces of any substance, including wood, metal, or plastic, connected by any chain, rope, leather, or other flexible material not exceeding 24 inches in length.

(3) (i) "Pepper mace" means an aerosol propelled combination of highly disabling irritant pepper-based products.

(ii) "Pepper mace" is also known as oleoresin capsicum (o.c.) spray.

(4) "Star knife" means a device used as a throwing weapon, consisting of several sharp or pointed blades arrayed as radially disposed arms about a central disk.

(5) (i) "Weapon" includes a dirk knife, bowie knife, switchblade knife, star knife, sandclub, metal knuckles, razor, and nunchaku.

(ii) "Weapon" does not include:

1. a handgun; or

2. a penknife without a switchblade.

...
(c) Prohibited.-

(1) A person may not wear or carry a dangerous weapon of any kind concealed on or about the person.

(2) A person may not wear or carry a dangerous weapon, chemical mace, pepper mace, or a tear gas device openly with the intent or purpose of injuring an individual in an unlawful manner.

(3) (i) This paragraph applies in Anne Arundel County, Baltimore County, Caroline County, Cecil County, Harford County, Kent County, Montgomery County, Prince George's County, St. Mary's County, Talbot County, Washington County, and Worcester County.

(ii) A minor may not carry a dangerous weapon between 1 hour after sunset and 1 hour before sunrise, whether concealed or not, except while:

1. on a bona fide hunting trip; or

2. engaged in or on the way to or returning from a bona fide trap shoot, sport shooting event, or any organized civic or military activity.

(d) Penalties.-

(1) A person who violates this section is guilty of a misdemeanor and on conviction is subject to imprisonment not exceeding 3 years or a fine not exceeding $1,000 or both.

(2) For a person convicted under subsection (c)(1) or (2) of this section, if it appears from the evidence that the weapon was carried, concealed or openly, with the deliberate purpose of injuring or killing another, the court shall impose the highest sentence of imprisonment prescribed.

§ 4-102. Deadly weapons on school property.

...
(b) Prohibited.- A person may not carry or possess a firearm, knife, or deadly weapon of any kind on public school property.

...

27.4 Selected Caselaw

Bacon v. State, 586 A.2d 18 (Md. 1991) (holding folding knife with four to six inch locking blade carried openly with blade extended still falls within "penknife without switchblade" exception to dangerous weapon carry prohibition).

In re Daryl L., 511 A.2d 1108 (Md. Ct. Spec. App. 1986) (holding folding knife with locking blade falls within exception to dangerous weapon concealed carry prohibition).

27.5 Preemption Law

No knife law preemption, firearms law preemption only. *See*, MD. CODE § 4-209 (2005).

27.6 Places Off-Limits While Carrying

Maryland prohibits the carry of firearms, knives and other deadly weapons on public school property. *See*, MD. CODE § 4-102 (2005).

27.7 School/College Carry

Maryland prohibits the carry of firearms, knives and other deadly weapons on public school property. *See*, MD. CODE § 4-102 (2005).

27.8 Selected City Ordinances

Gaithersburg – Unlawful to carry razors or other dangerous weapons. *See*, GAITHERSBURG, MD., CODE OF ORDINANCES § 15-16 (2004).

Cumberland – Concealed carry of sword canes and dirks prohibited. *See*, CUMBERLAND, MD., CODE OF ORDINANCES § 11-91 (2004). Possession of switchblades prohibited. *See, id.* § 11-95.

27.9 State Resources

Maryland State Police
1201 Reisterstown Road
Pikesville, MD 21208
Phone: (410) 268-6101
Website: http://www.mdsp.org/

Attorney General of Maryland
200 St. Paul Place
Baltimore, MD 21202
Phone: (410) 576-6300
Website: http://www.oag.state.md.us/

28 Massachusetts – The Bay State

Area: 8,257 sq.mi. (Rank: 45th)   Population: 6,349,097 (Rank: 13th)
Violent Crime Rate (per 100,000 residents): 458.8 (Rank: 33rd Safest)
State Motto: *Ense Petit Placidam Sub Libertate Quietem (By the Sword We Seek Peace, But Peace Only Under Liberty)*

28.1 Knife Carry Law Summary

Note: Blade length limits, if any, in parentheses.

Knife Type	Open Carry	Concealed Carry	Notes
Folding Knives	Yes	Yes	See note[53]
Fixed Bladed Knives	Yes	Yes	See note[53]
Dirks, Daggers, & Stilettos	No	No	
Automatic Knives	No	No	See note[54]
Balisongs	Yes	Yes	See note[55]
Sword Canes	No	No	

28.2 Discussion

Being one of the original thirteen colonies, and the site of several key battles of the Revolutionary War that gave birth to this great Nation, one might be inclined to think that Massachusetts law would favor citizens' right to carry defensive tools. Indeed, the state motto, *Ense Petit Placidam Sub Libertate Quietem*, meaning "by the sword we seek peace, but peace only under liberty," harkens to a freedom-loving revolutionary spirit that embraces arms as the means to achieve both peace and liberty. Such notions, however, would be greatly at odds with current Massachusetts law, as the state strictly regulates both firearms and a wide variety of weapons, including knives.

There is no statutorily defined blade length limit for ordinary fixed or folding knives. Massachusetts prohibits folding knives equipped with certain types of assisted opening mechanisms that enable the blade to be drawn at a locked position. In addition, dirks, daggers, stilettos, and "switch knives" are likewise prohibited. State law would appear to allow automatic knives with blades of one and a half inches or less, although the statute also appears to ban switch knives, typically a synonym for an automatic-type knife, completely. The cautious traveler visiting the Bay State would do well to consider any automatic knife, of any length blade, off limits in the Commonwealth. Note that balisongs, while not specifically prohibited, may fall within the switchblade prohibition, as balisongs do in some states.

Carry of ordinary fixed and folding knives, while permissible under state law, may be independently regulated by towns and cities, and a number of municipalities have done so.

---

[53] Note that some cities regulate carry and blade length. In addition, certain assisted-opening mechanisms are prohibited, to wit, any mechanism "which enables a knife with a locking blade to be drawn at a locked position[.]" *See*, Mass. Gen. Laws ch. 269, § 10 (2005).

[54] The law appears to allow automatic knives whose blades do not exceed 1.5 inches in length. The statute wording is somewhat ambiguous, however, and appears to ban "switch knives", typically a synonym for automatic knives.

[55] Note that balisongs may fall under the switchblade prohibition, as balisongs do in some states, and thus be subject to the same restrictions or prohibitions as switchblades.

Some cities and towns variously prohibit the sale, possession, and carry of knives of certain types and/or certain blade lengths. For example, travelers to Boston should be aware that the Boston Municipal Code prohibits carry of any knife, fixed or folding, with a blade length over two and a half inches in length. Other Massachusetts cities and towns have similar ordinances prohibiting carry within town or city limits. Travelers visiting particular cities may wish to contact the local authorities in those cities to verify that the knife they plan on carrying will be acceptable.

State law prohibits carry of dangerous weapons in the buildings or upon the grounds of any elementary or secondary school, or college or university without written authorization from that educational institution.

28.3 Selected Statutes

Mass. Gen. Laws (2005)

Chapter 269: Section 10. Carrying dangerous weapons; possession of machine gun or sawed-off shotguns; possession of large capacity weapon or large capacity feeding device; punishment

...

(b) Whoever, except as provided by law, carries on his person, or carries on his person or under his control in a vehicle, any stiletto, dagger or a device or case which enables a knife with a locking blade to be drawn at a locked position, any ballistic knife, or any knife with a detachable blade capable of being propelled by any mechanism, dirk knife, any knife having a double-edged blade, or a switch knife, or any knife having an automatic spring release device by which the blade is released from the handle, having a blade of over one and one-half inches, or a slung shot, blowgun, blackjack, metallic knuckles or knuckles of any substance which could be put to the same use with the same or similar effect as metallic knuckles, nunchaku, zoobow, also known as klackers or kung fu sticks, or any similar weapon consisting of two sticks of wood, plastic or metal connected at one end by a length of rope, chain, wire or leather, a shuriken or any similar pointed starlike object intended to injure a person when thrown, or any armband, made with leather which has metallic spikes, points or studs or any similar device made from any other substance or a cestus or similar material weighted with metal or other substance and worn on the hand, or a manrikigusari or similar length of chain having weighted ends; or whoever, when arrested upon a warrant for an alleged crime, or when arrested while committing a breach or disturbance of the public peace, is armed with or has on his person, or has on his person or under his control in a vehicle, a billy or other dangerous weapon other than those herein mentioned and those mentioned in paragraph (a), shall be punished by imprisonment for not less than two and one-half years nor more than five years in the state prison, or for not less than six months nor more than two and one-half years in a jail or house of correction, except that, if the court finds that the defendant has not been previously convicted of a felony, he may be punished by a fine of not more than fifty dollars or by imprisonment for not more than two and one-half years in a jail or house of correction.

...

(j) Whoever, not being a law enforcement officer, and notwithstanding any license obtained by him under the provisions of chapter one hundred and forty, carries on his person a firearm as hereinafter defined, loaded or unloaded or other dangerous weapon in any building or on the grounds of any elementary or secondary school, college or university without the written authorization of the board or officer in charge of such elementary or secondary school, college or university shall be punished by a fine of not more than one thousand dollars or by imprisonment for not more than one year, or both. For the purpose of this paragraph, "firearm" shall mean any pistol, revolver, rifle or smoothbore arm from which a shot, bullet or pellet can be discharged by whatever means.

Any officer in charge of an elementary or secondary school, college or university or any faculty member or administrative officer of an elementary or secondary school, college or university failing to report violations of this paragraph shall be guilty of a misdemeanor and punished by a fine of not more than five hundred dollars.

Chapter 269: Section 12. Manufacturing and selling knives, slung shots, swords, bludgeons and similar weapons

Section 12. Whoever manufactures or causes to be manufactured, or sells or exposes for sale, an instrument or weapon of the kind usually known as a dirk knife, a switch knife or any knife having an automatic spring release device by which the blade is released from the handle, having a blade of over one and one-half inches or a device or case which enables a knife with a locking blade to be drawn at a locked position, any ballistic knife, or any knife with a detachable blade capable of being propelled by any mechanism, slung shot, sling shot, bean blower, sword cane, pistol cane, bludgeon, blackjack, nunchaku, zoobow, also known as klackers or kung fu sticks, or any similar weapon consisting of two sticks of wood, plastic or metal connected at one end by a length of rope, chain, wire or leather, a shuriken or any similar pointed starlike object intended to injure a person when thrown, or a manrikigusari or similar length of chain having weighted ends; or metallic knuckles or knuckles of any other substance which could be put to the same use and with the same or similar effect as metallic knuckles, shall be punished by a fine of not less than fifty nor more than one thousand dollars or by imprisonment for not more than six months; provided, however, that sling shots may be manufactured and sold to clubs or associations conducting sporting events where such sling shots are used.

28.4 Selected Caselaw

Commonwealth v. Sinforoso, 434 Mass. 320, 749 N.E.2d 128 (2001) at footnote 1 (noting violation of city ordinance prohibiting carry of "any weapon with a blade in excess of two and one-half inches in length")

Commonwealth v. Smith, 40 Mass. App. Ct. 770 (1996) (affirming conviction for carrying knife with double-edged blade).

28.5 Preemption Law

None.

28.6 Places Off-Limits While Carrying

Carry of "dangerous weapons" on school, college, or university property is prohibited without written authorization from the school, college, or university. *See*, Mass. Gen. Laws ch. 269, § 10(j) (2005).

28.7 School/College Carry

See above.

28.8 Selected City Ordinances

Boston – Carry on person or under person's control in vehicle of any knife with a blade over 2½ inches in length prohibited. *See*, Boston, Mass., Municipal Code, § 16-45 *et. seq.* (2005).

Revere – Carry on person or under person's control in vehicle of any knife with a blade over 2½ inches in length prohibited. *See*, Revere, Mass., Rev. Ord. § 9.20.020 (2004).

28.9 State Resources

Massachusetts State Police
470 Worcester Road
Framingham, MA 01702
Phone: (508) 820-2300
Website: http://www.mass.gov (Search for "State Police")

Attorney General of Massachusetts
1350 Main Street, 4th Floor
Springfield, MA 01103
Phone: (413) 784-1240
Fax: (413) 784-1244
Website: http://www.ago.state.ma.us/

29 Michigan – The Wolverine State

Area: 56,804 sq.mi. (Rank: 22nd)   Population: 10,050,446 (Rank: 8th)
Violent Crime Rate (per 100,000 residents): 490.2 (Rank: 34th Safest)
State Motto: *Si Quaeris Peninsulam Amoenam, Circum Spice (If You are Seeking an Amenable (Pleasant) Peninsula, Look Around You)*

29.1 Knife Carry Law Summary

Note: Blade length limits, if any, in parentheses.

Knife Type	Open Carry	Concealed Carry	Notes
Folding Knives	Yes	Yes (<= 3")	See notes[56,57]
Fixed Bladed Knives	Yes	Yes	See note[58]
Dirks, Daggers, & Stilettos	Yes	No	See note[58]
Automatic Knives	No	No	
Balisongs	No	No	See note[57]

29.2 Discussion

Visitors to the Wolverine State will find a perhaps somewhat surprisingly restrictive legal environment for knife carry. With respect to knives, ordinary folding pocket knives should pose no problem, carried either openly or concealed. Note, however, that the statutory definition of "dangerous weapon" under the state's "unlawful intent" statute includes knives with blades over three inches in length, and a corollary statute prohibits concealed carry of *per se* weapons. Thus, prudent travelers would be wise to avoid concealed carry of folding knives with blades over three inches long.

State law provides that dirks, daggers, stilettos, and knives with blades over three inches in length may be carried openly so long as the wearer does not intend to use such knife unlawfully against another. The careful traveler should realize that such "unlawful intent" statutes provide considerable discretion to law enforcement for arrest of persons carrying such knives. In addition, such knives may not be carried either openly or concealed in a vehicle. As such, it is recommended that travelers seriously consider alternatives to dirk, dagger, stiletto, and large fixed bladed knife carry. Fixed bladed knives such as hunting or fishing knives, however, may be carried concealed if legitimately engaged in those activities, subject to the vehicle carry prohibition.

State law prohibits automatic knives. Knives such as balisongs, while not specifically prohibited, may fall under the switchblade prohibition, as balisongs do in some states. In

---

[56] The state's "unlawful intent" statute includes in its definition of "dangerous weapon" any knife with a blade longer than three inches. *See*, MICH. COMP. LAWS § 750.226 (2005). A separate statute prohibits concealed carry of weapons, including dirks, daggers, stilettos, and "other dangerous weapon[s]". *See, id.* at § 750.227. Thus, folding pocket knives with blades greater than three inches likely fall under this prohibition.
[57] State law prohibits automatic knives, the definition of which includes any knife having "the appearance of a pocket knife, the blade or blades of which can be opened by the flick of a button, pressure on a handle or other mechanical contrivance[.]" *See*, MICH. COMP. LAWS § 750.226a (2005). Note that this definition may include balisongs and assisted opening folding knives.
[58] State law prohibits carry, whether concealed or open, in a vehicle. *See*, MICH. COMP. LAWS § 750.227 (2005).

addition, based on the broad statutory wording of the automatic knife prohibition, some assisted opening knives may also fall under the switchblade prohibition, and thus may be illegal to carry.

Other that a state law prohibition on any knife carry in the sterile (secure) area of commercial airports[59] (already prohibited under federal law), no general state-wide off-limits locations on legal knife carry exist. Note that state law does prohibit possession of dangerous weapons, including knives with blades over three inches, by students in schools or at school activities. In addition, cities and towns may pass their own ordinances restricting knife carry within their jurisdictions.

29.3 Selected Statutes

MICH. COMP. LAWS §§ (2005)

750.222a "Double-edged, nonfolding stabbing instrument" defined.

(1) As used in this chapter, "doubled-edged, nonfolding stabbing instrument" does not include a knife, tool, implement, arrowhead, or artifact manufactured from stone by means of conchoidal fracturing.

(2) Subsection (1) does not apply to an item being transported in a vehicle, unless the item is in a container and inaccessible to the driver.

750.226 Firearm or dangerous weapon; carrying with unlawful intent.

Carrying firearm or dangerous weapon with unlawful intent—Any person who, with intent to use the same unlawfully against the person of another, goes armed with a pistol or other firearm or dagger, dirk, razor, stiletto, or knife having a blade over 3 inches in length, or any other dangerous or deadly weapon or instrument, shall be guilty of a felony, punishable by imprisonment in the state prison for not more than 5 years or by a fine of not more than 2,500 dollars.

750.226a Pocket knife opened by mechanical device; unlawful sale or possession; persons exempted.

Any person who shall sell or offer to sell, or any person who shall have in his possession any knife having the appearance of a pocket knife, the blade or blades of which can be opened by the flick of a button, pressure on a handle or other mechanical contrivance shall be guilty of a misdemeanor, punishable by imprisonment in the county jail for not to exceed 1 year or by a fine of not to exceed $300.00, or both.

The provisions of this section shall not apply to any one-armed person carrying a knife on his person in connection with his living requirements.

750.227 Concealed weapons; carrying; penalty.

(1) A person shall not carry a dagger, dirk, stiletto, a double-edged nonfolding stabbing instrument of any length, or any other dangerous weapon, except a hunting knife adapted and carried as such, concealed on or about his or her person, or whether concealed or otherwise in any vehicle operated or occupied by the person, except in his or her dwelling house, place of business or on other land possessed by the person.

(2) A person shall not carry a pistol concealed on or about his or her person, or, whether concealed or otherwise, in a vehicle operated or occupied by the person, except in his or her dwelling house, place of business, or on other land possessed by the person, without a license to carry the pistol as provided by law and if licensed, shall not carry the pistol in a place or manner inconsistent with any restrictions upon such license.

---

[59] *See*, MICH. COMP. LAWS § 259.80f (2005).

(3) A person who violates this section is guilty of a felony, punishable by imprisonment for not more than 5 years, or by a fine of not more than $2,500.00.

29.4 Selected Caselaw

People v. Johnson, 437 N.W.2d 302 (Mich. Ct. App. 1989) (holding concealed weapons statute's wording of "other dangerous weapon" applies to edged weapons only, not to other classes of dangerous weapons, and finding determination of whether particular weapon falls within statute's ambit is question of law, not question for fact-finder).

People v. Lynn, 580 N.W.2d 472 (Mich. Ct. App. 1998) (holding statute prohibiting concealed weapons constitutional).

29.5 Preemption Law

No knife law preemption, firearms law preemption only. *See*, MICH. COMP. LAWS § 123.1102 (2005).

29.6 Places Off-Limits While Carrying

State law prohibits carry of knives in the sterile (secure) areas of commercial airports. *See*, MICH. COMP. LAWS § 259.80f (2005). Towns and cities may pass their own local ordinances prohibiting or otherwise restricting carry within their jurisdictions.

29.7 School/College Carry

State law prohibits possession of dangerous weapons by students on school grounds or at school activities. The definition of "dangerous weapon" includes dirks, daggers, stilettos, knives with blades over three inches long, or a "pocket knife opened by a mechanical device[.]" *See*, MICH. COMP. LAWS § 380.1313 (2005).

Note that towns and cities may pass their own additional restrictions of prohibitions on knife carry by non-students on school grounds.

29.8 Selected City Ordinances

Detroit – Possession of cane swords, umbrella swords, switchblades and other self-opening knives prohibited. *See*, DETROIT, MICH., CITY CODE § 38-10-40 (2006). Carry, openly or concealed, of knife with blade three inches or longer prohibited. *See, id.* at § 38-10-42. Possession of knives in public city buildings with blades over three inches in length prohibited. *See, id.* at § 38-4-11.

Lansing – Carry, concealed or otherwise, of any knife with blade over three inches in length prohibited. *See*, LANSING, MICH., CODIFIED ORDINANCES § 696.04 (2005). Possession of knives on college campus property prohibited. *See, id.* at § 696.05.

29.9 State Resources

Michigan Department of State Police
714 S. Harrison Road
East Lansing, MI 48823
Phone: (517) 332-2521
Website: http://www.michigan.gov/msp

Michigan Attorney General
525 W. Ottawa St.
Lansing, MI 48909
Phone: (517) 373-1110
Fax: (517) 373-3042
Website: http://www.michigan.gov/ag

30 Minnesota – The North Star State

Area: 79,610 sq.mi. (Rank: 14th)   Population: 5,019,720 (Rank: 21st)
Violent Crime Rate (per 100,000 residents): 269.6 (Rank: 13th Safest)
State Motto: *L'Etoile du Nord (The Star of the North)*

30.1 Knife Carry Law Summary

<u>Note</u>: Blade length limits, if any, in parentheses.

Knife Type	Open Carry	Concealed Carry	Notes
Folding Knives	Yes	Yes	See note[60]
Fixed Bladed Knives	Yes	Yes	See note[60]
Dirks, Daggers, & Stilettos	No	No	
Automatic Knives	No	No	
Balisongs	No	No	

30.2 Discussion

Travelers to Minnesota will find a fairly restrictive legal environment for knife carry, especially within the urban population areas.

With respect to knives, ordinary folding pocket knives should pose no problem. There is no statutorily defined blade length limit under state law, although at least one major city imposes a blade length limit for knives considered *per se* weapons. Automatic knives are prohibited under state law. Dirks, daggers and stilettos are prohibited under some city ordinances, and likely would be considered *per se* dangerous weapons under state law as well. Balisongs, while not specifically prohibited, may fall under the statutory switchblade prohibition, as balisongs do in some states.

State law prohibits carry of dangerous weapons in courthouses and on school property. Minnesota does not preempt its cities and towns from regulating knife carry, unlike the case for firearms, and so towns and cities may impose their own restrictions on knife carry.

30.3 Selected Statutes

MINN. STAT. §§ (2005)

609.02 Definitions.

...

Subd. 6.   Dangerous weapon. "Dangerous weapon" means any firearm, whether loaded or unloaded, or any device designed as a weapon and capable of producing death or great bodily harm, any combustible or flammable liquid or other device or instrumentality that, in the manner it is used or intended to be used, is calculated or likely to produce death or great bodily harm, or any fire that is used to produce death or great bodily harm.

...

609.66 Dangerous weapons.

---

[60] State law prohibits the carry of dangerous weapons for use as such unlawfully against another. *See*, MINN. STAT. § 609.66 (1)(a) (2005). The cautious traveler should avoid carry of "tactical" knives with weapon-like appearances or overly large knives. Knives such as hunting and fishing knives should only be carried while engaged in those activities, and certainly not within urban areas.

Subdivision 1. Misdemeanor and gross misdemeanor crimes. (a) Whoever does any of the following is guilty of a crime and may be sentenced as provided in paragraph (b):

...

(4) manufactures, transfers, or possesses metal knuckles or a switch blade knife opening automatically; or

(5) possesses any other dangerous article or substance for the purpose of being used unlawfully as a weapon against another; or

...

30.4 Selected Caselaw

In re the Welfare of C. R. M., 611 N.W.2d 802 (Minn. 2000) (holding that state must prove defendant knew he possessed knife on school grounds for conviction. Four inch folding knife may be dangerous weapon and may support conviction under statute).

30.5 Preemption Law

No knife law preemption, firearms law preemption only. *See,* Minn. Stat. § 471.633 (2005).

30.6 Places Off-Limits While Carrying

Minnesota state law prohibits the carry of dangerous weapons on school grounds and in courthouses, subject to certain limited exceptions. In addition, towns and cities may pass their own local ordinances restricting or prohibiting carry. Minneapolis, for example, explicitly prohibits carry of knives of any kind on school property, with certain exceptions not normally applicable to the average traveler.

30.7 School/College Carry

Minnesota state law prohibits the carry of dangerous weapons on school grounds, subject to certain limited exceptions. In addition, towns and cities may pass their own local ordinances restricting or prohibiting carry.

30.8 Selected City Ordinances

Minneapolis – Carry of weapons on or about the person within the city prohibited. *See,* Minneapolis, Minn., Code of Ordinances § 393.90 (2006). The definition of "weapon" normally excludes folding knives with blades four inches or less, unless such knife is actually used as a weapon. *See, id.* at § 393.10. Carry of weapons while intoxicated also prohibited. *See, id.* at § 393.50. Possession of knives on school property prohibited (limited exceptions exist). *See, id.* at § 393.60.

Duluth – Possession of daggers, stilettos, and switchblades prohibited. *See,* Duluth, Minn., Legislative Code § 49-10 (2005).

30.9 State Resources

Minnesota Department of Public Safety
444 Cedar Street
Saint Paul, MN 55101
Phone: (651) 282-6565
Website: http://www.dps.state.mn.us/

Minnesota Attorney General's Office
102 State Capitol
St. Paul, MN 55155
Phone: (651) 296-6196
Phone: (800) 657-3787
Website: http://www.ag.state.mn.us/

31 Mississippi – The Magnolia State

Area: 46,907 sq.mi. (Rank: 31st)　Population: 2,871,782 (Rank: 31st)
Violent Crime Rate (per 100,000 residents): 295.1 (Rank: 19th Safest)
State Motto: *Virtute et Armis (By Valor and Arms)*

31.1 Knife Carry Law Summary

Note: Blade length limits, if any, in parentheses.

Knife Type	Open Carry	Concealed Carry	Notes
Folding Knives	Yes	Yes	
Fixed Bladed Knives	Yes	No	
Dirks, Daggers, & Stilettos	Yes	No	
Automatic Knives	Yes	No	
Balisongs	Yes	No	

31.2 Discussion

Visitors to the Magnolia State will find a fairly permissive legal environment for open knife carry, with a more restrictive environment for concealed carry. Open or concealed carry of ordinary pocket knives should pose no problem. Fixed bladed knives may be carried openly, but travelers should exercise care when carrying such knives concealed. Mississippi state law prohibits concealed carry of bowie knives, dirks, butcher knives and switchblades, although state law does not define these types of knives. The statute prohibits concealment "in whole or in part."[61] As such, travelers should exercise considerable caution carrying any fixed bladed knife, lest they inadvertently run afoul of the statutory language and be accused of carrying one of the prohibited knife types.

Note that balisongs, while not specifically prohibited, may fall under the switchblade prohibition, as balisongs do in some states.

Unlike with firearms, no state-wide statutory prohibitions on off-limits locations for otherwise legal knife carry appear to exist, although travelers should be aware that cities and towns may pass their own ordinances restricting knife carry. Tupelo, for example, prohibits carry of knives with blades greater than three and a half inches in length in a wide variety of places within that city, such as in government buildings, in establishments that serve alcohol for on-premises consumption, and at political rallies or meetings, among others.

31.3 Selected Statutes

Miss. Code §§ (2005)

§ 97-37-1. Deadly weapons; carrying while concealed; use or attempt to use; penalties.

(1) Except as otherwise provided in Section 45-9-101, any person who carries, concealed in whole or in part, any bowie knife, dirk knife, butcher knife, switchblade knife, metallic knuckles, blackjack, slingshot, pistol, revolver, or any rifle with a barrel of less than sixteen (16) inches in length, or any shotgun with a barrel of less than eighteen

---

[61] See, Miss. Code § 97-37-1 (2005).

(18) inches in length, machine gun or any fully automatic firearm or deadly weapon, or any muffler or silencer for any firearm, whether or not it is accompanied by a firearm, or uses or attempts to use against another person any imitation firearm, shall upon conviction be punished as follows:

...

(2) It shall not be a violation of this section for any person over the age of eighteen (18) years to carry a firearm or deadly weapon concealed in whole or in part within the confines of his own home or his place of business, or any real property associated with his home or business or within any motor vehicle.

(3) It shall not be a violation of this section for any person to carry a firearm or deadly weapon concealed in whole or in part if the possessor of the weapon is then engaged in a legitimate weapon-related sports activity or is going to or returning from such activity. For purposes of this subsection, "legitimate weapon-related sports activity" means hunting, fishing, target shooting or any other legal sports activity which normally involves the use of a firearm or other weapon.

§ 97-37-17. Possession of weapons by students; aiding or encouraging.

(1) The following definitions apply to this section:

(a) "Educational property" shall mean any public or private school building or bus, public or private school campus, grounds, recreational area, athletic field, or other property owned, used or operated by any local school board, school, college or university board of trustees, or directors for the administration of any public or private educational institution or during a school related activity; provided however, that the term "educational property" shall not include any sixteenth section school land or lieu land on which is not located a school building, school campus, recreational area or athletic field.

(b) "Student" shall mean a person enrolled in a public or private school, college or university, or a person who has been suspended or expelled within the last five (5) years from a public or private school, college or university, whether the person is an adult or a minor.

(c) "Switchblade knife" shall mean a knife containing a blade or blades which open automatically by the release of a spring or a similar contrivance.

(d) "Weapon" shall mean any device enumerated in subsection (2) or (4) of this section.

...

(4) It shall be a misdemeanor for any person to possess or carry, whether openly or concealed, any BB gun, air rifle, air pistol, bowie knife, dirk, dagger, slingshot, leaded cane, switchblade knife, blackjack, metallic knuckles, razors and razor blades (except solely for personal shaving), and any sharp-pointed or edged instrument except instructional supplies, unaltered nail files and clips and tools used solely for preparation of food, instruction and maintenance on educational property. Any person violating this subsection shall be guilty of a misdemeanor and, upon conviction thereof, shall be fined not more than One Thousand Dollars ($1,000.00), or be imprisoned not exceeding six (6) months, or both.

(5) It shall be a misdemeanor for any person to cause, encourage or aid a minor who is less than eighteen (18) years old to possess or carry, whether openly or concealed, any BB gun, air rifle, air pistol, bowie knife, dirk, dagger, slingshot, leaded cane, switchblade, knife, blackjack, metallic knuckles, razors and razor blades (except solely for personal shaving) and any sharp-pointed or edged instrument except instructional supplies, unaltered nail files and clips and tools used solely for preparation of food, instruction and maintenance on educational property. Any person violating this subsection shall be guilty of a misdemeanor and, upon conviction thereof, shall be fined not more than One Thousand Dollars ($1,000.00), or be imprisoned not exceeding six (6) months, or both.

...

(7) This section shall not apply to:

...

(g) Any weapon not prescribed by Section 97-37-1 which is in a motor vehicle under the control of a parent, guardian or custodian, as defined in Section 43-21-105, which is used to bring or pick up a student at a school building, school property or school function.

(8) All schools shall post in public view a copy of the provisions of this section.

§ 97-37-19. Deadly weapons; exhibiting in rude, angry, or threatening manner.

If any person, having or carrying any dirk, dirk-knife, sword, sword-cane, or any deadly weapon, or other weapon the carrying of which concealed is prohibited, shall, in the presence of three or more persons, exhibit the same in a rude, angry, or threatening manner, not in necessary self-defense, or shall in any manner unlawfully use the same in any fight or quarrel, the person so offending, upon conviction thereof, shall be fined in a sum not exceeding five hundred dollars or be imprisoned in the county jail not exceeding three months, or both. In prosecutions under this section it shall not be necessary for the affidavit or indictment to aver, nor for the state to prove on the trial, that any gun, pistol, or other firearm was charged, loaded, or in condition to be discharged.

31.4 Selected Caselaw

Coleman v. State, 592 So.2d 517 (Miss. 1991) (discussing arrest for carrying concealed knife with blade greater than three inches long).

Osborne v. State, 404 So.2d 545 (Miss. 1981) (upholding conviction for carrying concealed weapon, butcher knife with handle and part of blade visible in pants at defendant's waist).

31.5 Preemption Law

No knife law preemption, firearms law preemption only. *See*, MISS. CODE § 45-9-51 (2005).

31.6 Places Off-Limits While Carrying

No state law limitation. Towns and cities, however, may pass their own local ordinances prohibiting or restricting carry.

31.7 School/College Carry

No state law limitation. Towns and cities, however, may pass their own local ordinances prohibiting carry on school grounds.

31.8 Selected City Ordinances

Jackson – Carry of firearms or deadly weapons as defined in state law prohibited at city council meetings, parades, political rallies, or other political meetings held in or on public buildings. *See*, JACKSON, MISS., CODE OF ORDINANCES § 86-12 (2005).

Tupelo – Carry of "dangerous weapons," the definition of which includes knives with blades greater than three and a half inches, prohibited in, on, or at public parks, public meetings, political rallies, parades, at school, college, or professional events, including concerts and lectures, financial institution premises, commercial retail establishments, including shopping malls and centers, on government owned buildings or property, and in establishments serving alcohol for on-premises consumption. *See*, TUPELO, MISS., CODE OF ORDINANCES § 19-4 (1999).

31.9 State Resources

Mississippi State Police
P. O. Box 958
Jackson, MS 39205
Phone: (601) 987-1212
Fax: (601) 987-1498
Website: http://www.dps.state.ms.us/

Attorney General of Mississippi
P.O. Box 220
Jackson, MS 39205-0220
Phone: (601) 987-1586
Fax: (601) 987-1547
Website: http://www.ago.state.ms.us/

32 Missouri – The Show Me State

Area: 66,886 sq.mi. (Rank: 18th)   Population: 5,672,579 (Rank: 17th)
Violent Crime Rate (per 100,000 residents): 490.5 (Rank: 35th Safest)
State Motto: *Salus Populi Suprema Lex Esto (The Welfare of the People Shall Be the Supreme Law)*

32.1 Knife Carry Law Summary

Note: Blade length limits, if any, in parentheses.

Knife Type	Open Carry	Concealed Carry	Notes
Folding Knives	Yes (<= 4")	Yes (<= 4")	
Fixed Bladed Knives	Yes	No	
Dirks, Daggers, & Stilettos	Yes	No	
Automatic Knives	No	No	
Balisongs	No	No	

32.2 Discussion

Visitors to the Show Me State will find that the legal environment for knife carry, in keeping with the state's nickname, strongly favors open, versus concealed, knife carry. (Firearms-carrying travelers with recognized permits should note that while open carry is permitted under state law, many municipalities restrict or prohibit such carry.)

With respect to knives, ordinary folding pocket knives with blades no longer than four inches may be carried openly or concealed. Under state law, fixed bladed knives, including dirks, daggers, and stilettos, may be carried openly, although travelers would be well advised to exercise caution whenever carrying such knives, especially in urban areas. Automatic knives are prohibited. Knives such as balisongs, while not specifically prohibited, may fall under the switchblade prohibition, as balisongs do in some states, and thus the careful traveler would do well to avoid carry of such knives.

State law prohibits carry of weapons in schools, school buses, and at school sponsored or sanctioned events. As is the case in many states, travelers should be aware that cities and towns may pass their own ordinances prohibiting or otherwise restricting knife carry within their jurisdictions.

32.3 Selected Statutes

Mo. Rev. Stat. §§ (2005)

571.010. As used in this chapter:

...

(10) "Knife" means any dagger, dirk, stiletto, or bladed hand instrument that is readily capable of inflicting serious physical injury or death by cutting or stabbing a person. For purposes of this chapter, "knife" does not include any ordinary pocketknife with no blade more than four inches in length;

...

(18) "Switchblade knife" means any knife which has a blade that folds or closes into the handle or sheath, and

(a) That opens automatically by pressure applied to a button or other device located on the handle; or

(b) That opens or releases from the handle or sheath by the force of gravity or by the application of centrifugal force.

571.020. 1. A person commits a crime if such person knowingly possesses, manufactures, transports, repairs, or sells:

...

(7) A switchblade knife;

...

571.030. 1. A person commits the crime of unlawful use of weapons if he or she knowingly:

(1) Carries concealed upon or about his or her person a knife, a firearm, a blackjack or any other weapon readily capable of lethal use; or

...

(4) Exhibits, in the presence of one or more persons, any weapon readily capable of lethal use in an angry or threatening manner; or

...

(10) Carries a firearm, whether loaded or unloaded, or any other weapon readily capable of lethal use into any school, onto any school bus, or onto the premises of any function or activity sponsored or sanctioned by school officials or the district school board.

...

3. Subdivisions (1), (5), (8), and (10) of subsection 1 of this section do not apply when the actor is transporting such weapons in a nonfunctioning state or in an unloaded state when ammunition is not readily accessible or when such weapons are not readily accessible. Subdivision (1) of subsection 1 of this section does not apply to any person twenty-one years of age or older transporting a concealable firearm in the passenger compartment of a motor vehicle, so long as such concealable firearm is otherwise lawfully possessed, nor when the actor is also in possession of an exposed firearm or projectile weapon for the lawful pursuit of game, or is in his or her dwelling unit or upon premises over which the actor has possession, authority or control, or is traveling in a continuous journey peaceably through this state. Subdivision (10) of subsection 1 of this section does not apply if the firearm is otherwise lawfully possessed by a person while traversing school premises for the purposes of transporting a student to or from school, or possessed by an adult for the purposes of facilitation of a school-sanctioned firearm-related event.

4. Subdivisions (1), (8), and (10) of subsection 1 of this section shall not apply to any person who has a valid concealed carry endorsement issued pursuant to sections 571.101 to 571.121 or a valid permit or endorsement to carry concealed firearms issued by another state or political subdivision of another state.

...

32.4 Selected Caselaw

State v. Baldwin, 571 S.W.2d 236 (Mo. 1978) (affirming, *inter alia*, conviction under predecessor statute for concealed carry of steak knife and upholding jury determination that knife was dangerous and deadly weapon).

State v. Smith, 897 S.W.2d 87 (Mo. Ct. App. 1995) (reversing conviction for carrying concealed weapon and holding saw with handle and six and one-eight inch serrated blade not "knife" under statute).

State v. Pelz, 831 S.W.2d 635 (Mo. Ct. App. 1992) (affirming conviction for unlawful use of weapon in carrying concealed weapon, large lock-back knife in vehicle).

32.5 Preemption Law

No knife law preemption, firearms law preemption only. *See*, Mo. Rev. Stat. § 21.750 (2005).

32.6 Places Off-Limits While Carrying

State law prohibits carry of weapons "readily capable of lethal use" in schools, school buses, and at school sponsored or sanctioned events. *See*, Mo. Rev. Stat. § 571.030 (2005). Municipal governments may also pass their own local ordinances prohibiting or otherwise restricting carry within their respective jurisdictions.

32.7 School/College Carry

State law prohibits carry of weapons "readily capable of lethal use" in schools, school buses, and at school sponsored or sanctioned events. *See*, Mo. Rev. Stat. § 571.030 (2005).

32.8 Selected City Ordinances

Independence – Possession of deadly weapons prohibited on school grounds, playgrounds, parks, and city buildings or facilities. The definition of "deadly weapon" includes knives with blades greater than four inches in length. *See*, Independence, Mo., Code of Ordinances § 12.03.001 (2004). Carry of knives, either openly or concealed, "into any public building or place open to the public, or on any public property" prohibited. *See, id.* at § 12.03.003.

Jackson – Carry of any weapon readily capable of lethal use prohibited in churches, schools, polling places on election day, or any government building. *See*, Jackson, Mo., Code of Ordinances § 45-502 (2005).

32.9 State Resources

Department of Public Safety
Truman State Office Building, Rm. 870
Jefferson City, MO 65102-0749
Phone: (888) FYI-MDPS
Fax: (573) 751-5399
Website: http://www.dps.state.mo.us/home/dpshome.htm

Attorney General of Missouri
Supreme Court Building
207 W. High Street
Jefferson City, MO 65102
Phone: (573) 751-3321
Fax: (573) 751-0774
Website: http://www.ago.state.mo.us/index.htm

33 Montana – The Treasure State

Area: 145,552 sq.mi. (Rank: 4th)   Population: 909,453 (Rank: 44th)
Violent Crime Rate (per 100,000 residents): 293.8 (Rank: 18th Safest)
State Motto: *Oro y Plata (Gold and Silver)*

33.1 Knife Carry Law Summary

<u>Note:</u> Blade length limits, if any, in parentheses.

Knife Type	Open Carry	Concealed Carry	Notes
Folding Knives	Yes	Yes (< 4")	
Fixed Bladed Knives	Yes	Yes (< 4")	
Dirks, Daggers, & Stilettos	Yes	No	
Automatic Knives	No	No	
Balisongs	Yes	Yes (< 4")	

33.2 Discussion

First-time visitors to Montana will no doubt wonder at the state's natural beauty, from the rolling plains in the Eastern half of the state, to the state's Western snow-capped mountains. As the license plates proclaim, this *is* Big Sky Country. Perhaps not surprisingly, with few urban population centers of any appreciable size, the state's firearm and knife carry laws tend to be fairly unburdened with restrictions on law-abiding citizens.

With respect to knives, state law has a bias towards open carry. Knives with blades four inches or greater in length must be carried openly. Ordinary pocket knives with blades less than four inches long may be carried concealed. Fixed bladed knives, other than dirks, daggers, and stilettos, with blades less than four inches may also be carried concealed. Possession of automatic knives of any kind, however, is prohibited. Travelers should note that balisongs, while not specifically prohibited, may also fall under the switchblade prohibition, as balisongs do in some states.

State law specifically prohibits carry of concealed weapons while intoxicated. In addition, state law prohibits carry of concealed weapons in government buildings, financial institutions, and places serving alcohol. Note that, unlike the case for firearms, municipalities may pass and enforce their own restrictions on knife carry within their jurisdictions.

33.3 Selected Statutes

MONT. CODE ANN. §§ (2005)

45-2-101. General definitions. Unless otherwise specified in the statute, all words must be taken in the objective standard rather than in the subjective, and unless a different meaning plainly is required, the following definitions apply in this title:

...

(79) "Weapon" means an instrument, article, or substance that, regardless of its primary function, is readily capable of being used to produce death or serious bodily injury.

...

45-8-315. Definition. "Concealed weapon" means any weapon mentioned in 45-8-316 through 45-8-318 and 45-8-321 through 45-8-328 that is wholly or partially covered by the clothing or wearing apparel of the person carrying or bearing the weapon, except that for purposes of 45-8-321 through 45-8-328, concealed weapon means a handgun or a knife with a blade 4 or more inches in length that is wholly or partially covered by the clothing or wearing apparel of the person carrying or bearing the weapon.

45-8-316. Carrying concealed weapons. (1) Every person who carries or bears concealed upon his person a dirk, dagger, pistol, revolver, slingshot, sword cane, billy, knuckles made of any metal or hard substance, knife having a blade 4 inches long or longer, razor, not including a safety razor, or other deadly weapon shall be punished by a fine not exceeding $500 or imprisonment in the county jail for a period not exceeding 6 months, or both.

(2) A person who has previously been convicted of an offense, committed on a different occasion than the offense under this section, in this state or any other jurisdiction for which a sentence to a term of imprisonment in excess of 1 year could have been imposed and who carries or bears concealed upon his person any of the weapons described in subsection (1) shall be punished by a fine not exceeding $1,000 or imprisoned in the state prison for a period not exceeding 5 years, or both.

45-8-317. Exceptions. (1) Section 45-8-316 does not apply to:
...
(g) a person issued a permit under 45-8-321 or a person with a permit recognized under 45-8-329;
...
(i) a person who is outside the official boundaries of a city or town or the confines of a logging, lumbering, mining, or railroad camp or who is lawfully engaged in hunting, fishing, trapping, camping, hiking, backpacking, farming, ranching, or other outdoor activity in which weapons are often carried for recreation or protection; or

(j) the carrying of arms on one's own premises or at one's home or place of business.
...

45-8-327. Carrying a concealed weapon while under the influence. A person commits the offense of carrying a concealed weapon while under the influence if he purposely or knowingly carries a concealed weapon while under the influence of an intoxicating substance. It is not a defense that the person had a valid permit to carry a concealed weapon. A person convicted of the offense shall be imprisoned in the county jail for a term not to exceed 6 months or fined an amount not to exceed $500, or both.

45-8-328. Carrying concealed weapon in prohibited place -- penalty. (1) A person commits the offense of carrying a concealed weapon in a prohibited place if the person purposely or knowingly carries a concealed weapon in:

(a) portions of a building used for state or local government offices and related areas in the building that have been restricted;

(b) a bank, credit union, savings and loan institution, or similar institution during the institution's normal business hours. It is not an offense under this section to carry a concealed weapon while:

(i) using an institution's drive-up window, automatic teller machine, or unstaffed night depository; or

(ii) at or near a branch office of an institution in a mall, grocery store, or other place unless the person is inside the enclosure used for the institution's financial services or is using the institution's financial services.

(c) a room in which alcoholic beverages are sold, dispensed, and consumed under a license issued under Title 16 for the sale of alcoholic beverages for consumption on the premises.

(2) It is not a defense that the person had a valid permit to carry a concealed weapon. A person convicted of the offense shall be imprisoned in the county jail for a term not to exceed 6 months or fined an amount not to exceed $500, or both.

45-8-331. Switchblade knives. (1) Every person who carries or bears upon his person, who carries or bears within or on any motor vehicle or other means of conveyance owned or operated by him, or who owns, possesses, uses, stores, gives away, sells, or offers for sale a switchblade knife shall be punished by a fine not exceeding $500 or by imprisonment in the county jail for a period not exceeding 6 months or by both such fine and imprisonment.

(2) A bona fide collector whose collection is registered with the sheriff of the county in which said collection is located is hereby exempted from the provisions of this section.

(3) For the purpose of this section a switchblade knife is defined as any knife which has a blade 1 1/2 inches long or longer which opens automatically by hand pressure applied to a button, spring, or other device in the handle of the knife.

45-8-361. Possession or allowing possession of weapon in school building -- exceptions -- penalties -- seizure and forfeiture or return authorized -- definitions. (1) A person commits the offense of possession of a weapon in a school building if the person purposely and knowingly possesses, carries, or stores a weapon in a school building.

(2) A parent or guardian of a minor commits the offense of allowing possession of a weapon in a school building if the parent or guardian purposely and knowingly permits the minor to possess, carry, or store a weapon in a school building.

(3) (a) Subsection (1) does not apply to law enforcement personnel.

(b) The trustees of a district may grant persons and entities advance permission to possess, carry, or store a weapon in a school building.

(4) (a) A person convicted under this section shall be fined an amount not to exceed $500, imprisoned in the county jail for a term not to exceed 6 months, or both. The court shall consider alternatives to incarceration that are available in the community.

(b) (i) A weapon in violation of this section may be seized and, upon conviction of the person possessing or permitting possession of the weapon, may be forfeited to the state or returned to the lawful owner.

(ii) If a weapon seized under the provisions of this section is subsequently determined to have been stolen or otherwise taken from the owner's possession without permission, the weapon must be returned to the lawful owner.

(5) As used in this section:

(a) "school building" means all buildings owned or leased by a local school district that are used for instruction or for student activities. The term does not include a home school provided for in 20-5-109.

(b) "weapon" means any type of firearm, a knife with a blade 4 or more inches in length, a sword, a straight razor, a throwing star, nun-chucks, or brass or other metal knuckles. The term also includes any other article or instrument possessed with the purpose to commit a criminal offense.

33.4 Selected Caselaw

State v. George, 203 Mont. 124, 660 P.2d 97, (1983) (affirming conviction for aggravated assault using dull knife as weapon).

State v. Sanders, 208 Mont. 283, 676 P.2d 1312 (1984) (upholding constitutionality of concealed weapons statute).

33.5 Preemption Law

No knife law preemption, firearms law preemption only. *See*, MONT. CODE ANN. § 45-8-351 (2005).

33.6 Places Off-Limits While Carrying

Montana prohibits the carry of concealed weapons in state or local government offices, banks and financial institutions, and alcohol-serving establishments. *See*, MONT. CODE ANN. § 45-8-328 (2005).

33.7 School/College Carry

No state law limitation. Towns and cities, however, may pass their own local ordinances prohibiting carry on school grounds.

33.8 Selected City Ordinances

Billings – Possession or carry of weapons at city council meetings prohibited. The definition of "weapon" includes dirks, daggers, swords, and razors. *See*, BILLINGS, MONT., CITY CODE § 18-204 (2005).

33.9 State Resources

Montana Highway Patrol
2550 Prospect Ave.
Helena, MT 59620-1419
Phone: (406) 444-7000
Fax: (406) 444-4169
Website: http://www.doj.state.mt.us/department/highwaypatroldivision.asp

Montana Attorney General
P.O. Box 201401
Helena, MT 59620-1401
Phone: (406) 444-2026
Fax: (406) 444-3549
Website: http://www.doj.state.mt.us/default.asp

34 Nebraska – The Cornhusker State

Area: 76,872 sq.mi. (Rank: 15th)   Population: 1,729,180 (Rank: 38th)
Violent Crime Rate (per 100,000 residents): 308.7 (Rank: 21st Safest)
State Motto: *Equality Before the Law*

34.1 Knife Carry Law Summary

<u>Note:</u> Blade length limits, if any, in parentheses.

Knife Type	Open Carry	Concealed Carry	Notes
Folding Knives	Yes	Yes(<= 3½")	
Fixed Bladed Knives	Yes	No	
Dirks, Daggers, & Stilettos	No	No	
Automatic Knives	No	No	
Balisongs	Yes	Yes(<= 3½")	

34.2 Discussion

Travelers to Nebraska should be prepared to encounter a fairly restrictive legal environment for knife carry, particularly as it relates to concealed carry in urban areas. Nebraska state law contains a general prohibition against concealed carry of weapons, and the Nebraska Supreme Court has upheld and broadly interpreted the law, and companion municipal ordinances, to apply to a wide variety of knives and situations. For example, the Nebraska Supreme Court has ruled that the person carrying concealed need not carry in public, but can be prosecuted (and convicted) for concealed carry while on private property as a guest in another's home.[62] Given this broad criminal statute, visitors to the Cornhusker State should exercise caution in the kinds and types of knives they carry. Although state law incorporates a three and a half inch blade length limit in the definition of "knife" applicable to the concealed weapon statute, the overall definition is sufficiently broad as to encompass virtually any type of knife, with any blade length. Thus, while the summary table above lists a three and a half inch blade length limit, the law-abiding traveler should be aware that individuals have been prosecuted, and convicted, for carrying concealed knives with blade lengths as short as three inches.[63]

Note that while open carry of knives does not trigger the concealed weapon statute, such carry, especially in urban environments, will often result in unwanted law enforcement attention.

While the state does not appear to have a switchblade prohibition, given the dim view the state courts have taken to ordinary folding pocketknives, the carry of automatic knives by the casual traveler is likely to engender a negative response from law enforcement and the courts. Carry of knives such as balisongs, which have a reputation as martial arts weapons, should be avoided for similar reasons.

---

[62] *See, State v. Conklin,* 545 N.W.2d 101, 108 (Neb. 1996) (affirming conviction and upholding constitutionality of Omaha's concealed weapon ordinance). The court, however, left for another day the question of whether the Omaha concealed weapon ordinance, or inferentially, the analogous state statute, would apply to persons in their own homes. *Id.*

[63] *See, id.* at 108 (upholding conviction for concealed carry of folding knife with three inch blade).

No state-wide statutory prohibitions on off-limits locations for otherwise legal knife carry appear to exist, although travelers should be aware that cities and towns may pass their own ordinances restricting knife carry.

34.3 Selected Statutes

Neb. Rev. Stat. §§ (2005)

Section 28-109 – Terms, defined.

For purposes of the Nebraska Criminal Code, unless the context otherwise requires:

...

(7) Deadly weapon shall mean any firearm, knife, bludgeon, or other device, instrument, material, or substance, whether animate or inanimate, which in the manner it is used or intended to be used is capable of producing death or serious bodily injury;

...

Section 28-1201 – Terms, defined.

For purposes of sections 28-1201 to 28-1212, unless the context otherwise requires:

...

(4) Knife shall mean any dagger, dirk, knife, or stiletto with a blade over three and one-half inches in length or any other dangerous instrument capable of inflicting cutting, stabbing, or tearing wounds;

...

Section 28-1202 – Carrying concealed weapon; penalty; affirmative defense.

(1) Except as provided in subsection (2) of this section, any person who carries a weapon or weapons concealed on or about his or her person such as a revolver, pistol, bowie knife, dirk or knife with a dirk blade attachment, brass or iron knuckles, or any other deadly weapon commits the offense of carrying a concealed weapon.

(2) It shall be an affirmative defense that the defendant was engaged in any lawful business, calling, or employment at the time he or she was carrying any weapon or weapons and the circumstances in which such person was placed at the time were such as to justify a prudent person in carrying the weapon or weapons for the defense of his or her person, property, or family.

(3) Carrying a concealed weapon is a Class I misdemeanor.

(4) In the case of a second or subsequent conviction under this section, carrying a concealed weapon is a Class IV felony.

...

Section 28-1205 – Using a deadly weapon to commit a felony; penalty; separate and distinct offense.

(1) Any person who uses a firearm, a knife, brass or iron knuckles, or any other deadly weapon to commit any felony which may be prosecuted in a court of this state or who unlawfully possesses a firearm, a knife, brass or iron knuckles, or any other deadly weapon during the commission of any felony which may be prosecuted in a court of this state commits the offense of using a deadly weapon to commit a felony.

34.4 Selected Caselaw

State v. Pierson, 239 Neb. 350, 476 N.W.2d 544 (1991) (affirming concealed weapons conviction for carrying fixed bladed knife with three and a half inch blade, and folding knife with approximately three and a half inch blade).

State v. Conklin, 249 Neb. 727, 545 N.W.2d 101 (1996) (upholding constitutionality of Omaha concealed weapon ordinance, and affirming conviction for concealed carry of folding knife with three inch blade while defendant was guest in another's private home).

34.5 Preemption Law

No knife law preemption.

34.6 Places Off-Limits While Carrying

No state law limitation. Towns and cities, however, may pass their own local ordinances restricting or prohibiting carry.

34.7 School/College Carry

No state law limitation, although state law does incorporate penalties for students who possess or carry dangerous weapons on school grounds. *See*, NEB. REV. STAT. §§ 79-267, 79-283 (2005). Towns and cities may pass additional local ordinances prohibiting or otherwise restricting knife carry by non-students on school grounds.

34.8 Selected City Ordinances

Omaha – Carry of concealed weapons expressly forbidden. *See*, OMAHA, NEB., MUNICIPAL CODE §§ 20-192, 20-206 (2005). City mayor may prohibit carry (open or concealed) of knives during time of declared emergency. *See, id.* at § 8-85.

North Platte – Carry of weapons, whether open or concealed, prohibited in or on city parks, pathways, and recreation facilities. See, NORTH PLATTE, NEB., CODE OF ORDINANCES § 38-5 (2005).

34.9 State Resources

Nebraska State Patrol
P.O. Box 94907
Lincoln, NE 68509
Phone: (402) 471-4545
Website: http://www.nsp.state.ne.us/default.asp

Nebraska Attorney General
2115 State Capitol
Lincoln, NE 68507
Phone: (402) 471-2682
Fax: (402) 471-3297
Website: http://www.ago.state.ne.us/

35 Nevada – The Silver State

Area: 109,826 sq.mi. (Rank: 7th)   Population: 2,173,491 (Rank: 35th)
Violent Crime Rate (per 100,000 residents): 615.9 (Rank: 43rd Safest)
State Motto: *All for Our Country*

35.1 Knife Carry Law Summary

<u>Note:</u> Blade length limits, if any, in parentheses.

Knife Type	Open Carry	Concealed Carry	Notes
Folding Knives	Yes	Yes	
Fixed Bladed Knives	Yes	Yes	No concealed machetes
Dirks, Daggers, & Stilettos	Yes	No	
Automatic Knives	Yes (< 2")	Yes (< 2")	
Balisongs	Yes (< 2")	Yes (< 2")	See note[64]

35.2 Discussion

Visitors to the Silver State will find a fairly knife-friendly legal environment. Ordinary folding pocket knives should pose no problem and may be carried openly or concealed. Fixed bladed knives may also be carried openly or concealed, although state law prohibits dirks, daggers, and machetes from being carried concealed. As such, large fixed bladed knives, such as bowies, should probably not be carried concealed, lest such knives fall under the "machete" prohibition. As in most states, visitors to urban areas will likely encounter increased law enforcement attention if openly carrying any large knife. In addition, visitors to the state's numerous casinos should be aware that those establishments may impose their own restrictions on knife carry on their property.

State law prohibits possession, and hence carry of any kind, of automatic knives with blades two inches or longer. Note that knives such as balisongs, while not specifically listed as prohibited, may fall under switchblade prohibition, as balisongs do in some states. In addition, the statutory definition of a switchblade is fairly broadly worded, and will likely support a finding that a balisong falls under the switchblade definition.

Nevada prohibits carry, whether open or concealed, of dirks, daggers, or switchblades, in or on schools or colleges. In addition, municipal governments may pass their own ordinances restricting or prohibiting knife carry.

35.3 Selected Statutes

Nev. Rev. Stat. §§ (2005)

NRS 202.265 Possession of dangerous weapon on property or in vehicle of school; penalty; exceptions.

---

[64] The statutory definition of "switchblade" under state law includes any "knife having the appearance of a pocket knife, any blade of which is 2 or more inches long and which can be released automatically by a flick of a button, pressure on the handle or other mechanical device, or is released by any type of mechanism." *See,* Nev. Rev. Stat. § 202.350 (2005). This definition will likely support a finding that a balisong is a statutory switchblade, and thus subject to the switchblade restrictions.

1. Except as otherwise provided in this section, a person shall not carry or possess, while on the property of the Nevada System of Higher Education or a private or public school or while in a vehicle of a private or public school:

(a) An explosive or incendiary device;

(b) A dirk, dagger or switchblade knife;

(c) A nunchaku or trefoil;

(d) A blackjack or billy club or metal knuckles; or

(e) A pistol, revolver or other firearm.

2. Any person who violates subsection 1 is guilty of a gross misdemeanor.

3. This section does not prohibit the possession of a weapon listed in subsection 1 on the property of a private or public school by a:

(a) Peace officer;

(b) School security guard; or

(c) Person having written permission from the president of a branch or facility of the Nevada System of Higher Education or the principal of the school to carry or possess the weapon.

4. For the purposes of this section:

(a) "Firearm" includes:

(1) Any device used to mark the clothing of a person with paint or any other substance; and

(2) Any device from which a metallic projectile, including any ball bearing or pellet, may be expelled by means of spring, gas, air or other force.

(b) "Nunchaku" has the meaning ascribed to it in NRS 202.350.

(c) "Switchblade knife" has the meaning ascribed to it in NRS 202.350.

(d) "Trefoil" has the meaning ascribed to it in NRS 202.350.

(e) "Vehicle" has the meaning ascribed to "school bus" in NRS 484.148.

(Added to NRS by 1989, 656; A 1993, 364; 1995, 1151; 2001, 806)

NRS 202.350 Manufacture, importation, possession or use of dangerous weapon or silencer; carrying concealed weapon without permit; penalties; issuance of permit to carry concealed weapon; exceptions.

1. Except as otherwise provided in this section and NRS 202.355 and 202.3653 to 202.369, inclusive, a person within this State shall not:

(a) Manufacture or cause to be manufactured, or import into the State, or keep, offer or expose for sale, or give, lend or possess any knife which is made an integral part of a belt buckle or any instrument or weapon of the kind commonly known as a switchblade knife, blackjack, slungshot, billy, sand-club, sandbag or metal knuckles;

(b) Manufacture or cause to be manufactured, or import into the State, or keep, offer or expose for sale, or give, lend, possess or use a machine gun or a silencer, unless authorized by federal law;

(c) With the intent to inflict harm upon the person of another, possess or use a nunchaku or trefoil; or

(d) Carry concealed upon his person any:

(1) Explosive substance, other than ammunition or any components thereof;

(2) Dirk, dagger or machete;

(3) Pistol, revolver or other firearm, or other dangerous or deadly weapon; or

(4) Knife which is made an integral part of a belt buckle.

...

3. Except as otherwise provided in this subsection, the sheriff of any county may, upon written application by a resident of that county showing the reason or the purpose for which a concealed weapon is to be carried, issue a permit authorizing the applicant to carry in this State the concealed weapon described in the permit. The sheriff shall not issue a permit to a person to carry a switchblade knife. This subsection does not authorize the sheriff to issue a permit to a person to carry a pistol, revolver or other firearm.

...

8. As used in this section:

(a) "Concealed weapon" means a weapon described in this section that is carried upon a person in such a manner as not to be discernible by ordinary observation.

...

(d) "Nunchaku" means an instrument consisting of two or more sticks, clubs, bars or rods connected by a rope, cord, wire or chain used as a weapon in forms of Oriental combat.

...

(h) "Switchblade knife" means a spring-blade knife, snap-blade knife or any other knife having the appearance of a pocket knife, any blade of which is 2 or more inches long and which can be released automatically by a flick of a button, pressure on the handle or other mechanical device, or is released by any type of mechanism. The term does not include a knife which has a blade that is held in place by a spring if the blade does not have any type of automatic release.

(i) "Trefoil" means an instrument consisting of a metal plate having three or more radiating points with sharp edges, designed in the shape of a star, cross or other geometric figure and used as a weapon for throwing.

NRS 202.320 Drawing deadly weapon in threatening manner.

1. Unless a greater penalty is provided in NRS 202.287, a person having, carrying or procuring from another person any dirk, dirk-knife, sword, sword cane, pistol, gun or other deadly weapon, who, in the presence of two or more persons, draws or exhibits any of such deadly weapons in a rude, angry or threatening manner not in necessary self-defense, or who in any manner unlawfully uses that weapon in any fight or quarrel, is guilty of a misdemeanor.

2. A sheriff, deputy sheriff, marshal, constable or other peace officer shall not be held to answer, under the provisions of subsection 1, for drawing or exhibiting any of the weapons mentioned therein while in the lawful discharge of his duties.

35.4 Selected Caselaw

Huebner v. State, 103 Nev. 29, 731 P.2d 1330 (1987) (affirming conviction for concealed carry of disguised dirk knife with spring loaded, four and a half inch stabbing point).

35.5 Preemption Law

No knife law preemption, firearms law preemption only. *See*, Nev. Rev. Stat. §§ 244.364 (counties), 268.418 (cities), 269.222 (towns) (2005).

35.6 Places Off-Limits While Carrying

State law prohibits the carry of dirks, daggers, or switchblades on school property. *See*, NEV. REV. STAT. § 202.265 (2005). Note that municipalities may pass their own local ordinances further restricting or prohibiting carry. For example, Reno prohibits carry of weapons in municipal courthouses. *See*, RENO, NEV. MUNICIPAL CODE § 8.12.160 (2005).

35.7 School/College Carry

State law prohibits the carry of dirks, daggers, or switchblades on school property. *See*, NEV. REV. STAT. § 202.265 (2005). Note that municipalities may pass their own local ordinances further restricting or prohibiting carry.

35.8 Selected City Ordinances

Las Vegas – Loitering while carrying concealed dangerous or deadly weapon prohibited. The definition of dangerous or deadly weapon includes dirks, daggers, switchblades, straight razors, ice picks or similar stabbing instruments, any knife with a blade three inches or longer, or any "cutting, stabbing or bludgeoning weapon or device capable of inflicting grievous bodily harm[.]" *See*, LAS VEGAS, NEV., MUNICIPAL CODE § 10.70.020 (2006).

Reno – Possession of any knife with blade length two inches or greater while violating any park or recreational facility ordinance is separate misdemeanor. *See*, RENO, NEV., MUNICIPAL CODE § 8.23.140 (2005). Ordinance defines blade length measured "from the tip of the knife which is customarily sharpened to the unsharpened extension of the blade which forms the hinge connecting the blade to the handle." *See, id.* Possession of weapons in Reno Municipal courthouse prohibited. *See, id.* at § 8.12.160.

35.9 State Resources

Nevada Department of Public Safety
555 Wright Way
Carson City, NV 89711-0900
Phone: (775) 684-4808
Fax: (775) 684-4809
Website: http://dps.nv.gov/index.htm

Attorney General of Nevada
Office of the Attorney General
100 North Carson St.
Carson City, NV 89701-4717
Phone: (775) 684-1100
Website: http://ag.state.nv.us/

36 New Hampshire – The Granite State

Area: 8,968 sq.mi. (Rank: 44th)   Population: 1,275,056 (Rank: 41st)
Violent Crime Rate (per 100,000 residents): 167.0 (Rank: 4th Safest)
State Motto: *Live Free or Die!*

36.1 Knife Carry Law Summary

Note: Blade length limits, if any, in parentheses.

Knife Type	Open Carry	Concealed Carry	Notes
Folding Knives	Yes	Yes	
Fixed Bladed Knives	Yes	Yes	
Dirks, Daggers, & Stilettos	No	No	
Automatic Knives	No	No	
Balisongs	Yes	Yes	See note[65]

36.2 Discussion

Nestled in the northeast corner of the country, New Hampshire prides itself on its dedication to personal liberties. New Hampshire patriots like Daniel Webster, and Patrick Henry, whose famous words "give me liberty, or give me death!" form the basis for the state's motto, "Live Free or Die," reflect a fiercely independent and freedom-loving streak that persists to this day. This respect for personal freedoms is notably reflected in the state's liberal firearms laws, unusual for an Eastern state.

With respect to knives, visitors will find a somewhat permissive legal environment for knife carry. Ordinary fixed and folding pocket knives should pose no problem, and may be carried openly or concealed, although carry of large fixed blades should be avoided in urban areas, as such carry will likely result in unwanted law enforcement attention. There is no statutorily defined blade length limit. Dirks, daggers, stilettos, and automatic knives, however, are prohibited. Note that knives such as balisongs, while not specifically prohibited, may fall under the switchblade prohibition, as balisongs do in some states.

Apart from courthouses, no state-wide statutory prohibitions on off-limits locations for otherwise legal knife carry exist, although travelers should be aware that cities and towns may pass their own ordinances restricting knife carry. New Hampshire does not preempt its cities and towns from regulating knife carry, unlike the case for firearms, where the state has prohibited cities and towns from enacting their own firearms carry restrictions, ensuring uniform state-wide firearms laws. As such, towns and cities may enact ordinances regulating knife carry in such areas as school property within their jurisdictions.

36.3 Selected Statutes

N.H. Rev. Stat. Ann. §§ (2005)

---

[65] No explicit statutory prohibition; however could possibly fall under the state's prohibition on "switch knives", as balisongs do in some states, although the author has found no case law directly interpreting whether a balisong or "butterfly"-type knife would fall under such a prohibition.

159:16 Carrying or Selling Weapons. – Whoever, except as provided by the laws of this state, sells, has in his possession with intent to sell, or carries on his person any stiletto, switch knife, blackjack, dagger, dirk-knife, slung shot or metallic knuckles shall be guilty of a misdemeanor; and such weapon or articles so carried by him shall be confiscated to the use of the state.

625:11 General Definitions. – The following definitions apply to this code.

...

V. "Deadly weapon" means any firearm, knife or other substance or thing which, in the manner it is used, intended to be used, or threatened to be used, is known to be capable of producing death or serious bodily injury.

...

159:19 Courthouse Security. –

I. No person shall knowingly carry a loaded or unloaded pistol, revolver, or firearm or any other deadly weapon as defined in RSA 625:11, V, whether open or concealed or whether licensed or unlicensed, upon the person or within any of the person's possessions owned or within the person's control in a courtroom or area used by a court. Whoever violates the provisions of this paragraph shall be guilty of a class B felony.

...

36.4 Selected Caselaw

State v. Piper, 117 N.H. 64, 66, 369 A.2d 199, 201 (1977) (holding phrase "dangerous weapons" not unconstitutionally vague when applied to defendant arrested in possession of four-inch dirk knife).

36.5 Preemption Law

No knife law preemption, firearms law preemption only. *See*, N.H. Rev. Stat. Ann. § 159:26 (2005).

36.6 Places Off-Limits While Carrying

New Hampshire prohibits the carry of firearms and other deadly weapons, the definition of which includes knives, in courthouses. *See*, N.H. Rev. Stat. Ann. § 159:19 (2005).

36.7 School/College Carry

No state law limitation. Towns and cities, however, may pass their own local ordinances prohibiting carry on school grounds.

36.8 Selected City Ordinances

Manchester – Carry of "dangerous weapons" on school grounds prohibited. The definition of "dangerous weapons" specifically includes knives. Manchester, N.H., Code § 130.41 (1999).

36.9 State Resources

Department of Safety
New Hampshire State Police
33 Hazen Drive
Concord, NH 03305
Phone: (603) 271-2575

Fax: (603) 271-2527
Website: http://webster.state.nh.us/safety/nhsp/

Attorney General of New Hampshire
New Hampshire Department of Justice
33 Capitol Street
Concord, NH 03301
Phone: (603) 271-3658
Fax: (603) 271-2110
Website: http://www.state.nh.us/nhdoj/index.html

37 New Jersey – The Garden State

Area: 7,417 sq.mi. (Rank: 46th)   Population: 8,590,300 (Rank: 9th)
Violent Crime Rate (per 100,000 residents): 355.7 (Rank: 25th Safest)
State Motto: *Liberty and Prosperity*

37.1 Knife Carry Law Summary

<u>Note:</u> Blade length limits, if any, in parentheses.

Knife Type	Open Carry	Concealed Carry	Notes
Folding Knives	Yes	Yes	See note[66]
Fixed Bladed Knives	Yes	No	See note[67]
Dirks, Daggers, & Stilettos	No	No	
Automatic Knives	No	No	
Balisongs	No	No	

37.2 Discussion

Visitors to the Garden State will find a generally hostile legal environment for knife carry. The statutory definition of weapon encompasses virtually all knives, and state law requires that possession of any knife "under circumstances not manifestly appropriate for such lawful uses as it may have is" a crime.[68] Thus, the law-abiding traveler with even a folding pocket knife had better have a good, plausible reason for carrying that utility tool with a sharpened edge, and the proffered reason had better match the type of knife being carried. That all black, "tactical" knife with the large tanto point blade will be a hard sell as an all-around utility knife and apple peeler. Similarly, a fixed bladed hunting or fishing knife should be fine if you're actually out hunting or fishing, with the appropriate hunting or fishing licenses, but will likely get you in trouble if carried in the city.

Dirks, daggers, stilettos and automatic knives (switchblades and gravity knives) are *per se* weapons under New Jersey law, and are, for all practical purposes, prohibited. Technically, possession may be possible with an "explainable lawful purpose,"[69] but should you rely on this caveat, you (or the lawyer you're paying for) will likely be doing your explaining to a jury. Good luck.

Given this generally hostile legal environment, travelers should also be wary of carrying balisongs, as these knives may fall under the switchblade prohibition, as balisongs do in some states. In addition, balisongs are often associated with, and perceived as being, martial arts weapons, and thus may be prohibited under one of more of the state's weapon statutes.

Finally, New Jersey prohibits the carry of weapons on school, college, or other educational institution property.

---

[66] New Jersey law prohibits the carry of weapons to use unlawfully against another. *See,* N.J. STAT. § 2C:39-4(d) (2005). Travelers should avoid carry of "tactical" knives or knives with aggressive, weapon-like appearances.
[67] While the relevant statutes do not explicitly discuss concealment, travelers should be aware that concealment is often one of the factors considered in determining whether a knife is carried as a weapon for unlawful use against another (which is prohibited under state law). *See, e.g.,* N.J. STAT. §§ 2C:39-4(d), 2C:39-5(d) (2005).
[68] *See,* N.J. STAT. § 2C:39-5(d) (2005).
[69] *See, id.* at § 2C:39-3.

37.3 Selected Statutes

N.J. Stat. §§ (2006)

2C:39-1. Definitions. The following definitions apply to this chapter and to chapter 58:

...

h. "Gravity knife" means any knife which has a blade which is released from the handle or sheath thereof by the force of gravity or the application of centrifugal force.

...

p. "Switchblade knife" means any knife or similar device which has a blade which opens automatically by hand pressure applied to a button, spring or other device in the handle of the knife.

...

r. "Weapon" means anything readily capable of lethal use or of inflicting serious bodily injury. The term includes, but is not limited to, all (1) firearms, even though not loaded or lacking a clip or other component to render them immediately operable; (2) components which can be readily assembled into a weapon; (3) gravity knives, switchblade knives, daggers, dirks, stilettos, or other dangerous knives, billies, blackjacks, bludgeons, metal knuckles, sandclubs, slingshots, cesti or similar leather bands studded with metal filings or razor blades imbedded in wood; and (4) stun guns; and any weapon or other device which projects, releases, or emits tear gas or any other substance intended to produce temporary physical discomfort or permanent injury through being vaporized or otherwise dispensed in the air.

...

u. "Ballistic knife" means any weapon or other device capable of lethal use and which can propel a knife blade.

2C:39-3. Prohibited weapons and devices

...

e. Certain weapons. Any person who knowingly has in his possession any gravity knife, switchblade knife, dagger, dirk, stiletto, billy, blackjack, metal knuckle, sandclub, slingshot, cestus or similar leather band studded with metal filings or razor blades imbedded in wood, ballistic knife, without any explainable lawful purpose, is guilty of a crime of the fourth degree.

...

2C:39-4. Possession of weapons for unlawful purposes

...

d. Other weapons. Any person who has in his possession any weapon, except a firearm, with a purpose to use it unlawfully against the person or property of another is guilty of a crime of the third degree.

...

2C:39-5. Unlawful possession of weapons

...

d. Other weapons. Any person who knowingly has in his possession any other weapon under circumstances not manifestly appropriate for such lawful uses as it may have is guilty of a crime of the fourth degree.

...

(2) Any person who knowingly possesses any weapon enumerated in paragraphs (3) and (4) of subsection r. of N.J.S.2C:39-1 or any components which can readily be assembled into a firearm or other weapon enumerated in subsection r. of N.J.S.2C:39-1 or any other weapon under circumstances not manifestly appropriate for such lawful use as it may have, while in or upon any part of the buildings or grounds of any school, college, university or other educational institution without the written authorization of the governing officer of the institution is guilty of a crime of the fourth degree.

...

2C:39-9. Manufacture, transport, disposition and defacement of weapons and dangerous instruments and appliances

...

d. Weapons. Any person who manufactures, causes to be manufactured, transports, ships, sells or disposes of any weapon, including gravity knives, switchblade knives, ballistic knives, daggers, dirks, stilettos, billies, blackjacks, metal knuckles, sandclubs, slingshots, cesti or similar leather bands studded with metal filings, or in the case of firearms if he is not licensed or registered to do so as provided in chapter 58, is guilty of a crime of the fourth degree. Any person who manufactures, causes to be manufactured, transports, ships, sells or disposes of any weapon or other device which projects, releases or emits tear gas or other substances intended to produce temporary physical discomfort or permanent injury through being vaporized or otherwise dispensed in the air, which is intended to be used for any purpose other than for authorized military or law enforcement purposes by duly authorized military or law enforcement personnel or the device is for the purpose of personal self-defense, is pocket-sized and contains not more than three-quarters of an ounce of chemical substance not ordinarily capable of lethal use or of inflicting serious bodily injury, or other than to be used by any person permitted to possess such weapon or device under the provisions of subsection d. of N.J.S.2C:39-5, which is intended for use by financial and other business institutions as part of an integrated security system, placed at fixed locations, for the protection of money and property, by the duly authorized personnel of those institutions, is guilty of a crime of the fourth degree.

...

2C:39-9.1. Sale of knives to minors; crime of the fourth degree; exceptions

...

4. A person who sells any hunting, fishing, combat or survival knife having a blade length of five inches or more or an overall length of 10 inches or more to a person under 18 years of age commits a crime of the fourth degree; except that the establishment by a preponderance of the evidence of all of the following facts by a person making the sale shall constitute an affirmative defense to any prosecution therefor: a. that the purchaser falsely represented his age by producing a driver's license bearing a photograph of the licensee, or by producing a photographic identification card issued pursuant to section 2 of P.L.1980, c. 47 (C.39:3-29.3), or by producing a similar card purporting to be a valid identification card indicating that he was 18 years of age or older, and b. that the appearance of the purchaser was such that an ordinary prudent person would believe him to be 18 years of age or older, and c. that the sale was made in good faith relying upon the indicators of age listed in a. and b. above.

...

2C:39-6 Exemptions.

...

f. Nothing in subsections b., c. and d. of N.J.S.2C:39-5 shall be construed to prevent:

...

(2) A person carrying a firearm or knife in the woods or fields or upon the waters of this State for the purpose of hunting, target practice or fishing, provided that the firearm or knife is legal and appropriate for hunting or fishing purposes in this State and he has in his possession a valid hunting license, or, with respect to fresh water fishing, a valid fishing license;

...

(3) A person transporting any firearm or knife while traveling:

(a) Directly to or from any place for the purpose of hunting or fishing, provided the person has in his possession a valid hunting or fishing license; or

...

g. All weapons being transported under paragraph (2) of subsection b., subsection e., or paragraph (1) or (3) of subsection f. of this section shall be carried unloaded and contained in a closed and fastened case, gunbox, securely tied package, or locked in the trunk of the automobile in which it is being transported, and in the course of travel shall include only such deviations as are reasonably necessary under the circumstances.

37.4 Selected Caselaw

State v. Green, 62 N.J. 547, 303 A.2d 312 (1973) (reversing convictions under predecessor weapons statute and holding whether knife of type not *per se* weapon is "dangerous knife" is factual question for jury).

State v. Ebron, 122 N.J.Super. 552, 301 A.2d 167 (N.J. Super. Ct. App. Div., 1973) (affirming conviction under predecessor statute for carrying dangerous knife with five inch fixed blade).

37.5 Preemption Law

Limited firearms and knife law preemption. *See*, N.J. Stat. § 2C:1-5 (2006).

37.6 Places Off-Limits While Carrying

New Jersey state law prohibits the carry of weapons, the definition of which likely includes virtually all knives, on school, college or other educational institution grounds. *See,* N.J. STAT. § 2C:39-5 (2006).

37.7 School/College Carry

New Jersey state law prohibits the carry of weapons, the definition of which likely includes virtually all knives, on school, college or other educational institution grounds.

37.8 Selected City Ordinances

Hamilton – Possession of any weapon "potentially harmful to wildlife and dangerous to human safety" prohibited in public parks or recreation areas. *See,* HAMILTON TOWNSHIP, N.J., CODE OF ORDINANCES § 98-1 (2005).

Randolph – Carry of weapons in public parks or recreation areas prohibited. *See,* RANDOLPH TOWNSHIP, N.J., REV. ORDINANCES § 34-34 (2005).

37.9 State Resources

New Jersey State Police
P O Box 7068
West Trenton, NJ 08628
Phone: (609) 882-2000
Fax: (609) 292-3508
Website: http://www.njsp.org/front.html

Attorney General of New Jersey
Department of Law & Public Safety
Hughes Justice Complex
Trenton, NJ 08625-0080
Phone: (609) 292-8740
Fax: (609) 292-3508
Website: http://www.state.nj.us/lps/

38 New Mexico – Land of Enchantment

Area: 121,356 sq.mi. (Rank: 5th)   Population: 1,855,059 (Rank: 36th)
Violent Crime Rate (per 100,000 residents): 687.3 (Rank: 46th Safest)
State Motto: *Crescit Eundo (It Grows as It Goes)*

38.1 Knife Carry Law Summary

<u>Note:</u> Blade length limits, if any, in parentheses.

Knife Type	Open Carry	Concealed Carry	Notes
Folding Knives	Yes	Yes	
Fixed Bladed Knives	Yes	Yes	See note[70]
Dirks, Daggers, & Stilettos	No	No	
Automatic Knives	No	No	
Balisongs	No	No	See note[71]
Sword Canes	No	No	

38.2 Discussion

Visitors to New Mexico will find a legal environment that is fairly, and somewhat surprisingly, restrictive of knife carry. This is somewhat surprising, given the large, lightly populated rural nature of this beautiful Western state.

With respect to knives, ordinary folding pocket knives should pose no problem, and may be carried openly or concealed. There is no statutorily defined blade length limit. Dirks, daggers, stilettos, and automatic knives (switchblades), however, are prohibited. The state's courts have held that balisongs (butterfly knives) are statutory switchblades, and thus fall under the switchblade prohibition. Thus, balisongs are prohibited.

In addition, while fixed blades may be carried openly or concealed, state law prohibits carry of certain *per se* deadly weapons in public, including such large fix-bladed knives as bowie knives, butcher knives, and sword canes. Thus travelers should exercise care when carrying knives that may fall under a prohibited category.

State law prohibits carry of deadly weapons on school premises. In addition, local court rules in some judicial districts prohibit knife carry in courts and courthouses.

38.3 Selected Statutes

N.M. Stat. §§ (2005)

30-1-12. Definitions. (1963)

---

[70] State law prohibits carry of certain *per se* deadly weapons in public, including such large fix bladed knives as bowie knives, butcher knives, and sword canes. *See*, N.M. Stat. § 30-7-2 (2005). Law-abiding travelers should exercise caution when carrying any large fix blade, lest they run afoul of the cited statute (or a judge or jury's interpretation thereof).

[71] The New Mexico Court of Appeals has ruled that butterfly knives (balisongs) are switchblades under the law, and thus fall under the state's switchblade prohibition. *See*, *State v. Riddall*, 811 P.2d 576, 582 (N.M. Ct. App. 1991).

As used in the Criminal Code [30-1-1 NMSA 1978]:

...

B.   "deadly weapon" means any firearm, whether loaded or unloaded; or any weapon which is capable of producing death or great bodily harm, including but not restricted to any types of daggers, brass knuckles, switchblade knives, bowie knives, poniards, butcher knives, dirk knives and all such weapons with which dangerous cuts can be given, or with which dangerous thrusts can be inflicted, including swordcanes, and any kind of sharp pointed canes, also slingshots, slung shots, bludgeons; or any other weapons with which dangerous wounds can be inflicted;

...

30-7-2. Unlawful carrying of a deadly weapon. (2001)

A.   Unlawful carrying of a deadly weapon consists of carrying a concealed loaded firearm or any other type of deadly weapon anywhere, except in the following cases:

(1)   in the person's residence or on real property belonging to him as owner, lessee, tenant or licensee;

(2)   in a private automobile or other private means of conveyance, for lawful protection of the person's or another's person or property;

...

(5)   by a person in possession of a valid concealed handgun license issued to him by the department of public safety pursuant to the provisions of the Concealed Handgun Carry Act [29-19-1 NMSA 1978].

B.   Nothing in this section shall be construed to prevent the carrying of any unloaded firearm.

C.   Whoever commits unlawful carrying of a deadly weapon is guilty of a petty misdemeanor.

30-7-2.1. Unlawful carrying of a deadly weapon on school premises. (1994)

A.   Unlawful carrying of a deadly weapon on school premises consists of carrying a deadly weapon on school premises except by:

(1)   a peace officer;

(2)   school security personnel;

(3)   a student, instructor or other school-authorized personnel engaged in army, navy, marine corps or air force reserve officer training corps programs or state-authorized hunter safety training instruction;

(4)   a person conducting or participating in a school-approved program, class or other activity involving the carrying of a deadly weapon; or

(5)   a person older than nineteen years of age on school premises in a private automobile or other private means of conveyance, for lawful protection of the person's or another's person or property.

B.   As used in this section, "school premises" means:

(1)   the buildings and grounds, including playgrounds, playing fields and parking areas and any school bus of any public elementary, secondary, junior high or high school in or on which school or school-related activities are being operated under the supervision of a local school board; or

(2)   any other public buildings or grounds, including playing fields and parking areas that are not public school property, in or on which public school-related and sanctioned activities are being performed.

C.   Whoever commits unlawful carrying of a deadly weapon on school premises is guilty of a fourth degree felony.

30-7-8. Unlawful possession of switchblades. (1963)

Unlawful possession of switchblades consists of any person, either manufacturing, causing to be manufactured, possessing, displaying, offering, selling, lending, giving away or purchasing any knife which has a blade which opens automatically by hand pressure applied to a button, spring or other device in the handle of the knife, or any knife having a blade which opens or falls or is ejected into position by the force of gravity or by any outward or centrifugal thrust or movement.

Whoever commits unlawful possession of switchblades is guilty of a petty misdemeanor.

30-7-13. Carrying weapons prohibited. (1979)

A.   It is unlawful for any person without prior approval from the company to board or attempt to board a bus while in possession of a firearm or other deadly weapon upon his person or effects and readily accessible to him while on the bus. Any person who violates the provisions of this subsection is guilty of a misdemeanor.

B.   Subsection A of this section does not apply to duly elected or appointed law enforcement officers or commercial security personnel in the lawful discharge of their duties.

38.4 Selected Caselaw

State v. Riddall, 112 N.M. 78, 811 P.2d 576 (N.M. Ct. App. 1991) (affirming conviction and holding butterfly knife falls under switchblade prohibition)

State v. Salazar, 123 N.M. 347 , 940 P.2d 195 (N.M. Ct. App. 1997) (holding whether deadly weapon "readily accessible" under unlawful carry on school premises statute question of fact for jury).

38.5 Preemption Law

No knife law preemption.

38.6 Places Off-Limits While Carrying

New Mexico prohibits the carry of firearms and other deadly weapons in schools and on school grounds, or at school-sanctioned events, with certain limited exceptions for, e.g., firearms-related programs. State law also prohibits the readily accessible possession of firearms and other deadly weapons on buses.

Note that local court rules for various courts may also prohibit carry of deadly weapons, including knives, into courts or courthouses in those judicial districts. *See, e.g.*, DIST. CT. (2D JUDICIAL DIST.), LOCAL R. 2-108.

38.7 School/College Carry

New Mexico prohibits the carry of firearms and other deadly weapons in schools and on school grounds, or at school-sanctioned events, with certain limited exceptions for, e.g., firearms-related programs. *See*, N.M. STAT. § 30-7-2.1 (2005).

38.8 Selected City Ordinances

No relevant ordinances imposing additional restrictions beyond that embodied in state law. A number of municipalities have enacted local ordinances that mimic state law with respect to knife and deadly weapon offenses. *See, e.g.*, ALAMOGORDO, N.M., CODE OF ORDINANCES § 11-05-350 (2005) (Unlawful carrying of deadly weapon); CARLSBAD, N.M., CODE OF ORDINANCES

§ 32-2 (2000) (List of petty misdemeanors includes unlawful carry of deadly weapon); FARMINGTON, N.M., CITY CODE § 18-5-43 (2006) (Switchblades prohibited).

38.9 State Resources

New Mexico Department of Public Safety
P.O. Box 1628
Santa Fe, NM 87504
Phone: (505) 841-8053
Website: http://www.dps.nm.org/

Attorney General of New Mexico
407 Galisteo Street
Santa Fe, NM 87110
Phone: (505) 827-6000
Fax: (505) 827-5826
Website: http://www.ago.state.nm.us/

39 New York – The Empire State

Area: 47,214 sq.mi. (Rank: 30th)   Population: 19,157,532 (Rank: 3rd)
Violent Crime Rate (per 100,000 residents): 441.6 (Rank: 30th Safest)
State Motto: *Excelsior (Ever Upwards)*

39.1 Knife Carry Law Summary

<u>Note</u>: Blade length limits, if any, in parentheses.

New York (excluding New York City)

Knife Type	Open Carry	Concealed Carry	Notes
Folding Knives	Yes	Yes	See note[72]
Fixed Bladed Knives	Yes	Yes	See note[72]
Dirks, Daggers, & Stilettos	No	No	See note[72]
Automatic Knives	No	No	
Balisongs	Yes	Yes	See notes[72, 73]
Sword Canes	No	No	

New York City

Knife Type	Open Carry	Concealed Carry	Notes
Folding Knives	No	Yes (< 4")	See note[72]
Fixed Bladed Knives	No	Yes (< 4")	See note[72]
Dirks, Daggers, & Stilettos	No	No	
Automatic Knives	No	No	
Balisongs	No	Yes (< 4")	See notes[72, 73]
Sword Canes	No	No	

39.2 Discussion

Visitors to the Empire State will find important differences in the legal climate for knife carry, depending on whether their travels take them to New York City or to locations outside the Big Apple.

---

[72] State law prohibits carry of weapons with intent to use unlawfully against another, and creates a legal presumption that a dangerous knife is being carried for unlawful use against another. *See,* N.Y. PENAL LAW § 265.01 (2005). Whether a knife is a "dangerous knife" under the statute depends on several factors, including whether the knife is designed or adapted as a weapon, or whether the circumstances surrounding the possession of the knife evince an intention to use the same unlawfully against another. *See,* In the Matter of Jamie D., 466 N.Y.S.2d 286 (N.Y. 1983) Cautious travelers should avoid carry of any knife with overly aggressive or weapon-like appearance.

[73] While a few cases have addressed the issue of whether a balisong, or butterfly knife, is a gravity knife under the state's gravity knife statute and have held that a butterfly knife is not a gravity knife under the statute, the state's highest court has, to date, *not* taken a position on the issue. *See, e.g.,* selected cases cited, § 39.4, *infra.* As a result, cautious travelers should avoid carry of balisongs at this time, especially in NYC, given the aggressive enforcement and prosecution environment. Don't be a test case!

In New York City, open carry of any knife is prohibited, and thus travelers to NYC should ensure that any knife they carry, including folding pocket knives, are completely concealed from ordinary observation, including the pocket clip. In addition, carry of any knife with a blade four inches or longer is prohibited. The city has also enacted a prohibition on the possession of box cutters in public by anyone under the age of twenty-one, and on school premises by anyone under the age of twenty-two, with certain limited exceptions. The N.Y.C. Administrative Code defines box cutters as any "knife consisting of a razor blade, retractable, non-retractable, or detachable in segments, attached to or contained within a plastic or metal housing, including utility knives, snap-off knives, and box cart cutters."[74] Travelers should note that, as is the case in every other state, the city's more restrictive knife carry ordinances simply supplement, rather than supercede, state law. Thus, for example, the switchblade prohibition under state law also applies in New York City, despite the fact that the city does not have its own separate switchblade prohibition.

Travelers should further be aware that NYC has reportedly been very aggressive in its interpretation and enforcement of the state's gravity knife statute, which defines a "gravity knife" as any knife with a locking blade released from the handle by gravity or the application of centrifugal force.[75] Thus, knives that can be "flipped open" by holding the handle *or the blade* with a flick of the wrist, technically could be held to be a "gravity knife" under the statute. This insidious interpretation of the statute encompasses virtually all folding pocket knives without closed-position locks. While the typical knife collector or average pocket knife user would hardly consider the ordinary folding pocket knife with a locking blade to be a gravity knife, as that term is generally understood, such is the risk one runs in New York City.

Note that a number of other states and jurisdictions have similar gravity knife prohibitions, yet few prosecutions appear to exist in those other states for carry of ordinary pocket knives with locking blades under the gravity knife statutes of those other states. If you carry a folding pocket knife in NYC, be careful!

Outside of New York City, and under New York state law, no statutorily defined blade length limit exists. Ordinary folding pocket knives may be carried openly or concealed. Similarly, ordinary fix bladed knives may be carried openly or concealed. In any event, regardless of the type of knife, the knife must not be carried with intent to use unlawfully against another. Furthermore, under state law, carry of "any dagger, dirk, stiletto, dangerous knife or any other weapon, instrument, ..., made or adapted for use primarily as a weapon, is presumptive evidence of intent to use the same unlawfully against another."[76] That is, the law *presumes* that knives such as daggers, dirks and stilettos are carried as weapons for unlawful use. Carry of other "dangerous kni[ves]," such as hunting knives, not primarily designed or specially adapted as weapons, may still violate state law if the circumstances surrounding such carry leads a fact-finder, such as a jury, to conclude that the knife was being carried as a weapon for unlawful use.[77]

---

[74] *See,* N.Y.C. ADMIN. CODE § 10-134.1 (2005).
[75] *See,* N.Y. PENAL LAW § 265.00 subdiv.5 (2005).
[76] *See,* N.Y. PENAL LAW § 265.15 subdiv.4 (2005).
[77] *See,* In the Matter of Jamie D., 466 N.Y.S.2d 286 (N.Y. 1983). In this case, the Court of Appeals of New York, the state's highest court, ruled that "the circumstances of its possession, although there has been no modification of the implement, may permit a finding that on the occasion of its possession it was essentially a weapon rather than a utensil." *Id.* at 288.

With regard to balisongs, or butterfly knives, while a few cases have addressed the issue of whether such knives are gravity knives under the state's gravity knife statute and have held that butterfly knives are not statutory gravity knives, travelers should be aware that the state's highest court has, to date, *not* taken a position on the issue. As a result, cautious travelers should avoid carry of balisongs at this time, especially given the public, and possibly judicial, perception of balisongs as martial arts weapons.

39.3 Selected Statutes

39.3.1   New York State

N.Y. Penal Law §§ (2005)

§ 265.00 Definitions.

...

4. "Switchblade knife" means any knife which has a blade which opens automatically by hand pressure applied to a button, spring or other device in the handle of the knife.

5. "Gravity knife" means any knife which has a blade which is released from the handle or sheath thereof by the force of gravity or the application of centrifugal force which, when released, is locked in place by means of a button, spring, lever or other device.

5-a. "Pilum ballistic knife" means any knife which has a blade which can be projected from the handle by hand pressure applied to a button, lever, spring or other device in the handle of the knife.

5-b. "Metal knuckle knife" means a weapon that, when closed, cannot function as a set of metal knuckles, nor as a knife and when open, can function as both a set of metal knuckles as well as a knife.

...

§ 265.01 Criminal possession of a weapon in the fourth degree.

A person is guilty of criminal possession of a weapon in the fourth degree when:

(1) He possesses any firearm, electronic dart gun, electronic stun gun, gravity knife, switchblade knife, pilum ballistic knife, metal knuckle knife, cane sword, billy, blackjack, bludgeon, metal knuckles, chuka stick, sand bag, sandclub, wrist-brace type slingshot or slungshot, shirken or "Kung Fu star"; or

(2) He possesses any dagger, dangerous knife, dirk, razor, stiletto, imitation pistol, or any other dangerous or deadly instrument or weapon with intent to use the same unlawfully against another; or

...

§ 265.15 Presumptions of possession, unlawful intent and defacement.

...

2. The presence in any stolen vehicle of any weapon, instrument, appliance or substance specified in sections 265.01, 265.02, 265.03, 265.04 and 265.05 is presumptive evidence of its possession by all persons occupying such vehicle at the time such weapon, instrument, appliance or substance is found.

3. The presence in an automobile, other than a stolen one or a public omnibus, of any firearm, large capacity ammunition feeding device, defaced firearm, defaced rifle or shotgun, defaced large capacity ammunition feeding device, firearm silencer, explosive or incendiary bomb, bombshell, gravity knife, switchblade knife, pilum ballistic knife, metal knuckle knife, dagger, dirk, stiletto, billy, blackjack, metal knuckles, chuka stick, sandbag, sandclub or slungshot is presumptive evidence of its possession by all persons occupying such automobile at the time such weapon, instrument or appliance is found, except under the following circumstances: (a) if such weapon, instrument or appliance is found upon the person of one of the occupants therein; (b) if such weapon, instrument or appliance is found in an automobile which is being operated for hire by a duly licensed driver in the due, lawful and proper pursuit of his or her trade, then such presumption shall not apply to the driver; or (c) if the weapon so found is a

pistol or revolver and one of the occupants, not present under duress, has in his or her possession a valid license to have and carry concealed the same.

4. The possession by any person of the substance as specified in section 265.04 is presumptive evidence of possessing such substance with intent to use the same unlawfully against the person or property of another if such person is not licensed or otherwise authorized to possess such substance. The possession by any person of any dagger, dirk, stiletto, dangerous knife or any other weapon, instrument, appliance or substance designed, made or adapted for use primarily as a weapon, is presumptive evidence of intent to use the same unlawfully against another.

39.3.2   *New York City*

NEW YORK CITY ADMINISTRATIVE CODE §§ (2005)

§ 10-133 Possession of knives or instruments. a. Legislative findings. It is hereby declared and found that the possession in public places, streets and parks of the city, of large knives is a menace to the public health, peace, safety and welfare of the people of the city; that the possession in public places, streets and parks of such knives has resulted in the commission of many homicides, robberies, maimings and assaults of and upon the people of the city; that this condition encourages and fosters the commission of crimes, and contributes to juvenile delinquency, youth crime and gangsterism; that unless the possession or carrying in public places, streets and parks of the city of such knives without a lawful purpose is prohibited, there is danger of an increase in crimes of violence and other conditions detrimental to public peace, safety and welfare. It is further declared and found that the wearing or carrying of knives in open view in public places while such knives are not being used for a lawful purpose is unnecessary and threatening to the public and should be prohibited.

b. It shall be unlawful for any person to carry on his or her person or have in such person's possession, in any public place, street, or park any knife which has a blade length of four inches or more.

c. It shall be unlawful for any person in a public place, street or park, to wear outside of his or her clothing or carry in open view any knife with an exposed or unexposed blade unless such person is actually using such knife for a lawful purpose as set forth in subdivision d of this section.
...

§ 10-134 Prohibition on sale of certain knives. a. Legislative findings. It is hereby declared and found that the possession in public places, streets and parks of the city, of folding knives which lock upon opening, is a menace to the public health, peace, safety and welfare of the people of the city; that the possession in public places, streets and parks of such knives has resulted in the commission of many homicides, robberies, maimings and assaults of and upon the people of the city, that this condition encourages and fosters the commission of crimes, and contributes to juvenile delinquency, youth crime and gangsterism; that if this situation is not addressed, then there is a danger of an increase in crimes of violence, and other conditions detrimental to public peace, safety and welfare. It has been found that folding knives with a blade of four (4) inches or more that locks in an open position are designed and used almost exclusively for the purpose of stabbing or the threat thereof. Therefore for the safety of the city, such weapons should be prohibited from sale within the jurisdiction of the city of New York.

b. It shall be unlawful for any person to sell, or offer for sale within the jurisdiction of the city of New York, any folding knife with a blade length of four or more inches which is so constructed that when it is opened it is locked in an open position and cannot be closed without depressing or moving a release mechanism.
...

§ 10-134.1 Prohibition on sale of box cutters to persons under twenty-one years of age, open displays of box cutters by sellers, and possession of box cutters in a public place, or on school premises by persons under twenty-two years of age. a. Legislative findings. The council hereby finds that the number of school safety incidents which take place in the city's schools are disturbingly high and are rising, and that these incidents place students and staff at unacceptable risk of injury and disrupt the learning environment. Board of education statistics reveal that for the first half of the 1994-95 school year, 8,333 school safety incidents occurred, representing a 27.6 percent increase as compared with the same period in the prior year. Board of education statistics also reveal that for the entire 1994-95 school year, 19,814 school safety incidents were reported, representing an increase of 16 percent as compared to the prior school year. The council further finds that the board of education's school safety statistics reveal that over 2,000 box cutters and other similar implements were seized during the 1994-95 school year, indicating that these instruments have become the "weapon of choice" in the city's schools. These implements are used as weapons by students as they are relatively inexpensive, readily available, and easily deployable. Used as weapons, box cutters and similar instruments can cause great injury. It is the council's belief that banning the sale of box cutters to minors under eighteen years of age, requiring that those who sell box cutters ensure that they are not displayed in a manner that increases opportunities for minors to steal them, and banning the possession of box cutters by persons under twenty-two years of age on school premises, will significantly help in reducing the number of violent school safety incidents and in ensuring that schools are the safe havens of knowledge and education that children need and deserve.

b. Definitions. For purposes of this section:

(1) "Box cutter" means any knife consisting of a razor blade, retractable, non-retractable, or detachable in segments, attached to or contained within a plastic or metal housing, including utility knives, snap-off knives, and box cart cutters.

(2) "Person" means any natural person, corporation, partnership, firm, organization or other legal entity.

(3) "Public place" means a place to which the public or a substantial group of persons has access, and includes, but is not limited to, any street, highway, parking lot, plaza, transportation facility, school, place of amusement, park, playground, and any hallway, lobby and other portion of an apartment house or hotel not constituting a room or apartment designed for actual residence.

(4) "School premises" means the buildings, grounds, or facilities, or any portion thereof, owned, occupied by, or under the custody or control of public and private institutions for the primary purpose of providing educational instruction to students, and any vehicles owned, operated or leased by such institutions which are used to transport such students or the personnel of such institutions.

c. It shall be unlawful for any person to sell or offer to sell or cause any person to sell or offer to sell a box cutter to any individual under twenty-one years of age.

d. No person who sells or offers for sale box cutters shall place such box cutters on open display so that such implements are accessible to the public without the assistance of such seller, or his or her employee or other agent, offering such implement for sale; provided, however, that the restrictions of this subdivision shall not apply to those box cutters on open display (1) which are clearly and fully visible from a place of payment for goods or services or customer information at which such seller or an employee or other agent of such seller is usually present during hours when the public is invited or (2) which are in a package, box or other container provided by the manufacturer, importer or packager that is larger than 41 square inches.

e. It shall be unlawful for any person under twenty-two years of age to possess a box cutter on school premises, and unlawful for any person under twenty-one years of age to possess a box cutter while in a public place; provided, however, that nothing in this subdivision shall preclude: [list of certain exceptions and affirmative defenses]

...

39.4 Selected Caselaw

In the Matter of Jamie D., 466 N.Y.S.2d 286, 59 N.Y.2d 589 (N.Y. 1983) (upholding conviction for possession of dangerous knife, steak knife with five inch blade)

People v. Zuniga, 303 A.D.2d 773; 759 N.Y.S.2d 86 (N.Y. App. Div. 2003) (holding butterfly knife not gravity knife and dismissing indictment)

People v. Dolson, 142 Misc.2d 779, 538 N.Y.S.2d 393 (N.Y. Co. Ct., 1989) (holding butterfly knife not gravity knife under statute and reversing conviction)

People v. Hunter, 402 N.Y.S.2d 604, 61 A.D.2d 990 (N.Y. App. Div. 1978) (holding presumption of intent to use dangerous knife unlawfully may be overcome in self-defense situation)

People v. Hawkins, 2003 N.Y. Slip Op. 51516(U) (N.Y. Crim. Ct. 2003) (denying motion to dismiss gravity knife possession charge in New York City for knife "that opened and locked when flipped")

In Re Patrick L., 665 N.Y.S.2d 70, 244 A.D.2d 244 (N. Y. App. Div. 1997) (affirming family court juvenile delinquent adjudication for possession of box cutter and razor blade by minor)

39.5 Preemption Law

No knife law preemption, limited firearms licensing law preemption only. *See*, N.Y. PENAL LAW § 400.00(6) (2005).

39.6 Places Off-Limits While Carrying

New York City prohibits carry of box cutters in public places by anyone under twenty-one years of age, and in schools by anyone under the age of twenty-two. Certain limited exceptions and affirmative defenses exist. *See*, N.Y.C. ADMIN. CODE § 10-134.1 (2005).

39.7 School/College Carry

New York City prohibits carry of box cutters in public places by anyone under twenty-one years of age, and in schools by anyone under the age of twenty-two. Certain limited exceptions and affirmative defenses exist.

39.8 Selected City Ordinances

New York City – Unlawful to carry knife with blade four inches or longer. *See*, N.Y.C. ADMIN. CODE § 10-133 (2005). Open carry of knives prohibited. *See, id.* Carry of box cutters on school premises by person under twenty-two years of age prohibited; carry of box cutters in public place by person under twenty-one years of age prohibited (certain limited exceptions and affirmative defenses apply). *See, id.* at § 10-134.1.

39.9 State Resources

New York State Police
Public Information Office
Albany, NY 12226
Phone: (518) 457-2180
Website: http://www.troopers.state.ny.us/

Attorney General of New York
The Capitol
Albany, NY 12224-0341
Phone: (518) 474-7330
Website: http://www.oag.state.ny.us/home.html

40 North Carolina – The Tar Heel State

Area: 48,711 sq.mi. (Rank: 29th)   Population: 8,320,146 (Rank: 11th)
Violent Crime Rate (per 100,000 residents): 447.8 (Rank: 31st Safest)
State Motto: *Esse Quam Videri (To Be, Rather Than to Seem)*

40.1 Knife Carry Law Summary

Note: Blade length limits, if any, in parentheses.

Knife Type	Open Carry	Concealed Carry	Notes
Folding Knives	Yes	Yes	
Fixed Bladed Knives	Yes	No	
Dirks, Daggers, & Stilettos	Yes	No	
Automatic Knives	Yes	No	
Balisongs	Yes	No	

40.2 Discussion

Visitors to the Tar Heel State will find a fairly friendly legal environment for knife carry. State law prohibits concealed carry of any knife other than an ordinary pocket knife, but otherwise permits open carry of a wide variety of other knives. Ballistic knives, however, are strictly prohibited, and may not be possessed even by law enforcement. There is no statutorily defined blade length limit under state law, although municipalities may impose their own restrictions in this regard, as well as the types of knives that may be carried. For example, some municipalities prohibit possession of automatic knives (switchblades), which are otherwise legal under state law. Other municipalities have enacted blade length limit restrictions, and placed restrictions on carry in public city government buildings.

Under state law, knives may not be carried on educational institution property, with certain limited exceptions not generally applicable to visitors to the state. In addition, state law prohibits carry of deadly weapons on state government property or in courthouses. Finally, state law prohibits possession of deadly weapons by anyone participating in, affiliated with, or present as a spectator at parades, funeral processions, picket lines, or demonstrations at private health care facilities or public places under the control of the state or any municipality.

40.3 Selected Statutes

N.C. Gen. Stat. §§ (2005)

§ 14-269. Carrying concealed weapons.

(a) It shall be unlawful for any person willfully and intentionally to carry concealed about his person any bowie knife, dirk, dagger, slung shot, loaded cane, metallic knuckles, razor, shurikin, stun gun, or other deadly weapon of like kind, except when the person is on the person's own premises.

...

(d) This section does not apply to an ordinary pocket knife carried in a closed position. As used in this section, "ordinary pocket knife" means a small knife, designed for carrying in a pocket or purse, that has its cutting edge and point entirely enclosed by its handle, and that may not be opened by a throwing, explosive, or spring action.

§ 14-269.2. Weapons on campus or other educational property.

(a) The following definitions apply to this section:

(1) Educational property. – Any school building or bus, school campus, grounds, recreational area, athletic field, or other property owned, used, or operated by any board of education or school board of trustees, or directors for the administration of any school.

(1a) Employee. – A person employed by a local board of education or school whether the person is an adult or a minor.

(1b) School. – A public or private school, community college, college, or university.

(2) Student. – A person enrolled in a school or a person who has been suspended or expelled within the last five years from a school, whether the person is an adult or a minor.

(3) Switchblade knife. – A knife containing a blade that opens automatically by the release of a spring or a similar contrivance.

(4) Weapon. – Any device enumerated in subsection (b), (b1), or (d) of this section.
...
(d) It shall be a Class 1 misdemeanor for any person to possess or carry, whether openly or concealed, any BB gun, stun gun, air rifle, air pistol, bowie knife, dirk, dagger, slungshot, leaded cane, switchblade knife, blackjack, metallic knuckles, razors and razor blades (except solely for personal shaving), firework, or any sharp-pointed or edged instrument except instructional supplies, unaltered nail files and clips and tools used solely for preparation of food, instruction, and maintenance, on educational property.

(e) It shall be a Class 1 misdemeanor for any person to cause, encourage, or aid a minor who is less than 18 years old to possess or carry, whether openly or concealed, any BB gun, stun gun, air rifle, air pistol, bowie knife, dirk, dagger, slungshot, leaded cane, switchblade knife, blackjack, metallic knuckles, razors and razor blades (except solely for personal shaving), firework, or any sharp-pointed or edged instrument except instructional supplies, unaltered nail files and clips and tools used solely for preparation of food, instruction, and maintenance, on educational property.
...

§ 14-269.4. Weapons on State property and in courthouses.

It shall be unlawful for any person to possess, or carry, whether openly or concealed, any deadly weapon, not used solely for instructional or officially sanctioned ceremonial purposes in the State Capitol Building, the Executive Mansion, the Western Residence of the Governor, or on the grounds of any of these buildings, and in any building housing any court of the General Court of Justice. If a court is housed in a building containing nonpublic uses in addition to the court, then this prohibition shall apply only to that portion of the building used for court purposes while the building is being used for court purposes.
...

§ 14-269.6. Possession and sale of spring-loaded projectile knives prohibited.

(a) On and after October 1, 1986, it shall be unlawful for any person including law-enforcement officers of the State, or of any county, city, or town to possess, offer for sale, hold for sale, sell, give, loan, deliver, transport, manufacture or go armed with any spring-loaded projectile knife, a ballistic knife, or any weapon of similar character. Except that it shall be lawful for a law-enforcement agency to possess such weapons solely for evidentiary, education or training purposes.

(b) Any person violating the provisions of this section shall be guilty of a Class 1 misdemeanor.

§ 14-277.2. Weapons at parades, etc., prohibited.

(a) It shall be unlawful for any person participating in, affiliated with, or present as a spectator at any parade, funeral procession, picket line, or demonstration upon any private health care facility or upon any public place owned or under the control of the State or any of its political subdivisions to willfully or intentionally possess or have immediate access to any dangerous weapon. Violation of this subsection shall be a Class 1 misdemeanor. It shall be presumed that any rifle or gun carried on a rack in a pickup truck at a holiday parade or in a funeral procession does not violate the terms of this act.

(b) For the purposes of this section the term "dangerous weapon" shall include those weapons specified in G.S. 14-269, 14-269.2, 14-284.1, or 14-288.8 or any other object capable of inflicting serious bodily injury or death when used as a weapon.

...

40.4 Selected Caselaw

In the Matter of Dale B., 385 S.E.2d 521, 96 N.C.App. 375 (N.C. Ct. App. 1989) (holding folding knife with closed length of four and a half inches was ordinary pocket knife within meaning of concealed weapon statute).

State v. Torain, 316 N.C. 111, 340 S.E.2d 465 (N.C. 1986) (affirming conviction and trial court determination that, as matter of law, utility knife with one inch blade was "dangerous or deadly weapon" as used by rapist).

State v. Mills, No. COA05-852 (Unpublished Op., N.C. Ct. App. 2006) (affirming probation revocation for concealment in bag of two knives not ordinary pocket knives under statute).

40.5 Preemption Law

No knife law preemption, firearms law preemption only. *See*, N.C. GEN. STAT. § 14-409.40 (2005).

40.6 Places Off-Limits While Carrying

North Carolina prohibits the carry, whether openly or concealed, of bowie knives, dirks, daggers, switchblades, razors and razor blades, or "any sharp-pointed or edged instrument" in schools or on school property. *See*, N.C. GEN. STAT. § 14-269.2(d) (2005). Certain limited exceptions do exist for instructional supplies and use, food preparation, and maintenance. *See, id.* State law also prohibits any form of carry of deadly weapons in state government buildings, and in courthouses. *See*, N.C. GEN. STAT. § 14-269.4 (2005).

State law prohibits possession of deadly weapons by anyone participating in, affiliated with, or present as a spectator at parades, funeral processions, picket lines, or demonstrations at private health care facilities or public places under the control of the state or any municipality. *See*, N.C. GEN. STAT. § 14-277.2 (2005).

Note that municipalities may pass their own local ordinances prohibiting or otherwise restricting knife carry within their jurisdictions.

40.7 School/College Carry

North Carolina prohibits the carry, whether openly or concealed, of bowie knives, dirks, daggers, switchblades, razors and razor blades, or "any sharp-pointed or edged instrument" in schools or on school property. *See*, N.C. GEN. STAT. § 14-269.2(d) (2005). Certain limited exceptions do exist for instructional supplies and use, food preparation, and maintenance. *See, id.* Note that municipalities may pass their own local ordinances prohibiting or otherwise restricting knife carry within their jurisdictions.

40.8 Selected City Ordinances

Cary – Carry, whether openly or concealed, of any knife with blade three inches or greater prohibited in city parks. Exception exists for use in public exhibitions and with permit from director of parks and recreation. *See*, CARY, N.C., CODE OF ORDINANCES § 24-10 (2006).

Charlotte – Possession or carry of any kind of any knife with blade greater than three and a half inches on city property prohibited. Exception exists for knives used solely for food preparation, instruction, or maintenance, and for razors and razor blades used solely for personal shaving. *See*, CHARLOTTE, N.C., CODE OF ORDINANCES § 15-14 (2005)

Durham – Possession of dangerous weapons on or in city government property, including parks and recreation facilities, prohibited. The definition of dangerous weapon includes bowie knives, dirks, daggers, razors, and switchblades. *See*, DURHAM, N.C., CODE OF ORDINANCES § 12-22 (2005).

Winston-Salem – Possession of switchblades prohibited. *See*, WINSTON-SALEM, N.C., CODE OF ORDINANCES § 38-12 (2006).

40.9 State Resources

North Carolina State Highway Patrol
512 N. Salisbury Street
Raleigh, NC 27699-4702
Phone: (919) 733-7952
Website: http://www.nccrimecontrol.org/

Office of the Attorney General
North Carolina Department of Justice
Raleigh, NC 27602-0629
Phone: (919) 716-6400
Fax: (919) 716-6750
Website: http://www.ncdoj.com/default.jsp

41 North Dakota – The Peace Garden State

Area: 68,976 sq.mi. (Rank: 17th)   Population: 634,110 (Rank: 48th)
Violent Crime Rate (per 100,000 residents): 79.4 (Rank: Safest (1st))
State Motto: *Liberty and Union, Now and Forever, One and Inseparable*

41.1 Knife Carry Law Summary

Note: Blade length limits, if any, in parentheses.

Knife Type	Open Carry	Concealed Carry	Notes
Folding Knives	Yes	Yes (< 5")	See note[78]
Fixed Bladed Knives	Yes	Yes (< 5")	See note[78]
Dirks, Daggers, & Stilettos	Yes	No	
Automatic Knives	Yes	No	
Balisongs	Yes	No	See note[79]

41.2 Discussion

Visitors to North Dakota will no doubt be moved by its rugged beauty, and will appreciate the state's generally knife friendly legal environment. Under state law, a wide variety of knives may be legally carried openly, including automatic knives, daggers, stilettos, etc. Concealed carry of knives deemed dangerous weapons, however, is prohibited without a recognized concealed weapons permit. The definition of "dangerous weapon" includes automatic knives such as switchblades and gravity knives, machetes, scimitars, stilettos, swords and daggers, and any knife with a blade five inches or longer.[80] Note that while such knives are *per se* dangerous weapons, other knives not specifically enumerated, or with blades less than five inches may also qualify as dangerous weapons if, for example, the knife is designed (or marketed) or specially adapted or modified for use as a weapon, with little or no other non-weapon uses. For instance, the Supreme Court of North Dakota has held, in affirming a conviction under the state's concealed weapon statute, that a straight razor with a two and three-quarter inch blade and certain weapon-like features that made the razor unsuitable for shaving, was a dangerous weapon under the statute.[81]

The definition of dangerous weapon also specifically includes any "martial arts weapon."[82] As such, balisongs (butterfly knives), which are often associated with, and perceived as martial arts weapons, could quite likely be deemed a dangerous weapon, and thus should not be

---

[78] While the definition of "dangerous weapon" under state law includes knives with blades five inches or longer, the North Dakota Supreme Court has held that a knife with weapon-like features and a blade two and three-quarter inches long was in fact a "dangerous weapon", and upheld a conviction for concealed carry of a dangerous weapon on this basis. *See*, State v. Vermilya, 423 N.W.2d 153, 155 (N.D. 1988). Thus, careful travelers would do well to avoid carrying "tactical" folders and fixed bladed with overly aggressive, weapon-like features, even those with blades less than the statutory five inches in length, lest they run afoul of such a determination.

[79] State law includes "martial arts weapon" under the definition of "dangerous weapon." *See*, N.D. CENT. CODE § 62.1-01-01 (2005). Travelers should note that balisongs (butterfly knives) are often perceived as martial arts weapons, and thus cautious travelers would be wise to avoid carrying any balisong concealed, even those with blades less than five inches long, without a recognized concealed weapon permit.

[80] *See*, N.D. CENT. CODE § 62.1-01-01 (2005).

[81] *See*, State v. Vermilya, 423 N.W.2d 153 (N.D. 1988).

[82] *See*, N.D. CENT. CODE § 62.1-01-01 (2005).

carried concealed without a recognized permit. In addition, balisongs may be deemed to be statutory switchblades, as balisongs are in some states, and so would be subject to the same restrictions as switchblades, which require a recognized permit for concealed carry.

Fortunately, North Dakota is a "shall issue" state for concealed weapons permits, and both issues permits to non-residents, as well as recognizes a number of other states' permits. Those travelers with recognized permits may carry firearms and dangerous weapons concealed, subject to North Dakota law.

State law prohibits carry of firearms or dangerous weapons in establishments selling alcoholic beverages, or on gaming sites. Note that towns and cities may enact their own ordinances further restricting or prohibiting knife carry, and some of the larger cities have in fact done so.

41.3 Selected Statutes

N.D. Cent. Code §§ (2005)

62.1-01-01. General definitions. As used in this title, unless the context otherwise requires:

1. "Dangerous weapon" includes any switchblade or gravity knife, machete, scimitar, stiletto, sword, dagger, or knife with a blade of five inches [12.7 centimeters] or more; any throwing star, nunchaku, or other martial arts weapon; any billy, blackjack, sap, bludgeon, cudgel, metal knuckles, or sand club; any slungshot; any bow and arrow, crossbow, or spear; any stun gun; any weapon that will expel, or is readily capable of expelling, a projectile by the action of a spring, compressed air, or compressed gas including any such weapon, loaded or unloaded, commonly referred to as a BB gun, air rifle, or CO2 gun; and any projector of a bomb or any object containing or capable of producing and emitting any noxious liquid, gas, or substance.
...

62.1-02-04. Possession of firearm or dangerous weapon in liquor establishment or gaming site prohibited - Penalty - Exceptions. Any person who enters or remains in that part of the establishment that is set aside for the retail sale in an establishment engaged in the retail sale of alcoholic beverages or used as a gaming site while in the possession of a firearm or dangerous weapon is guilty of a class A misdemeanor. This section does not apply to:

1. A law enforcement officer.

2. The proprietor.

3. The proprietor's employee.

4. A designee of the proprietor when the designee is displaying an unloaded firearm or dangerous weapon as a prize or sale item in a raffle or auction.

5. Private security personnel while on duty for the purpose of delivering or receiving moneys used at the liquor establishment or gaming site.

62.1-04-01. Definition of concealed. A firearm or dangerous weapon is concealed if it is carried in such a manner as to not be discernible by the ordinary observation of a passerby. There is no requirement that there be absolute invisibility of the firearm or dangerous weapon, merely that it not be ordinarily discernible. A firearm or dangerous weapon is considered concealed if it is not secured, and is worn under clothing or carried in a bundle that is held or carried by the individual, or transported in a vehicle under the individual's control or direction and available to the individual, including beneath the seat or in a glove compartment. A firearm or dangerous weapon is not considered concealed if it is:

1. Carried in a belt holster which is wholly or substantially visible or carried in a case designed for carrying a firearm or dangerous weapon and which is wholly or substantially visible;

2. Locked in a closed trunk or luggage compartment of a motor vehicle;

3. Carried in the field while lawfully engaged in hunting, trapping, or target shooting, whether visible or not; or

4. Carried by any person permitted by law to possess a handgun unloaded and in a secure wrapper from the place of purchase to that person's home or place of business, or to a place of repair, or back from those locations.

5. A bow and arrow, an unloaded rifle or shotgun, or an unloaded weapon that will expel, or is readily capable of expelling, a projectile by the action of a spring, compressed air, or compressed gas including any such weapon commonly referred to as a BB gun, air rifle, or CO2 gun, while carried in a motor vehicle.

62.1-04-02. Carrying concealed firearms or dangerous weapons prohibited. No person, other than a law enforcement officer, may carry any firearm or dangerous weapon concealed unless the person is licensed to do so or exempted pursuant to this chapter. For purposes of this chapter, dangerous weapon does not mean a spray or aerosol containing CS (ortho-chlorobenzamalonitrile), CN (alpha-chloroacetophenone), or other irritating agent intended for use in the defense of a person.

41.4 Selected Caselaw

State v. Vermilya, 423 N.W.2d 153, 155 (N.D. 1988) (affirming conviction for carrying concealed dangerous weapon, straight razor "unsuitable for shaving" and with blade approx. two and three quarter inches long, and holding intent to use as weapon may be inferred if knife design "peculiarly suitable for use as weapon")

41.5 Preemption Law

No knife law preemption, firearms law preemption only. *See*, N.D. CENT. CODE § 62.1-01-03 (2005).

41.6 Places Off-Limits While Carrying

North Dakota state law prohibits the carry of firearms and other dangerous weapons, the definition of which includes a broad variety of knives, such as switchblades, gravity knives, machetes, stilettos, swords, daggers, etc., and any knife with a blade five inches or longer, in liquor establishments or gaming sites. *See*, N.D. CENT. CODE § 62.1-02-04 (2005).

Note that local towns and cities may pass their own local ordinances prohibiting or restricting knife possession or carry in their jurisdictions.

41.7 School/College Carry

State law prohibits firearm or weapon possession by students on school property or at school functions. *See*, N.D. CENT. CODE § 15.1-19-10 (2005). No state law limitation appears to exists for non-students. Towns and cities, however, may pass their own local ordinances prohibiting carry on school grounds by non-students.

41.8 Selected City Ordinances

Grand Forks – Possession of dangerous weapons, the definition of which includes switchblades, gravity knives, machetes, stilettos, swords, daggers, etc., and any knife with a blade five inches or longer, prohibited in public parks. *See*, GRAND FORKS, N.D., CITY CODE § 9-0204 (2006).

Minot – Possession of unsheathed or uncased knives prohibited in public, in places selling alcoholic beverages, places of public accommodations or public assembly, or on private property without permission of the property owner. *See,* MINOT, N.D., CODE OF ORDINANCES § 23-66 (2006). Possession of *per se* weapons other than firearms prohibited in public, in places selling alcoholic beverages, or on private property without permission of the property owner. The ordinance defines "weapon" as "any device or substance which is designed or subsequently modified to disable, to wound, or to kill a human being which device or substance as designed or subsequently modified is not customarily used for any other purpose." *See, id.* at § 23-67.

41.9 State Resources

Bureau of Criminal Investigation
Bismarck, ND 58502-1054
Phone: (701) 328-5500
Fax: (701) 328-5510
Website: http://www.ag.state.nd.us/BCI/BCI.htm

Office of the Attorney General
600 E Boulevard Ave Dept 125
Bismarck, ND 58505-0040
Phone: (701) 328-2210
TDD: (701) 328-3409
Fax: (701) 328-2226
Website: http://www.ag.state.nd.us/

42 Ohio – The Buckeye State

Area: 40,948 sq.mi. (Rank: 35th)   Population: 11,421,267 (Rank: 7th)
Violent Crime Rate (per 100,000 residents): 341.8 (Rank: 23rd Safest)
State Motto: *With God, All Things Are Possible*

42.1 Knife Carry Law Summary

<u>Note:</u> Blade length limits, if any, in parentheses.

Knife Type	Open Carry	Concealed Carry	Notes
Folding Knives	Yes	Yes	See note[83]
Fixed Bladed Knives	Yes	No	See note[84]
Dirks, Daggers, & Stilettos	Yes	No	
Automatic Knives	No	No	
Balisongs	Yes	No	See note[85]

42.2 Discussion

Visitors to the Buckeye State will find a fairly restrictive legal environment for knife carry. State law prohibits carrying a concealed deadly weapon, defined as "any instrument, device, or thing capable of inflicting death, and designed or specially adapted for use as a weapon, or possessed, carried, or used as a weapon."[86] While the state recently enacted "shall-issue" licensing for concealed handguns, no such provision or permit exists for knives.

Most knives may be carried openly, with the exception of automatic knives such as switchblades or gravity knives, sales of which are strictly prohibited except to law enforcement personnel. Ballistic knives are included in the definition of "dangerous ordnance," and are subject to a wide range of statutory restrictions.

Ordinary folding pocket knives may be carried openly or concealed, although travelers should avoid carry of "tactical" folders with overly aggressive, weapon-like appearance or features, lest such knives be deemed deadly weapons, and hence prohibited from concealed carry. Note that "concealed" under Ohio law means either concealed on the person, or concealed ready at hand (readily accessible). While there is no statutorily defined blade length limit, readers should note that blade length often factors into whether a particular knife is determined to be a deadly weapon.

---

[83] State law prohibits concealed carry of deadly weapons, so any knife carried concealed must not be either "designed or specially adapted for use as a weapon," or actually "possessed, carried, or used as a weapon" in order to be legally carried concealed. *See,* OHIO REV. CODE ANN. §§ 2923.12 (Anderson 2005).

[84] Readers should note that while some fixed bladed knives may be deemed not to be deadly weapons, as that term is defined in Ohio law, there appear to exist numerous cases where fixed bladed knives have been ruled deadly weapons, thus resulting in convictions for carrying concealed weapons. *See, e.g.,* selected cases cited, Section 42.4, *infra.*

[85] Balisongs have been held to be deadly weapons, and hence prohibited from concealed carry. *See,* City of Columbus v. Dawson, 501 N.E.2d 677, 679 (Ohio Ct. App. 1986).

[86] *See,* OHIO REV. CODE ANN. §§ 2923.11(A), 2923.12 (Anderson 2005).

The Ohio Court of Appeals has ruled that balisongs (butterfly knives) are deadly weapons, and hence may not be carried concealed.[87]

State law prohibits possession or carry of deadly weapons in "school safety zones," courthouses and buildings containing a courtroom. In addition, "home rule" municipalities may enact their own ordinances restricting or prohibiting knife carry.

42.3 Selected Statutes

OHIO REV. CODE ANN. §§ (Anderson 2005)

§ 2923.11. Definitions.

As used in sections 2923.11 to 2923.24 of the Revised Code:

(A) "Deadly weapon" means any instrument, device, or thing capable of inflicting death, and designed or specially adapted for use as a weapon, or possessed, carried, or used as a weapon.
...
(J) "Ballistic knife" means a knife with a detachable blade that is propelled by a spring-operated mechanism.

(K) "Dangerous ordnance" means any of the following, except as provided in division (L) of this section:

(1) Any automatic or sawed-off firearm, zip-gun, or ballistic knife;
...

§ 2923.12. Carrying concealed weapons.

(A) No person shall knowingly carry or have, concealed on the person's person or concealed ready at hand, any of the following:

(1) A deadly weapon other than a handgun;

(2) A handgun other than a dangerous ordnance;

(3) A dangerous ordnance.

(B) No person who has been issued a license or temporary emergency license to carry a concealed handgun under section 2923.125 [2923.12.5] or 2923.1213 [2923.12.13] of the Revised Code or a license to carry a concealed handgun that was issued by another state with which the attorney general has entered into a reciprocity agreement under section 109.69 of the Revised Code, who is stopped for a law enforcement purpose, and who is carrying a concealed handgun shall fail to promptly inform any law enforcement officer who approaches the person after the person has been stopped that the person has been issued a license or temporary emergency license to carry a concealed handgun and that the person then is carrying a concealed handgun.
...

[§ 2923.12.2] § 2923.122. Illegal conveyance or possession of deadly weapon or dangerous ordnance or illegal possession of object indistinguishable from firearm in school safety zone.

(A) No person shall knowingly convey, or attempt to convey, a deadly weapon or dangerous ordnance into a school safety zone.

(B) No person shall knowingly possess a deadly weapon or dangerous ordnance in a school safety zone.
...

[§ 2923.12.3] § 2923.123. Illegal conveyance of deadly weapon or dangerous ordnance into courthouse; illegal possession or control in courthouse.

---

[87] *See,* City of Columbus v. Dawson, 501 N.E.2d 677, 679 (Ohio Ct. App. 1986).

(A) No person shall knowingly convey or attempt to convey a deadly weapon or dangerous ordnance into a courthouse or into another building or structure in which a courtroom is located.

(B) No person shall knowingly possess or have under the person's control a deadly weapon or dangerous ordnance in a courthouse or in another building or structure in which a courtroom is located.

...

§ 2923.20. Unlawful transaction in weapons.

(A) No person shall:

(1) Recklessly sell, lend, give, or furnish any firearm to any person prohibited by section 2923.13 or 2923.15 of the Revised Code from acquiring or using any firearm, or recklessly sell, lend, give, or furnish any dangerous ordnance to any person prohibited by section 2923.13, 2923.15, or 2923.17 of the Revised Code from acquiring or using any dangerous ordnance;

(2) Possess any firearm or dangerous ordnance with purpose to dispose of it in violation of division (A) of this section;

(3) Manufacture, possess for sale, sell, or furnish to any person other than a law enforcement agency for authorized use in police work, any brass knuckles, cestus, billy, blackjack, sandbag, switchblade knife, springblade knife, gravity knife, or similar weapon;

...

§ 2923.24. Possessing criminal tools.

(A) No person shall possess or have under the person's control any substance, device, instrument, or article, with purpose to use it criminally.

(B) Each of the following constitutes prima-facie evidence of criminal purpose:

(1) Possession or control of any dangerous ordnance, or the materials or parts for making dangerous ordnance, in the absence of circumstances indicating the dangerous ordnance, materials, or parts are intended for legitimate use;

(2) Possession or control of any substance, device, instrument, or article designed or specially adapted for criminal use;

(3) Possession or control of any substance, device, instrument, or article commonly used for criminal purposes, under circumstances indicating the item is intended for criminal use.

(C) Whoever violates this section is guilty of possessing criminal tools. Except as otherwise provided in this division, possessing criminal tools is a misdemeanor of the first degree. If the circumstances indicate that the substance, device, instrument, or article involved in the offense was intended for use in the commission of a felony, possessing criminal tools is a felony of the fifth degree.

42.4 Selected Caselaw

City of Columbus v. Dawson, 28 Ohio App. 3d 45, 501 N.E.2d 677 (Ohio Ct. App. 1986) (affirming conviction for concealed carry of balisong knife and upholding fact-finder determination that balisong knife designed as weapon).

State v. Johns, 2005 Ohio 1694 (Ohio Ct. App. 2005) (affirming conviction for carrying concealed weapon, "K-bar" knife found under driver's seat and upholding determination that knife designed for use as weapon).

State v. Warnement, 2000 OH 47968 (Ohio Ct. App. 2000) (affirming vehicle driver's conviction for carrying concealed weapon, sheathed hunting knife stored in unlocked glove compartment of vehicle).

State v. Anderson, 2 Ohio App. 3d 71, 440 N.E.2d 814 (Ohio Ct. App. 1981) (reversing conviction for carrying concealed weapon, folding knife with four inch locking blade and difficult to open one-handed, and holding state did not prove knife designed or adapted for use as weapon, nor knife carried, possessed, or used as weapon).

State v. Cathel, 127 Ohio App.3d 408, 713 N.E.2d 52 (Ohio Ct. App. 1998) (reversing conviction for carrying concealed weapon, folding knife with "Deerslayer" marked on four inch blade requiring two hands to open, for failure to prove knife either designed or adapted for use as weapon, or knife carried, possessed, or used as weapon).

42.5 Preemption Law

No knife law preemption, limited firearms law preemption for concealed handgun licensing only. *See*, 125th Ohio Gen. Assy. Am. Sub H.B. 12 § 9 (2004).

42.6 Places Off-Limits While Carrying

Ohio state law prohibits the possession of deadly weapons in "school safety zones" and courthouses and buildings containing a courtroom. *See*, OHIO REV. CODE ANN. §§ 2923.122, 2923.123 (Anderson 2005). Note that "home rule" municipalities may enact their own restrictions or prohibitions on knife carry.

42.7 School/College Carry

State law prohibits possession of deadly weapons in "school safety zones." *See*, OHIO REV. CODE ANN. §§ 2923.122, 2923.123 (Anderson 2005). Note that "home rule" municipalities may enact their own restrictions or prohibitions on knife carry.

42.8 Selected City Ordinances

Cincinnati – Possession of deadly weapons on school property prohibited. *See*, CINCINNATI, OHIO, MUNICIPAL CODE § 708-39 (2006). Carry of deadly or dangerous weapon in city buildings, including handguns, prohibited "notwithstanding the possession of a permit to carry a concealed handgun pursuant to Section 2923.125 of the Ohio Revised Code." *See, id.* at § 708-41. City manager empowered during "public danger or emergency" to restrict or prohibit possession or carry of weapons, including knives, in public. *See, id.* at Art. XVIII, § 7.

Dayton – Carrying concealed deadly weapons prohibited. *See*, Dayton, Ohio, Code of Ordinances § 138.02 (2005).

42.9 State Resources

Ohio State Highway Patrol
Customer Service Center West
1970 West Broad Street
Columbus, OH 43223
phone: (614) 995-5353
Website: http://www.statepatrol.ohio.gov/index.htm

Attorney General of Ohio
State Office Tower
Columbus, OH 43215-3428
Phone: (614) 466-4320
Website: http://www.ag.state.oh.us/

43 Oklahoma – The Sooner State

Area: 68,667 sq.mi. (Rank: 19th)   Population: 3,493,714 (Rank: 28th)
Violent Crime Rate (per 100,000 residents): 500.5 (Rank: 37th Safest)
State Motto: *Labor omnia vincit (Labor Conquers All Things)*

43.1 Knife Carry Law Summary

Note: Blade length limits, if any, in parentheses.

Knife Type	Open Carry	Concealed Carry	Notes
Folding Knives	Yes	Yes	
Fixed Bladed Knives	Yes	Yes	See note[88]
Dirks, Daggers, & Stilettos	No	No	
Automatic Knives	No	No	
Balisongs	No	No	See note[89]
Sword Canes	No	No	

43.2 Discussion

Visitors to Oklahoma will find a fairly restrictive legal environment for knife carry. Ordinary folding pocket knives should pose no problem, and may be carried openly or concealed. Fixed bladed knives may be carried openly or concealed as well, although readers should note that bowie knives are specifically prohibited. As a result, visitors should avoid carry of large fix bladed knives, especially in urban areas, lest their knives be deemed bowies for purposes of prosecution. State law does provide an explicit exception for knives carried for bona fide hunting, fishing, or recreational uses. Thus, hunting or fishing knives may be carried openly or concealed while on a legal, bona fide hunting or fishing trip.

There is no statutorily defined blade length limit. Dirks, daggers, stilettos, and automatic knives, however, are prohibited. Note that balisongs, while not specifically prohibited, may fall under the switchblade prohibition, as balisongs do in some states. Thus, visitors should avoid carry of balisongs in the Sooner State.

Oklahoma prohibits the carry of firearms and other deadly weapons, including daggers, dirks, switchblades, sword canes, and bowie knives, in establishments that serve alcoholic beverages, and in schools or on school property. Violation of either of these prohibitions is a felony. In addition, municipalities may pass their own local ordinances prohibiting or further restricting knife carry in their jurisdictions.

43.3 Selected Statutes

OKLA. STAT. tit. 21 §§ (2005)

---

[88] State law prohibits carry, whether openly or concealed, of bowie knives. *See,* OKLA. STAT. tit. 21 § 1272 (2005). Thus, travelers should exercise care when carrying any large, fixed bladed knife, lest they run afoul of this prohibition.

[89] Balisongs may fall under the state's prohibition on switchblades, as balisongs do in some states. Therefore, travelers would do well to avoid carrying balisongs.

§21-1272. Unlawful carry.

A. It shall be unlawful for any person to carry upon or about his or her person, or in a purse or other container belonging to the person, any pistol, revolver, shotgun or rifle whether loaded or unloaded or any dagger, bowie knife, dirk knife, switchblade knife, spring-type knife, sword cane, knife having a blade which opens automatically by hand pressure applied to a button, spring, or other device in the handle of the knife, blackjack, loaded cane, billy, hand chain, metal knuckles, or any other offensive weapon, whether such weapon be concealed or unconcealed, except this section shall not prohibit:

1. The proper use of guns and knives for hunting, fishing, educational or recreational purposes;

2. The carrying or use of weapons in a manner otherwise permitted by statute or authorized by the Oklahoma Self-Defense Act;

...

§21-1272.1. Carrying firearms where liquor is consumed.

A. It shall be unlawful for any person to carry or possess any weapon designated in Section 1272 of this title in any establishment where low-point beer, as defined by Section 163.2 of Title 37 of the Oklahoma Statutes, or alcoholic beverages, as defined by Section 506 of Title 37 of the Oklahoma Statutes, are consumed. This provision shall not apply to a peace officer, as defined in Section 99 of this title, or to private investigators with a firearms authorization when acting in the scope and course of employment, and shall not apply to an owner or proprietor of the establishment having a pistol, rifle, or shotgun on the premises. Provided however, a person possessing a valid concealed handgun license pursuant to the provisions of the Oklahoma Self-Defense Act, Section 1290.1 et seq. of this title may carry the concealed handgun into any restaurant or other establishment licensed to dispense low-point beer or alcoholic beverages where the sale of low-point beer or alcoholic beverages does not constitute the primary purpose of the business.

Provided further, nothing in this section shall be interpreted to authorize any peace officer in actual physical possession of a weapon to consume low-point beer or alcoholic beverages, except in the authorized line of duty as an undercover officer.

Nothing in this section shall be interpreted to authorize any private investigator with a firearms authorization in actual physical possession of a weapon to consume low-point beer or alcoholic beverages in any establishment where low-point beer or alcoholic beverages are consumed.

B. Any person violating the provisions of this section shall be punished as provided in Section 1272.2 of this title.

§21-1272.2. Penalty for firearm in liquor establishment.

Any person who intentionally or knowingly carries on his or her person any weapon in violation of Section 1272.1 of this title, shall, upon conviction, be guilty of a felony punishable by a fine not to exceed One Thousand Dollars ($1,000.00), or imprisonment in the State Penitentiary for a period not to exceed two (2) years, or both such fine and imprisonment.

Any person convicted of violating the provisions of this section after having been issued a concealed handgun license pursuant to the provisions of the Oklahoma Self-Defense Act, Sections 1290.1 through 1290.26 of this title, shall have the license revoked by the Oklahoma State Bureau of Investigation after a hearing and determination that the person is in violation of Section 1272.1 of this title.

§21-1278. Unlawful intent to carry.

Any person in this state who carries or wears any deadly weapons or dangerous instrument whatsoever with the intent or for the avowed purpose of unlawfully injuring another person, upon conviction, shall be guilty of a felony punishable by a fine not exceeding Five Thousand Dollars ($5,000.00), by imprisonment for a period not exceeding two (2) years, or by both such fine and imprisonment. The mere possession of such a weapon or dangerous instrument, without more, however, shall not be sufficient to establish intent as required by this section.

Any person convicted of violating the provisions of this section after having been issued a concealed handgun license pursuant to the provisions of the Oklahoma Self-Defense Act, Section 1290.1 et seq. of this title, shall have the license permanently revoked and shall be liable for an administrative fine of One Thousand Dollars ($1,000.00) upon a hearing and determination by the Oklahoma State Bureau of Investigation that the person is in violation of the provisions of this section.

§21-1280.1. Possession of firearm on school property.

A. It shall be unlawful for any person to have in his or her possession on any public or private school property or while in any school bus or vehicle used by any school for transportation of students or teachers any firearm or weapon designated in Section 1272 of this title, except as provided in subsection C of this section or as otherwise authorized by law.

B. "School property" means any publicly or privately owned property held for purposes of elementary, secondary or vocational-technical education, and shall not include property owned by public school districts or private educational entities where such property is leased or rented to an individual or corporation and used for purposes other than educational.

C. Firearms and weapons are allowed on school property and deemed not in violation of subsection A of this section as follows:

1. A gun or knife designed for hunting or fishing purposes kept in a privately owned vehicle and properly displayed or stored as required by law, or a handgun carried in a vehicle pursuant to a valid handgun license authorized by the Oklahoma Self-Defense Act, provided such vehicle containing said gun or knife is driven onto school property only to transport a student to and from school and such vehicle does not remain unattended on school property;

2. A gun or knife used for the purposes of participating in the Oklahoma Department of Wildlife Conservation certified hunter training education course or any other hunting, fishing, safety or firearms training courses, or a recognized firearms sports event, team shooting program or competition, or living history reenactment, provided the course or event is approved by the principal or chief administrator of the school where the course or event is offered, and provided the weapon is properly displayed or stored as required by law pending participation in the course, event, program or competition; and

3. Weapons in the possession of any peace officer or other person authorized by law to possess a weapon in the performance of their duties and responsibilities.

D. Any person violating the provisions of this section shall, upon conviction, be guilty of a felony punishable by a fine not to exceed Five Thousand Dollars ($5,000.00), and imprisonment for not more than two (2) years. Any person convicted of violating the provisions of this section after having been issued a concealed handgun license pursuant to the provisions of the Oklahoma Self-Defense Act shall have the license permanently revoked and shall be liable for an administrative fine of One Hundred Dollars ($100.00) upon a hearing and determination by the Oklahoma State Bureau of Investigation that the person is in violation of the provisions of this section.

43.4 Selected Caselaw

Beeler v. State, 334 P.2d 799 (Okla. Crim. App. 1959) (affirming conviction and trial court ruling of chain as *per se* dangerous weapon, and holding judge may declare instrument *per se* dangerous weapon where "the weapon used appears to have been designed as a weapon of combat and is capable by its description or appearance of producing death or serious bodily injury").

43.5 Preemption Law

No knife law preemption, firearms law preemption only. *See*, OKLA. STAT. tit. 21 § 1289.24 (2005).

43.6 Places Off-Limits While Carrying

Oklahoma prohibits the carry of firearms and other deadly weapons, including daggers, dirks, switchblades, sword canes, and bowie knives, in establishments that serve alcoholic beverages, and in schools or on school property. *See*, OKLA. STAT. tit. 21 §§ 1272.1, 1280.1 (2005). Violation of either of these prohibitions is a felony. *See, id.* at §§ 1272.2, 1280.1.

In addition, towns and cities may pass their own local ordinances prohibiting or further restricting knife carry in their jurisdictions.

43.7 School/College Carry

Oklahoma prohibits the carry of firearms and other deadly weapons, including daggers, dirks, switchblades, sword canes, and bowie knives, in schools or on school property. *See*, OKLA. STAT. tit. 21 § 1280.1 (2005). In addition, towns and cities may pass their own local ordinances prohibiting or restricting knife carry on school grounds.

43.8 Selected City Ordinances

Oklahoma City – Carry of handguns and other deadly weapons, including daggers, dirks, switchblades, sword canes, and bowie knives, prohibited in churches and religious assemblies, and any place "persons are assembled for public worship, for amusement, or for educational or scientific purposes, or into any circus, show or public exhibition of any kind, or into any ballroom, or to any social party or social gathering, or to any election, or to any political convention, or to any other public assembly[.]" *See*, OKLAHOMA CITY, OKLA., MUNICIPAL CODE § 30-303 (2006). Note that the city also prohibits the sale of switchblades and pocket knives with blades longer than four inches. *See, id.* at § 30-311.

43.9 State Resources

Oklahoma Highway Patrol
3600 North Martin Luther King Blvd.
Oklahoma City, OK 73111
Phone: (405) 425-7709
Website: http://www.dps.state.ok.us/ohp/

Attorney General of Oklahoma
2300 N. Lincoln Blvd
Oklahoma City, OK 73105
Phone: (405) 521-3921
Website: http://www.oag.state.ok.us/

44 Oregon – The Beaver State

Area: 95,997 sq.mi. (Rank: 10th)   Population: 3,521,515 (Rank: 27th)
Violent Crime Rate (per 100,000 residents): 298.3 (Rank: 20th Safest)
State Motto: *She Flies With Her Own Wings*

44.1 Knife Carry Law Summary

Note: Blade length limits, if any, in parentheses.

Knife Type	Open Carry	Concealed Carry	Notes
Folding Knives	Yes	Yes	
Fixed Bladed Knives	Yes	Yes	
Dirks, Daggers, & Stilettos	Yes	No	
Automatic Knives	Yes	No	
Balisongs	Yes	No	

44.2 Discussion

Visitors to the Beaver State will find a fairly friendly legal environment for knife carry, with a strong legal bias towards open carry. In fact, state law prohibits concealed carry of switchblades, dirks, daggers, ice picks, and similar instruments, but permits open carry of these knives. Concealed carry of folding pocket knives and ordinary fixed blades should pose no problem. There is no statutorily defined blade length limit. Note that state law makes carry or possession of any dangerous or deadly weapon with intent to use unlawfully against another a crime. In addition, note that balisongs may be considered statutory switchblades, as balisongs are in some states, and thus concealed carry would be prohibited.

The state prohibits carry or possession of dangerous weapons on or in public buildings and court facilities. The definition of public building, for purposes of this prohibition, includes hospitals, and educational institutions such as schools and colleges.

44.3 Selected Statutes

Or. Rev. Stat. §§ (2005)

161.015 General definitions. As used in chapter 743, Oregon Laws 1971, and ORS 166.635, unless the context requires otherwise:

(1) "Dangerous weapon" means any weapon, device, instrument, material or substance which under the circumstances in which it is used, attempted to be used or threatened to be used, is readily capable of causing death or serious physical injury.

(2) "Deadly weapon" means any instrument, article or substance specifically designed for and presently capable of causing death or serious physical injury.

...

166.220 Unlawful use of weapon. (1) A person commits the crime of unlawful use of a weapon if the person:

(a) Attempts to use unlawfully against another, or carries or possesses with intent to use unlawfully against another, any dangerous or deadly weapon as defined in ORS 161.015; or

(b) Intentionally discharges a firearm, blowgun, bow and arrow, crossbow or explosive device within the city limits of any city or within residential areas within urban growth boundaries at or in the direction of any person, building, structure or vehicle within the range of the weapon without having legal authority for such discharge.

(2) This section does not apply to:

(a) Police officers or military personnel in the lawful performance of their official duties;

(b) Persons lawfully defending life or property as provided in ORS 161.219;

(c) Persons discharging firearms, blowguns, bows and arrows, crossbows or explosive devices upon

public or private shooting ranges, shooting galleries or other areas designated and built for the purpose of target shooting; or

(d) Persons lawfully engaged in hunting in compliance with rules and regulations adopted by the State Department of Fish and Wildlife.

(3) Unlawful use of a weapon is a Class C felony. [Amended by 1975 c.700 §1; 1985 c.543 §1; 1991 c.797 §1]

166.240 Carrying of concealed weapons. (1) Except as provided in subsection (2) of this section, any person who carries concealed upon the person any knife having a blade that projects or swings into position by force of a spring or by centrifugal force, any dirk, dagger, ice pick, slingshot, metal knuckles, or any similar instrument by the use of which injury could be inflicted upon the person or property of any other person, commits a Class B misdemeanor.
...
166.360 Definitions for ORS 166.360 to 166.380. As used in ORS 166.360 to 166.380, unless the context requires otherwise:

(1) "Capitol building" means the Capitol, the State Office Building, the State Library Building, the Labor and Industries Building, the State Transportation Building, the Agriculture Building or the Public Service Building and includes any new buildings which may be constructed on the same grounds as an addition to the group of buildings listed in this subsection.

(2) "Court facility" means a courthouse or that portion of any other building occupied by a circuit court, the Court of Appeals, the Supreme Court or the Oregon Tax Court or occupied by personnel related to the operations of those courts, or in which activities related to the operations of those courts take place.
...
(4) "Public building" means a hospital, a capitol building, a public or private school, as defined in ORS 339.315, a college or university, a city hall or the residence of any state official elected by the state at large, and the grounds adjacent to each such building. The term also includes that portion of any other building occupied by an agency of the state or a municipal corporation, as defined in ORS 297.405, other than a court facility.

(5) "Weapon" means:

(a) A firearm;

(b) Any dirk, dagger, ice pick, slingshot, metal knuckles or any similar instrument or a knife other than an ordinary pocket knife, the use of which could inflict injury upon a person or property;

(c) Mace, tear gas, pepper mace or any similar deleterious agent as defined in ORS 163.211;

(d) An electrical stun gun or any similar instrument;

(e) A tear gas weapon as defined in ORS 163.211;

(f) A club, bat, baton, billy club, bludgeon, knobkerrie, nunchaku, nightstick, truncheon or any similar instrument, the use of which could inflict injury upon a person or property; or

(g) A dangerous or deadly weapon as those terms are defined in ORS 161.015. [1969 c.705 §1; 1977 c.769 §2; 1979 c.398 §1; 1989 c.982 §4; 1993 c.741 §2; 1999 c.577 §2; 1999 c.782 §6; 2001 c.201 §1]

166.370 Possession of firearm or dangerous weapon in public building or court facility;

exceptions; discharging firearm at school. (1) Any person who intentionally possesses a loaded or unloaded firearm or any other instrument used as a dangerous weapon, while in or on a public building, shall upon conviction be guilty of a Class C felony.

(2)(a) Except as otherwise provided in paragraph (b) of this subsection, a person who intentionally possesses:

(A) A firearm in a court facility is guilty, upon conviction, of a Class C felony. A person who intentionally possesses a firearm in a court facility shall surrender the firearm to a law enforcement officer.

(B) A weapon, other than a firearm, in a court facility may be required to surrender the weapon to a law enforcement officer or to immediately remove it from the court facility. A person who fails to comply with this subparagraph is guilty, upon conviction, of a Class C felony.

(b) The presiding judge of a judicial district may enter an order permitting the possession of specified weapons in a court facility.

(3) Subsection (1) of this section does not apply to:
...
(d) A person who is licensed under ORS 166.291 and 166.292 to carry a concealed handgun.
...
(f) Possession of a firearm on school property if the firearm:

(A) Is possessed by a person who is not otherwise prohibited from possessing the firearm; and

(B) Is unloaded and locked in a motor vehicle.

(4) The exceptions listed in subsection (3)(b) to (f) of this section constitute affirmative defenses to a charge of violating subsection (1) of this section.

(5)(a) Any person who knowingly, or with reckless disregard for the safety of another, discharges or attempts to discharge a firearm at a place that the person knows is a school shall upon conviction be guilty of a Class C felony.

(b) Paragraph (a) of this subsection does not apply to the discharge of a firearm:

(A) As part of a program approved by a school in the school by an individual who is participating in the program; or

(B) By a law enforcement officer acting in the officer's official capacity.

(6) Any weapon carried in violation of this section is subject to the forfeiture provisions of ORS 166.279.

(7) Notwithstanding the fact that a person's conduct in a single criminal episode constitutes a violation of both subsections (1) and (5) of this section, the district attorney may charge the person with only one of the offenses.

(8) As used in this section, "dangerous weapon" means a dangerous weapon as that term is defined in ORS 161.015. [1969 c.705 §§2,4; 1977 c.207 §2; 1979 c.398 §2; 1989 c.839 §22; 1989 c.982 §5; 1991 c.67 §39; 1993 c.625 §1; 1999 c.782 §7; 1999 c.1040 §4; 2001 c.666 §§24,36; 2003 c.614 §6]

44.4 Selected Caselaw

State v. Delgado, 298 Or. 395, 692 P.2d 610 (Or. 1984) (affirming reversal of conviction for possession of switchblade, and holding switchblade protected "arm" under Oregon Constitution).

State v. Pruett, 37 Or. App. 183, 586 P.2d 800 (Or. Ct. App. 1978) (reversing conviction for concealed carry of folding knife with three and a half inch locking blade, and holding knife at issue ordinary pocket knife under statute).

City of Portland v. Lodi, 782 P.2d 415, 308 Or. 468 (Or. 1989) (affirming invalidation and overturning of City of Portland penal ordinance prohibiting concealed carry of ordinary pocket knife with blade longer than three and a half inches)

44.5 Preemption Law

No knife law preemption, firearms law preemption only. *See*, OR. REV. STAT. § 166.170 (2005).

44.6 Places Off-Limits While Carrying

Oregon prohibits the carry of firearms and other dangerous weapons in public buildings, the definition of which includes schools and colleges, and in court facilities. *See*, OR. REV. STAT. § 166.370 (2005).

44.7 School/College Carry

Oregon prohibits the carry of firearms and other dangerous weapons in public buildings, the definition of which includes schools and colleges, and in court facilities. *See*, OR. REV. STAT. § 166.370 (2005).

44.8 Selected City Ordinances

Hillsboro – Concealed carry of dirk, dagger, stiletto, or any knife other than ordinary pocket knife prohibited. *See*, HILLSBORO, OR., MUNICIPAL CODE § 9.12.010 (2006).

44.9 State Resources

Oregon State Police
255 Capitol St. N.E.
Salem, OR 97310
Phone: (503) 378-3720
Fax: (503) 378-8282
Website: http://www.oregon.gov/OSP

Attorney General of Oregon
Department of Justice
1162 Court Street NE
Salem, OR 97310
Phone: (503) 378-4400
Fax: (503) 378-4017
Website: http://www.doj.state.or.us/

45 Pennsylvania – The Keystone State

Area: 44,817 sq.mi. (Rank: 32nd)   Population: 12,335,091 (Rank: 6th)
Violent Crime Rate (per 100,000 residents): 411.1 (Rank: 28th Safest)
State Motto: *Virtue, Liberty, and Independence*

45.1 Knife Carry Law Summary

Note: Blade length limits, if any, in parentheses.

Knife Type	Open Carry	Concealed Carry	Notes
Folding Knives	Yes	Yes	
Fixed Bladed Knives	Yes	Yes	
Dirks, Daggers, & Stilettos	No	No	See note[90]
Automatic Knives	No	No	
Balisongs	No	No	See note[91]

45.2 Discussion

Visitors to Pennsylvania will find a fairly restrictive legal environment for knife carry, perhaps reflecting a legislative compromise between the state's urban and rural areas. Ordinary fixed and folding knives may be carried openly or concealed. Note that state law prohibits concealed carry of any weapon "readily capable of lethal use" with intent to employ the weapon criminally.[92] There is no statutorily defined blade length limit. Dirks, daggers, stilettos, and automatic knives, however, are prohibited.

With regard to balisongs, readers should note that balisongs may fall under the switchblade prohibition, as balisongs do in some states. While one lower county court has held that balisongs are not prohibited offensive weapons, be aware this ruling only applies in that particular county. Given that no higher court with state-wide jurisdiction has apparently issued a published opinion on the issue of balisongs, cautious travelers would do well to avoid possession of balisongs in the state.

---

[90] The state law prohibition on offensive weapons lists a number of *per se* offensive weapons, including any "dagger, knife, razor or cutting instrument, the blade of which is exposed in an automatic way by switch, push-button, spring mechanism, or otherwise." *See*, 18 Pa. Cons. Stat. § 908 (2003). The Pennsylvania Supreme Court, in a decision from 1979, seems to indicate that "dagger" is modified by the automatic opening provision of the statute. *See*, Comm. v. Fisher, 400 A.2d 1284, 1286 (Pa. 1979) (citing Comm. v. Cartagena, 393 A.2d 350, 361 (Pa. 1978)). The case cited, however, does not include the term "dagger" as being modified by the automatic opening provision of the statute. *See*, Comm. v. Cartagena, 393 A.2d 350, 361 (Pa. 1978). A conservative reading of these opinions and the statute tends to lead to the conclusion that daggers are *per se* offensive weapons, and thus may not be possessed.

[91] Balisongs may fall under the switchblade prohibition, as balisongs do in some states. While at least one county court has concluded that balisongs (butterfly knives) are not prohibited offensive weapons, travelers should be aware that this lower court ruling would have binding effect only in the deciding court's jurisdiction, in this case, Bucks County. *See*, Comm. v. Miles, 7 Pa. D. & C.4th 67 (Bucks C., 1989). As such, a conservative view of the legal status of balisongs leads to listing its status as prohibited, absent a clarification in the statutory language, or an appropriate ruling from a higher court with statewide application on this issue.

[92] *See*, 18 Pa. Cons. Stat. § 907 (2003).

State law prohibits the carry of firearms and other weapons, the definition of which includes any knife, in or on elementary or secondary schools or school property, including school buses. In addition, state law prohibits the carry of firearms or dangerous weapons into court facilities. The definition of dangerous weapon applicable to this prohibition specifically includes daggers and switchblades. Note that municipalities may enact their own ordinances further restricting or prohibiting knife carry in their jurisdictions. In particular, travelers to the City of Brotherly Love should be aware that Philadelphia appears to have enacted a sweeping prohibition on "cutting weapons" in public, the penalty for violation of which is a minimum fine of at least $300, *and a minimum imprisonment* of ninety days.[93] Whether such a broad prohibition and/or penalty would in fact withstand judicial scrutiny is unclear, although you probably don't want to be the test case.

45.3 Selected Statutes

18 Pa. Cons. Stat. §§ (2003)

§ 2301. Definitions.

Subject to additional definitions contained in subsequent provisions of this article which are applicable to specific chapters or other provisions of this article, the following words and phrases, when used in this article shall have, unless the context clearly indicates otherwise, the meanings given to them in this section:

"Bodily injury." -- Impairment of physical condition or substantial pain.

"Deadly weapon." -- Any firearm, whether loaded or unloaded, or any device designed as a weapon and capable of producing death or serious bodily injury, or any other device or instrumentality which, in the manner in which it is used or intended to be used, is calculated or likely to produce death or serious bodily injury.

§ 907. Possessing instruments of crime.

(a) Criminal instruments generally.--A person commits a misdemeanor of the first degree if he possesses any instrument of crime with intent to employ it criminally.

(b) Possession of weapon.--A person commits a misdemeanor of the first degree if he possesses a firearm or other weapon concealed upon his person with intent to employ it criminally.

(c) Unlawful body armor.--A person commits a felony of the third degree if in the course of the commission of a felony or in the attempt to commit a felony he uses or wears body armor or has the control, custody or possession any body armor.

(d) Definitions.--As used in this section, the following words and phrases shall have the meanings given to them in this subsection:

"Body armor." -- Any protective covering for the body, or parts thereof, made of any polyaramid fiber or any resin-treated glass fiber cloth or any material or combination of materials made or designed to prevent, resist, deflect or deter the penetration thereof by ammunition, knife, cutting or piercing instrument or any other weapon.

"Instrument of crime." -- Any of the following:

1.   Anything specially made or specially adapted for criminal use.

2.   Anything used for criminal purposes and possessed by the actor under circumstances not manifestly appropriate for lawful uses it may have.

---

[93] See, Philadelphia, Pa., Code § 10-820 (2006).

"Weapon." -- Anything readily capable of lethal use and possessed under circumstances not manifestly appropriate for lawful uses which it may have. The term includes a firearm which is not loaded or lacks a clip or other component to render it immediately operable, and components which can readily be assembled into a weapon.

§ 908. Prohibited offensive weapons.

(a) Offense defined.--A person commits a misdemeanor of the first degree if, except as authorized by law, he makes repairs, sells, or otherwise deals in, uses, or possesses any offensive weapon.

(b) Exceptions.--

1.   It is a defense under this section for the defendant to prove by a preponderance of evidence that he possessed or dealt with the weapon solely as a curio or in a dramatic performance, or that, with the exception of a bomb, grenade or incendiary device, he complied with the National Firearms Act (26 U.S.C. 5801 et seq.), or that he possessed it briefly in consequence of having found it or taken it from an aggressor, or under circumstances similarly negativing any intent or likelihood that the weapon would be used unlawfully.

2.   This section does not apply to police forensic firearms experts or police forensic firearms laboratories. Also exempt from this section are forensic firearms experts or forensic firearms laboratories operating in the ordinary course of business and engaged in lawful operation who notify in writing, on an annual basis, the chief or head of any police force or police department of a city, and, elsewhere, the sheriff of a county in which they are located, of the possession, type and use of offensive weapons.

3.   This section shall not apply to any person who makes, repairs, sells or otherwise deals in, uses or possesses any firearm for purposes not prohibited by the laws of this Commonwealth.

(c) Definition.--As used in this section, the following words and phrases shall have the meanings given to them in this subsection:

"Firearm." -- Any weapon which is designed to or may readily be converted to expel any projectile by the action of an explosive or the frame or receiver of any such weapon.

"Offensive weapons." -- Any bomb, grenade, machine gun, sawed-off shotgun with a barrel less than 18 inches, firearm specially made or specially adapted for concealment or silent discharge, any blackjack, sandbag, metal knuckles, dagger, knife, razor or cutting instrument, the blade of which is exposed in an automatic way by switch, push-button, spring mechanism, or otherwise, or other implement for the infliction of serious bodily injury which serves no common lawful purpose.

(d) Exemptions.--The use and possession of blackjacks by the following persons in the course of their duties are exempt from this section:
...

§ 912. Possession of weapon on school property.

(a) Definition.--Notwithstanding the definition of "weapon" in section 907 (relating to possessing instruments of crime), "weapon" for purposes of this section shall include but not be limited to any knife, cutting instrument, cutting tool, nun-chuck stick, firearm, shotgun, rifle and any other tool, instrument or implement capable of inflicting serious bodily injury.

(b) Offense defined.--A person commits a misdemeanor of the first degree if he possesses a weapon in the buildings of, on the grounds of, or in any conveyance providing transportation to or from any elementary or secondary publicly-funded educational institution, any elementary or secondary private school licensed by the Department of Education or any elementary or secondary parochial school.

(c) Defense.--It shall be a defense that the weapon is possessed and used in conjunction with a lawful supervised school activity or course or is possessed for other lawful purpose.

§ 913. Possession of firearm or other dangerous weapon in court facility.

(a) Offense defined.--A person commits an offense if he:

1. knowingly possesses a firearm or other dangerous weapon in a court facility or knowingly causes a firearm or other dangerous weapon to be present in a court facility; or

2. knowingly possesses a firearm or other dangerous weapon in a court facility with the intent that the firearm or other dangerous weapon be used in the commission of a crime or knowingly causes a firearm or other dangerous weapon to be present in a court facility with the intent that the firearm or other dangerous weapon be used in the commission of a crime.

(b) Grading.--

1. Except as otherwise provided in paragraph (3), an offense under subsection (a)(1) is a misdemeanor of the third degree.

2. An offense under subsection (a)(2) is a misdemeanor of the first degree.

3. An offense under subsection (a)(1) is a summary offense if the person was carrying a firearm under section 6106(b) (relating to firearms not to be carried without a license) or 6109 (relating to licenses) and failed to check the firearm under subsection (e) prior to entering the court facility.

(c) Exceptions.--Subsection (a) shall not apply to:

...

(d) Posting of notice.--Notice of the provisions of subsections (a) and (e) shall be posted conspicuously at each public entrance to each courthouse or other building containing a court facility and each court facility, and no person shall be convicted of an offense under subsection (a)(1) with respect to a court facility if the notice was not so posted at each public entrance to the courthouse or other building containing a court facility and at the court facility unless the person had actual notice of the provisions of subsection (a).

(e) Facilities for checking firearms or other dangerous weapons.--Each county shall make available at or within the building containing the court facility by July 1, 2002, lockers or similar facilities at no charge or cost for the temporary checking of firearms by persons carrying firearms under section 6106(b) or 6109 or for the checking of other dangerous weapons that are not otherwise prohibited by law. Any individual checking a firearm, dangerous weapon or an item deemed to be a dangerous weapon at a court facility must be issued a receipt. Notice of the location of the facility shall be posted as required under subsection (d).

(f) Definitions.--As used in this section, the following words and phrases shall have the meanings given to them in this subsection:

"Court facility." -- The courtroom of a court of record; a courtroom of a community court; the courtroom of a district justice; a courtroom of the Philadelphia Municipal Court; a courtroom of the Pittsburgh Magistrates Court; a courtroom of the Traffic Court of Philadelphia; judge's chambers; witness rooms; jury deliberation rooms; attorney conference rooms; prisoner holding cells; offices of court clerks, the district attorney, the sheriff and probation and parole officers; and any adjoining corridors.

"Dangerous weapon." -- A bomb, grenade, blackjack, sandbag, metal knuckles, dagger, knife (the blade of which is exposed in an automatic way by switch, push-button, spring mechanism or otherwise) or other implement for the infliction of serious bodily injury which serves no common lawful purpose.

"Firearm." -- Any weapon, including a starter gun, which will or is designed to expel a projectile or projectiles by the action of an explosion, expansion of gas or escape of gas. The term does not include any device designed or used exclusively for the firing of stud cartridges, explosive rivets or similar industrial ammunition.

45.4 Selected Caselaw

Comm. v. Diliberto, 582 A.2d 690, 399 Pa.Super. 470 (Pa. Super. Ct. 1990) (affirming conviction for possession of switchblade).

Comm. v. Duxbury, 674 A.2d 1116, 449 Pa.Super. 640 (Pa. Super. Ct. 1996) (affirming conviction for sale of deadly weapon to minor, pen-knife with three inch blade)

Comm. v. Fisher, 400 A.2d 1284, 485 Pa. 8 (Pa. 1979) (reversing conviction for possession of prohibited offensive weapon, "Wyoming" knife with two blades, advertised for hunting and fishing uses).

Comm. v. Miles, 7 Pa. D. & C.4th 67 (Bucks C., 1989) (finding butterfly knife not a prohibited offensive weapon). Note that this is only a lower county court opinion.

45.5 Preemption Law

No knife law preemption, firearms law preemption only. *See*, 18 PA. CONS. STAT. § 6120 (2003).

45.6 Places Off-Limits While Carrying

State law prohibits the carry of firearms and other weapons, the definition of which includes any knife, in or on elementary or secondary schools or school property, including school buses. *See*, 18 PA. CONS. STAT. § 912 (2003).

State law also prohibits the carry of firearms or dangerous weapons into court facilities. The definition of dangerous weapon applicable to this prohibition specifically includes daggers and switchblades. *See*, 18 PA. CONS. STAT. § 913 (2003).

45.7 School/College Carry

State law prohibits the carry of firearms and other weapons, the definition of which includes any knife, in or on elementary or secondary schools or school property, including school buses. *See*, 18 PA. CONS. STAT. § 912 (2003).

45.8 Selected City Ordinances

Philadelphia – Carry of switchblades prohibited. *See*, PHILADELPHIA, PA., CODE § 10-810 (2006). Use or possession on public streets or on public property of any "cutting weapon", defined as "[a]ny *knife* or other cutting instrument which can be used as a weapon that has a cutting edge similar to that of a *knife*" prohibited, with exception for "tool or instrument commonly or ordinarily used in a trade, profession or calling" while "actually being used in the active exercise of that trade, profession or calling." *See, id.* at § 10-820. Violation penalty is *minimum* fine of $300 *and minimum* ninety day imprisonment. *Id.* Possession of weapons, the definition of which includes knives and cutting instruments, prohibited on or within 100 feet of any school, or in any conveyance providing transportation to or form school. *See, id.* at § 10-833.

45.9 State Resources

Pennsylvania State Police
Department Headquarters
Harrisburg, PA 17110
Phone: (717) 783-5599
Website: http://www.psp.state.pa.us/psp/site/default.asp

Attorney General of Pennsylvania
16th Floor, Strawberry Square
Harrisburg, PA 17120
Phone: (717) 787-3391
Website: http://www.attorneygeneral.gov/

46 Rhode Island – The Ocean State

Area: 1,045 sq.mi. (Rank: 50th)   Population: 1,069,725 (Rank: 43rd)
Violent Crime Rate (per 100,000 residents): 247.4 (Rank: 11th Safest)
State Motto: *Hope*

46.1 Knife Carry Law Summary

<u>Note:</u> Blade length limits, if any, in parentheses.

Knife Type	Open Carry	Concealed Carry	Notes
Folding Knives	Yes	Yes (<= 3")	
Fixed Bladed Knives	Yes	Yes (<= 3")	
Dirks, Daggers, & Stilettos	Yes	Yes (<= 3")	
Automatic Knives	Yes	Yes (<= 3")	
Balisongs	No	No	

46.2 Discussion

Visitors to the Ocean State will find a fairly permissive legal environment for knife carry, at least on paper. State law technically allows open carry of a wide spectrum of knives, and concealed carry of knives with blades three inches or shorter. Rhode Island is one of the few states that specifies how blade length is measured for purposes of the statute, to wit, "from the end of the handle where the blade is attached to the end of the blade[.]"[94] The Rhode Island Supreme Court has ruled that violation of the statutory blade limit for concealed carry does not require any showing of intent to use the knife unlawfully, and that mere concealed possession is sufficient for conviction.[95]

Technically, state law allows carry of dirks, daggers, stilettos, bowie knives and "sword-in-canes" (sword canes), so long as the wearer harbors no intent to use such knife unlawfully against another.[96] In practice, however, a visitor openly wearing a large dagger or bowie knife in this small, mostly urban Eastern state will likely encounter concerned, apprehensive looks from citizens, and considerable unwanted law enforcement attention.

In addition, readers should note that state law prohibits possession of so-called "Kung-Fu" weapons, and balisongs, which are often associated with, and perceived by the public as, martial arts weapons, may fall under this statutory ban on possession. Some limited exceptions and affirmative defenses exist, but are unlikely to apply to the typical traveler.

State law prohibits possession of firearms or other weapons on school grounds, or at school-sponsored events or while riding school-provided transportation. The penalty for violation of this prohibition is a felony, with a minimum prison sentence of one year, or a hefty fine. Note that municipalities may enact their own restrictions on knife carry beyond those in state law, although few appear to have done so.

---

[94] *See*, R.I. GEN. LAWS § 11-47-42 (2005).
[95] *See*, State v. Johnson, 414 A.2d 477, 480 (R.I. 1980).
[96] *See*, R.I. GEN. LAWS § 11-47-42 (2005).

46.3 Selected Statutes

R.I. Gen. Laws §§ (2005)

§ 11-47-42 Weapons other than firearms prohibited. – (a) No person shall carry or possess or attempt to use against another any instrument or weapon of the kind commonly known as a blackjack, slingshot, billy, sandclub, sandbag, metal knuckles, slap glove, bludgeon, stun-gun, or the so called "Kung-Fu" weapons, nor shall any person, with intent to use unlawfully against another, carry or possess a dagger, dirk, stiletto, sword-in-cane, bowie knife, or other similar weapon designed to cut and stab another, nor shall any person wear or carry concealed upon his person, any of the above-mentioned instruments or weapons, or any razor, or knife of any description having a blade of more than three (3) inches in length measuring from the end of the handle where the blade is attached to the end of the blade, or other weapon of like kind or description. Any person violating the provisions of this subsection shall be punished by a fine of not more than one thousand dollars ($1,000) or by imprisonment for not more than one year, or both, and the weapon so found shall be confiscated.

(2) Any person violating the provisions of this subsection while he or she is incarcerated within the confines of the adult correctional institutions shall be punished by a fine of not less than one thousand dollars ($1,000) nor more than three thousand dollars ($3,000), or by imprisonment for not less than one year nor more than five (5) years, or both, and the weapon so found shall be confiscated.

(b) No person shall sell to a person under eighteen (18) years of age, without the written authorization of the minor's parent or legal guardian, any stink bomb, blackjack, slingshot, bill, sandclub, sandbag, metal knuckles, slap glove, bludgeon, stungun, paint ball gun, so called "kung-fu" weapons, dagger, dirk, stiletto, sword-in-cane, bowie knife, razor, or knife of any description having a blade of more than three inches (3") in length as described in subsection (a) of this section, or any multi-pronged star with sharpened edges designed to be used as a weapon and commonly known as a Chinese throwing star, except that an individual who is actually engaged in the instruction of martial arts and licensed under § 5-43-1 may carry and possess any multi-pronged star with sharpened edges for the sole purpose of instructional use. Any person violating the provisions of this subsection shall be punished by a fine of not less than one thousand dollars ($1,000) nor more than three thousand dollars ($3,000), or by imprisonment for not less than one year nor more than five (5) years, or both, and the weapons so found shall be confiscated.

§ 11-47-43 Collectors and police officers exempt from § 11-47-42. – The provisions of § 11-47-42, so far as they forbid the possession of certain instruments or weapons, shall not apply to any person who possesses or is making a collection of the weapons as curios or for educational, professional, scientific, or any other lawful purpose, without intent to use the instrument or weapon unlawfully. Nor shall the provisions of § 11-47-42, so far as they relate to the possession or carrying of any billy, apply to sheriffs, constables, police, or other officers or guards whose duties require them to arrest or to keep and guard prisoners or property, nor to any person summoned by those officers to aid them in the discharge of their duties while actually engaged in their duties.

§ 11-47-59 Possession of knife during commission of crime. – No person shall commit or attempt to commit any crime of violence while having in his or her possession a knife with a blade more than three (3) inches long. Every person violating the provisions of this section shall, upon conviction, be sentenced for a term not less than one year nor more than five (5) years and/or fined not exceeding three thousand dollars ($3,000).

§ 11-47-60 Possession of firearms on school grounds. – (a) No person shall have in his or her possession any firearm or other weapons on school grounds.

(2) For the purposes of this section, "school grounds" means the property of a public or private elementary or secondary school or in those portions of any building, stadium, or other structure on school grounds which were, at the time of the violation, being used for an activity sponsored by or through a school in this state or while riding school provided transportation.

(3) Every person violating the provisions of this section shall, upon conviction, be sentenced to imprisonment for not less than one year nor more than five (5) years, or shall be fined not less than five hundred dollars ($500) nor more than five thousand dollars ($5,000).

(4) Any juvenile adjudicated delinquent pursuant to this statute shall, in addition to whatever other penalties are imposed by the family court, lose his or her license to operate a motor vehicle for up to six (6) months. If the juvenile has not yet obtained the necessary age to obtain a license, the court may impose as part of its sentence a delay in his or her right to obtain the license when eligible to do so, for a period of up to six (6) months.

(b) The provisions of this section shall not apply to any person who shall be exempt pursuant to the provisions of §§ 11-47-9, 11-47-11, and 11-47-18 or to the following activities when the activities are officially recognized and sanctioned by the educational institution:

(1) Firearm instruction and/or safety courses;

(2) Government-sponsored military-related programs such as ROTC;

(3) Interscholastic shooting and/or marksmanship events;

(4) Military history and firearms collection courses and/or programs; and

(5) The use of blank guns in theatrical and/or athletic events.

(c) The provisions of this section shall not apply to colleges, universities, or junior colleges.

46.4 Selected Caselaw

State v. Johnson, 414 A.2d 477 (R.I. 1980) (affirming conviction for concealed carry of knife with blade longer than three inches, and stating statute does not require showing of intent to use weapon unlawfully).

46.5 Preemption Law

No knife law preemption, firearms law preemption only. *See*, R.I. GEN. LAWS § 11-47-58 (2005).

46.6 Places Off-Limits While Carrying

Rhode Island prohibits the carry of firearms and other weapons on school grounds, or at school-sponsored events or while riding school-provided transportation. *See*, R.I. GEN. LAWS § 11-47-60 (2005).

46.7 School/College Carry

Rhode Island prohibits the carry of firearms and other weapons on school grounds, or at school-sponsored events or while riding school-provided transportation. *See*, R.I. GEN. LAWS § 11-47-60 (2005).

46.8 Selected City Ordinances

Newport – Possession of switchblades prohibited. *See*, NEWPORT, R.I., CODIFIED ORDINANCES § 9.16.030 (2006). Display of "any deadly weapon, or instrument or thing which by its appearance may be considered a deadly weapon, in any public place in a manner calculated or likely to alarm or frighten another or others" prohibited. *See, id.* at § 9.04.050.

46.9 State Resources

Rhode Island State Police
311 Danielson Pike
Scituate, RI 02857-1907
Phone: (401) 444-1000
Fax: (401) 444-1105
Website: http://www.risp.state.ri.us/

Attorney General of Rhode Island
150 South Main Street
Providence, RI 02903
Phone: (401) 274-4400
Fax: (401) 222-1331
Website: http://www.riag.state.ri.us/

47   South Carolina – The Palmetto State

Area: 30,109 sq.mi. (Rank: 40th)   Population: 4,107,183 (Rank: 25th)
Violent Crime Rate (per 100,000 residents): 784.2 (Rank: 50th Safest)
State Motto: *Dum Spiro Spero (While I Breathe, I Hope)*

47.1 Knife Carry Law Summary

Note: Blade length limits, if any, in parentheses.

Knife Type	Open Carry	Concealed Carry	Notes
Folding Knives	Yes	Yes	
Fixed Bladed Knives	Yes	Yes	
Dirks, Daggers, & Stilettos	Yes	No	
Automatic Knives	Yes	Yes	Some localities restrict
Balisongs	Yes	Yes	Some localities restrict

47.2 Discussion

Visitors to the Palmetto State will find a generally permissive legal environment for knife carry under state law. Carry, whether open or concealed, of most knives is generally permitted under state law. Note, however, that state law prohibits concealed carry of deadly weapons "usually used for the infliction of personal injury."[97] Thus, knives designed or specially adapted as weapons, such as daggers and swords, will likely fall under this prohibition. The statute, however, exempts from its scope dirks and razors unless they are used with intent to commit, or in furtherance of, a crime.[98]

State law prohibits carry of firearms and other weapons, the definition of which includes knives with blades over two inches long, on elementary or secondary school grounds. Although this prohibition seems straightforward, readers should be aware that the statute contains a catchall provision that, in at least one case, has been used to declare that possession of a razor with a one inch blade was a prohibited weapon.[99]

As is the case in most states, municipalities may enact their own local ordinances prohibiting or further restricting knife carry within their jurisdictions, and a number of cities and towns have done so. For example, the city of Columbia, the state capitol, prohibits carry of any kind of a number of types of knives, including dirks, butcher knives, and razors, as well as possession of switchblades.[100]

47.3 Selected Statutes

S.C. CODE §§ (2005)

SECTION 16-23-405. Definition of "weapon"; confiscation and disposition of weapons used in commission or in furtherance of crime.

---

[97] *See*, S.C. CODE § 16-23-460 (2005).
[98] *Id.*
[99] *See*, case(s) cited, Section 47.4, *infra*.
[100] *See*, COLUMBIA, S.C., CODE OF ORDINANCES §§ 14-102, 14-103 (2005).

(1) Except for the provisions relating to rifles and shotguns in Section 16-23-460, as used in this chapter, 'weapon' means firearm (rifle, shotgun, pistol, or similar device that propels a projectile through the energy of an explosive), a knife with a blade over two inches long, a blackjack, a metal pipe or pole, or any other type of device or object which may be used to inflict bodily injury or death.

(2) A person convicted of a crime, in addition to a penalty, shall have a weapon used in the commission or in furtherance of the crime confiscated. Each weapon must be delivered to the chief of police of the municipality or to the sheriff of the county if the violation occurred outside the corporate limits of a municipality. The law enforcement agency that receives the confiscated weapon may use it within the agency, transfer it to another law enforcement agency for the lawful use of that agency, trade it with a retail dealer licensed to sell pistols in this State for a pistol or other equipment approved by the agency, or destroy it. A weapon must not be disposed of in any manner until the results of any legal proceeding in which it may be involved are finally determined. A firearm seized by the State Law Enforcement Division may be kept by the division for use by its forensic laboratory.

SECTION 16-23-430. Carrying weapons on school property.

(1) It shall be unlawful for any person, except State, county or municipal law-enforcement officers or personnel authorized by school officials, to carry on his person, while on any elementary or secondary school property, a knife, with a blade over two inches long, a blackjack, a metal pipe or pole, firearms or any other type of weapon, device or object which may be used to inflict bodily injury or death.

(2) A person who violates the provisions of this section is guilty of a felony and, upon conviction, must be fined not more than one thousand dollars or imprisoned not more than five years, or both. Any weapon or object used in violation of this section may be confiscated by the law enforcement division making the arrest.

SECTION 16-23-460. Carrying concealed weapons; forfeiture of weapons.

Any person carrying a deadly weapon usually used for the infliction of personal injury concealed about his person is guilty of a misdemeanor, must forfeit to the county, or, if convicted in a municipal court, to the municipality the concealed weapon, and must be fined not less than two hundred dollars nor more than five hundred dollars or imprisoned not less than thirty days nor more than ninety days. Nothing herein contained may be construed to apply to (1) persons carrying concealed weapons upon their own premises or pursuant to and in compliance with Article 4 of Chapter 31 of Title 23, or (2) peace officers in the actual discharge of their duties. The provisions of this section do not apply to rifles, shotguns, dirks, slingshots, metal knuckles, or razors unless they are used with the intent to commit a crime or in furtherance of a crime.

SECTION 16-23-490. Additional punishment for possession of firearm or knife during commission of, or attempt to commit, violent crime.

(A) If a person is in possession of a firearm or visibly displays what appears to be a firearm or visibly displays a knife during the commission of a violent crime and is convicted of committing or attempting to commit a violent crime as defined in Section 16-1-60, he must be imprisoned five years, in addition to the punishment provided for the principal crime. This five-year sentence does not apply in cases where the death penalty or a life sentence without parole is imposed for the violent crime.

(B) Service of the five-year sentence is mandatory unless a longer mandatory minimum term of imprisonment is provided by law for the violent crime. The court may impose this mandatory five-year sentence to run consecutively or concurrently.

(C) The person sentenced under this section is not eligible during this five-year period for parole, work release, or extended work release. The five years may not be suspended and the person may not complete his term of imprisonment in less than five years pursuant to good-time credits or work credits, but may earn credits during this period.

(D) As used in this section, "firearm" means any machine gun, automatic rifle, revolver, pistol, or any weapon which will, or is designed to, or may readily be converted to expel a projectile; "knife" means an instrument or tool consisting of a sharp cutting blade whether or not fastened to a handle which is capable of being used to inflict a cut, slash, or wound.

(E) The additional punishment may not be imposed unless the indictment alleged as a separate count that the person was in possession of a firearm or visibly displayed what appeared to be a firearm or visibly displays a knife during the commission of the violent crime and conviction was had upon this count in the indictment. The penalties prescribed in this section may not be imposed unless the person convicted was at the same time indicted and convicted of a violent crime as defined in Section 16-1-60.

47.4 Selected Caselaw

In the Interest of Dave G., 477 S.E.2d 470, 324 S.C. 347 (S.C. Ct. App. 1996) (affirming conviction for possession of razor blade with one inch blade on school property, and upholding trial judge factual determination that razor was "weapon, device or object" capable of "inflicting bodily injury or death.")

47.5 Preemption Law

No knife law preemption, firearms law preemption only. *See*, S.C. CODE § 23-31-510 (2005).

47.6 Places Off-Limits While Carrying

State law prohibits the carry of firearms and other weapons, the definition of which includes knives with blades over two inches long, on elementary or secondary school property. *See*, S.C. CODE § 16-23-430 (2005). Readers should be aware that the statute contains a catchall provision that, in at least one case, has been used to declare a razor blade under the two inch limit to be a prohibited weapon.[101]

In addition, municipalities may pass their own local ordinances prohibiting or otherwise restricting knife carry within their jurisdictions.

47.7 School/College Carry

State law prohibits the carry of firearms and other weapons, the definition of which includes knives with blades over two inches long, on elementary or secondary school property. *See*, S.C. CODE § 16-23-430 (2005).

47.8 Selected City Ordinances

Charleston – Possession of martial arts weapons prohibited. *See*, CHARLESTON, S.C., CODE § 21-211 (2005). Concealed carry of "any ice pick, razor, knife, dagger or stiletto, the blade of which exceeds three (3) inches in length" prohibited. *See, id.* at § 21-215.

Columbia – Carry, whether open or concealed, of any "dirk, butcher knife, case knife, sword or spear, …, razors or other weapons of offense" prohibited. *See*, COLUMBIA, S.C., CODE OF ORDINANCES § 14-102 (2005). Possession of switchblades within the city prohibited. *See, id.* at § 14-103.

---

[101] *See*, In the Interest of Dave G., 477 S.E.2d 470, 471-72 (S.C. Ct. App. 1996).

Myrtle Beach – Carry, whether open or concealed, of dirks, razors, "or other deadly weapons used for the infliction of injury to person or property" prohibited. *See,* MYRTLE BEACH, S.C., CODE OF ORDINANCES § 14-102 (2005).

47.9 State Resources

South Carolina Law Enforcement Division
P.O. Box 21398
Columbia, SC 29221-1398
Phone: (803) 896-7216
Fax: (803) 896-7041
Website: http://www.sled.state.sc.us/

South Carolina Attorney General
1000 Assembly Street, Room 519
Columbia, SC 29201
Phone: (803) 734-4399
Fax: (803) 734-4323
Website: http://www.scattorneygeneral.org/

48 South Dakota – The Mount Rushmore State

Area: 75,885 sq.mi. (Rank: 16th)   Population: 761,063 (Rank: 46th)
Violent Crime Rate (per 100,000 residents): 171.5 (Rank: 5th Safest)
State Motto: *Under God the People Rule*

48.1 Knife Carry Law Summary

<u>Note:</u> Blade length limits, if any, in parentheses.

Knife Type	Open Carry	Concealed Carry	Notes
Folding Knives	Yes	Yes	
Fixed Bladed Knives	Yes	Yes	
Dirks, Daggers, & Stilettos	Yes	Yes	
Automatic Knives	Yes	Yes	See note[102]
Balisongs	Yes	Yes	See note[103]

48.2 Discussion

Visitors to South Dakota will find a permissive legal environment for knife carry. State law permits open or concealed carry of most knives. State law makes it a felony, however, to carry a concealed dangerous weapon, the definition of which includes any knife, with intent to commit a felony. There is no statutorily defined blade length limit. The legislature has repealed, effective July 1, 2006, two knife-related statutes prohibiting possession of ballistic knives, and prohibiting possession of butterfly or balisong knives by persons under the age of eighteen.

Apart from courthouses and schools, no other state-wide statutory prohibitions on off-limits locations for otherwise legal knife carry exist, although cities and towns may pass their own ordinances restricting knife carry. South Dakota does not preempt its cities and towns from regulating knife carry, unlike the case for firearms, where the state has prohibited local governments from enacting their own firearms carry restrictions, ensuring uniform state-wide firearms laws. As such, local governments may enact their own ordinances prohibiting or otherwise restricting knife carry within their jurisdictions.

48.3 Selected Statutes

S.D. CODIFIED LAWS §§ (2005)

22-1-2. (Text of section effective July 1, 2006) Definition of terms. Terms used in this title mean:
...
(10) "Dangerous weapon" or "deadly weapon," any firearm, stun gun, knife, or device, instrument, material, or substance, whether animate or inanimate, which is calculated or designed to inflict death or serious bodily harm, or by the manner in which it is used is likely to inflict death or serious bodily harm;
...

---

[102] Effective July 1, 2006, possession of ballistic knives is no longer prohibited. *See,* S.D. CODIFIED LAWS § 22-14-19 (2005) (repealed effective July 1, 2006).
[103] Effective July 1, 2006, possession of butterfly/balisong knives by minors is no longer prohibited. *See,* S.D. CODIFIED LAWS § 22-14-29 (2005) (repealed effective July 1, 2006).

22-14-8. (Text of section effective until July 1, 2006) **Concealment of weapon with intent to commit felony.** Any person who conceals on or about his person a controlled or dangerous weapon with intent to commit a felony is guilty of a Class 5 felony.

(Text of section effective July 1, 2006) **Concealment of weapon with intent to commit felony-- Felony.** Any person who conceals on or about his or her person a controlled or dangerous weapon with intent to commit a felony is guilty of a Class 5 felony.

Source: SL 1976, ch 158, § 14-5; SL 1977, ch 189, § 28; SL 2005, ch 120, § 246.

22-14-19. **Ownership, possession, or sale of ballistic knife prohibited--Ballistic knife defined- -Violation as misdemeanor.** No person may own, possess, or sell a ballistic knife. A ballistic knife is a knife encased in a tubular metal sheath which when removed, uncovers a detachable blade that can be propelled by a spring mechanism operated at the push of a button. A violation of this section is a Class 1 misdemeanor. **(This section is repealed effective July 1, 2006 pursuant to SL 2005, ch 120, § 258.)**

Source: SL 1987, ch 164.

22-14-23. (Text of section effective until July 1, 2006) **Possession in county courthouse as misdemeanor.** Except as provided in § 22-14-24, any person who knowingly possesses or causes to be present a firearm or other dangerous weapon, in any county courthouse, or attempts to do so, is guilty of a Class 1 misdemeanor.
  (Text of section effective July 1, 2006) **Possession in county courthouse--Misdemeanor.** Except as provided in § 22-14-24, any person who knowingly possesses or causes to be present any firearm or other dangerous weapon, in any county courthouse, or attempts to do so, is guilty of a Class 1 misdemeanor.

Source: SL 1993, ch 173, § 2; SL 2005, ch 120, § 262.

22-14-29. **Ownership, possession, or carrying of butterfly/balisong knife by minors prohibited--Misdemeanor.** No person under the age of eighteen may own, possess, or carry a butterfly/balisong knife. A butterfly/balisong knife is a knife which is encased in a metal, wooden, or plastic sheath which when removed, uncovers a detachable blade that can be opened automatically by operation of inertia, gravity, or both. A violation of this section is a Class 1 misdemeanor. **(This section is repealed effective July 1, 2006 pursuant to SL 2005, ch 120, § 266.)**

Source: SL 1994, ch 163.

13-32-7. **Possession of firearms on elementary or secondary school premises or vehicle as misdemeanor--Exceptions.** Any person, other than a law enforcement officer, who intentionally carries, has in his possession, stores, keeps, leaves, places, or puts into the possession of another person, any firearm, or air gun, whether or not the firearm or air gun is designed, adapted, used, or intended primarily for imitative or noisemaking purposes, or any dangerous weapon, on or in any elementary or secondary school premises, vehicle, or building or any premises, vehicle, or building used or leased for elementary or secondary school functions, whether or not any person is endangered by such actions, is guilty of a Class 1 misdemeanor. This section does not apply to starting guns while in use at athletic events, firearms, or air guns at firing ranges, gun shows, and supervised schools or sessions for training in the use of firearms. This section does not apply to the ceremonial presence of unloaded weapons at color guard ceremonies.

Source: SL 1961, ch 49; SL 1979, ch 120; SL 1982, ch 86, § 145; SL 1990, ch 129; SL 1991, ch 147, § 1; SL 1993, ch 142; SL 2002, ch 90, § 1.

48.4 Selected Caselaw

State v. Short Horn, 427 N.W.2d 361 (S.D. 1988) (affirming revocation of probation and upholding trial court determination that pocket knife was "offensive weapon" under statute).

48.5 Preemption Law

No knife law preemption, firearms law preemption only. *See*, S.D. CODIFIED LAWS §§ 7-18A-36 (Counties), 8-5-13 (Townships), 9-19-20 (Municipalities) (2005).

48.6 Places Off-Limits While Carrying

South Dakota prohibits the carry of firearms and other dangerous weapons on elementary or secondary school premises. *See*, S.D. CODIFIED LAWS § 13-32-7 (2005). State law also prohibits possession of firearms and dangerous weapons in county courthouses. *See, id.* at § 22-14-23.

48.7 School/College Carry

South Dakota prohibits the carry of firearms and other dangerous weapons on elementary or secondary school premises. *See*, S.D. CODIFIED LAWS § 13-32-7 (2005).

48.8 Selected City Ordinances

Aberdeen – Concealed carry of daggers, bowie knives, dirks, and other dangerous and deadly weapons prohibited. *See*, ABERDEEN, S.D., REVISED ORDINANCES § 19-76 (2005). Possession in licensed alcoholic beverage establishments of any "sharp or dangerous weapon" prohibited, except a folding pocket knife (kept in closed position) with blade less than three inches. *See, id.* § 4-4.

Rapid City – Concealed carry of "any knife with a blade exceeding 3 inches in length, or any sharp or dangerous weapon such as is usually employed in attack or defense of the person" prohibited. *See*, RAPID CITY, S.D., CODE OF ORDINANCES § 9.28.030 (2004). Carry, whether open or concealed, of any weapon or "sharp or dangerous object," other than a folding knife carried in the closed position with a blade less than three inches in length, prohibited in all alcoholic beverage establishments except those solely selling beer for off-premises consumption. *See, id.* at § 9.27.040.

Sioux Falls – Concealed carry of daggers, bowie knives, razors, dirks and other dangerous and deadly weapons prohibited. *See*, SIOUX FALLS, S.D., REVISED ORDINANCES § 26-51 (2006). Drawing of deadly weapons, including knives, so that weapon "may be used against or upon another person" prohibited, except for self-defense purpose. *See, id.* at § 26-52. Carry in "threatening or menacing manner, without authority of law, any pistol, revolver, dagger, razor, dangerous knife, stiletto, …, or other dangerous weapon" prohibited. *See, id.* at § 26-25.

48.9 State Resources

South Dakota Highway Patrol
500 East Capitol
Pierre, SD 57501-5070
Phone: (605) 773-3105
Fax: (605) 773-6046
Website: http://hp.state.sd.us/

Attorney General of South Dakota
500 East Capitol Ave.
Pierre, SD 57501-5070
Phone: (605) 773-3215
Fax: (605) 773-4106
Website: http://www.state.sd.us/attorney/index.asp

49   Tennessee – The Volunteer State

Area: 41,217 sq.mi. (Rank: 34th)   Population: 5,797,289 (Rank: 16th)
Violent Crime Rate (per 100,000 residents): 695.2 (Rank: 47th Safest)
State Motto: *Agriculture and Commerce*

49.1 Knife Carry Law Summary

<u>Note:</u> Blade length limits, if any, in parentheses.

Knife Type	Open Carry	Concealed Carry	Notes
Folding Knives	Yes (< 4")	Yes (< 4")	
Fixed Bladed Knives	Yes (< 4")	Yes (< 4")	
Dirks, Daggers, & Stilettos	Yes (< 4")	Yes (< 4")	
Automatic Knives	No	No	
Balisongs	Yes (< 4")	Yes (< 4")	See note[104]

49.2 Discussion

Visitors to the Volunteer State will find a fairly permissive legal environment for knife carry. State law prohibits carry with any intent to go armed, that is, with the intent to use the knife carried as a weapon, of any knife with a blade greater than four inches in length. Fixed and folding knives, with blades four inches or less, may be carried openly or concealed. Switchblades are prohibited. Note that balisongs may fall under the switchblade prohibition, as balisongs do in some states. As such, cautious travelers would be wise to avoid carry of balisongs in this state.

State law prohibits carry of any "bowie knife, hawk bill knife, ice pick, dagger, …, switchblade knife, … or any other weapon of like kind" on public or private school grounds. The statute defines "weapon of like kind" as encompassing "razors and razor blades, except those used solely for personal shaving, and any sharp pointed or edged instrument," and provides limited exceptions for instructional, food preparation, and maintenance uses.[105] In addition, Tennessee prohibits possession of weapons, including switchblades, in court facilities.[106]

As in many states, local governments may enact their own ordinances prohibition or otherwise restricting the carry of knives within their jurisdictions.

49.3 Selected Statutes

TENN. CODE §§ (2005)

39-17-1301. Part definitions.

As used in this part, unless the context otherwise requires:

…

---

[104] State law prohibits possession of switchblades. *See*, TENN. CODE § 39-17-1302(7) (2005). Note that balisongs may fall under the switchblade prohibition, as balisongs do in some states. As such, cautious travelers would be wise to avoid carry of balisongs.
[105] *See*, TENN. CODE § 39-17-1309 (2005).
[106] *See*, TENN. CODE § 39-17-1306 (2005).

(7) "Knife" means any bladed hand instrument that is capable of inflicting serious bodily injury or death by cutting or stabbing a person with the instrument;

...

(14) "Switchblade knife" means any knife that has a blade which opens automatically by:

(A) Hand pressure applied to a button or other device in the handle; or

(B) Operation of gravity or inertia; and

...

39-17-1302. Prohibited weapons.

(a) A person commits an offense who intentionally or knowingly possesses, manufactures, transports, repairs or sells:

...

(7) A switchblade knife or knuckles; or

(8) Any other implement for infliction of serious bodily injury or death which has no common lawful purpose.

...

(c) It is an affirmative defense to prosecution under this section which the person must prove by a preponderance of the evidence that:

(2) The person's conduct was relative to dealing with the weapon solely as a curio, ornament or keepsake, and if the weapon is a type described in subdivisions (a)(1)-(5), that it was in a nonfunctioning condition and could not readily be made operable; or

(3) The possession was brief and occurred as a consequence of having found the weapon or taken it from an aggressor.

(d) ...

(4) An offense under subdivisions (a)(7)-(8) is a Class A misdemeanor.

39-17-1306. Carrying weapons during judicial proceedings.

(a) No person shall intentionally, knowingly, or recklessly carry on or about the person while inside any room in which judicial proceedings are in progress any weapon prohibited by § 39-17-1302(a), for the purpose of going armed; provided, that if the weapon carried is a firearm, the person is in violation of this section regardless of whether such weapon is carried for the purpose of going armed.

(b) Any person violating subsection (a) commits a Class E felony.

(c) The provisions of subsection (a) shall not apply to any person who:

...

(2) Has been directed by a court to bring the firearm for purposes of providing evidence.

39-17-1307. Unlawful carrying or possession of a weapon.

(a) (1) A person commits an offense who carries with the intent to go armed a firearm, a knife with a blade length exceeding four inches (4"), or a club.

(2) An offense under subdivision (a)(1) is a Class C misdemeanor, except it is a Class A misdemeanor if the person's carrying of a handgun occurred at a place open to the public where one (1) or more persons were present.

...

(c) (1) A person commits an offense who possesses any deadly weapon with intent to employ it in the commission of or escape from an offense.

(2) An offense under subdivision (c)(1) is a Class E felony.

39-17-1308. Defenses to unlawful possession or carrying of a weapon.

(a) It is a defense to the application of § 39-17-1307 if the possession or carrying was:

...

(2) By a person authorized to possess or carry a firearm pursuant to § 39-17-1315 or § 39-17-1351;

(3) At the person's:

(A) Place of residence;

(B) Place of business; or

(C) Premises;

(4) Incident to lawful hunting, trapping, fishing, camping, sport shooting or other lawful activity;

...

(9) By any person possessing a club/baton who holds a certificate that the person has had training in the use of a club/baton for self-defense which is valid and issued by a certified person authorized to give training in the use of clubs/batons, and is not prohibited from purchasing a firearm under any local, state or federal laws; or

...

(b) The defenses described in this section are not available to persons described in § 39-17-1307(b)(1).

39-17-1309. Carrying weapons on school property.

(a) As used in this section, "weapon of like kind" includes razors and razor blades, except those used solely for personal shaving, and any sharp pointed or edged instrument, except unaltered nail files and clips and tools used solely for preparation of food, instruction and maintenance.

(b) (1) It is an offense for any person to possess or carry, whether openly or concealed, with the intent to go armed, any firearm, explosive, explosive weapon, bowie knife, hawk bill knife, ice pick, dagger, slingshot, leaded cane, switchblade knife, blackjack, knuckles or any other weapon of like kind, not used solely for instructional or school-sanctioned ceremonial purposes, in any public or private school building or bus, on any public or private school campus, grounds, recreation area, athletic field or any other property owned, used or operated by any board of education, school, college or university board of trustees, regents or directors for the administration of any public or private educational institution.

(2) A violation of this subsection (b) is a Class E felony.

(c) (1) It is an offense for any person to possess or carry, whether openly or concealed, any firearm, not used solely for instructional or school-sanctioned ceremonial purposes, in any public or private school building or bus, on any public or private school campus, grounds, recreation area, athletic field or any other property owned, used or operated by any board of education, school, college or university board of trustees, regents or directors for the administration of any public or private educational institution. It is not an offense under this subsection (c) for a nonstudent adult to possess a firearm, if such firearm is contained within a private vehicle operated by the adult and is not handled by such adult, or by any other person acting with the expressed or implied consent of such adult, while such vehicle is on school property.

(2) A violation of this subsection (c) is a Class B misdemeanor.

(d) (1) Each chief administrator of a public or private school shall display in prominent locations about the school a sign, at least six inches (6") high and fourteen inches (14") wide, stating:

FELONY. STATE LAW PRESCRIBES A MAXIMUM PENALTY OF SIX (6) YEARS IMPRISONMENT AND A FINE NOT TO EXCEED THREE THOUSAND DOLLARS ($3,000) FOR CARRYING WEAPONS ON SCHOOL PROPERTY.

(2) As used in this subsection (d), "prominent locations" about a school includes, but is not limited to, sports arenas, gymnasiums, stadiums and cafeterias.

(e) The provisions of subsections (b) and (c) do not apply to the following persons:

...

(5) Any pupils who are members of the reserve officers training corps or pupils enrolled in a course of instruction or members of a club or team, and who are required to carry arms or weapons in the discharge of their official class or team duties;

...

39-17-1310. Affirmative defense to carrying weapons on school property.

It is an affirmative defense to prosecution under § 39-17-1309(a)-(d) that the person's behavior was in strict compliance with the requirements of one (1) of the following classifications:

(1)   A person hunting during the lawful hunting season on lands owned by any public or private educational institution and designated as open to hunting by the administrator of the educational institution;

(2)   A person possessing unloaded hunting weapons while transversing the grounds of any public or private educational institution for the purpose of gaining access to public or private lands open to hunting with the intent to hunt on such public or private lands unless the lands of the educational institution are posted prohibiting such entry;

(3)   A person possessing guns or knives when conducting or attending "gun and knife shows" and such program has been approved by the administrator of the educational institution; or

(4)   A person entering the property for the sole purpose of delivering or picking up passengers and who does not remove, utilize or allow to be removed or utilized any weapon from the vehicle.

39-17-1311. Carrying weapons on public parks, playgrounds, civic centers and other public recreational buildings and grounds.

(a) It is an offense for any person to possess or carry, whether openly or concealed, with the intent to go armed, any weapon prohibited by § 39-17-1302(a), not used solely for instructional, display or sanctioned ceremonial purposes, in or on the grounds of any public park, playground, civic center or other building facility, area or property owned, used or operated by any municipal, county or state government, or instrumentality thereof, for recreational purposes.

(b) The provisions of subsection (a) shall not apply to the following persons:

...

(5) Any pupils who are members of the reserve officers training corps or pupils enrolled in a course of instruction or members of a club or team, and who are required to carry arms or weapons in the discharge of their official class or team duties;

...

(7) Also, only to the extent a person strictly conforms such person's behavior to the requirements of one (1) of the following classifications:

(A)   A person hunting during the lawful hunting season on lands owned by any municipality, county, state or instrumentality thereof and designated as open to hunting by law or by the appropriate official;

(B)   A person possessing unloaded hunting weapons while transversing the grounds of any such public recreational building or property for the purpose of gaining access to public or private lands open to hunting with the intent to hunt on the public or private lands unless the public recreational building or property is posted prohibiting such entry;

(C)   A person possessing guns or knives when conducting or attending "gun and knife shows" when such program has been approved by the administrator of the recreational building or property;

(D)   A person entering the property for the sole purpose of delivering or picking up passengers and who does not remove any weapon from the vehicle or utilize it in any manner;

(E)   A person who possesses or carries a firearm for the purpose of sport or target shooting and sport or target shooting is permitted in such park or recreational area; or

...

At such time as such person's behavior no longer strictly conforms to one (1) of such classifications, such person shall be subject to the provisions of subsection (a).

(c) (1)   Each chief administrator of public recreational property shall display in prominent locations about such place a sign, at least six inches (6") high and fourteen inches (14") wide, stating:

MISDEMEANOR. STATE LAW PRESCRIBES A MAXIMUM PENALTY OF ELEVEN (11) MONTHS AND TWENTY-NINE (29) DAYS AND A FINE NOT TO EXCEED TWO THOUSAND FIVE HUNDRED DOLLARS ($2,500) FOR CARRYING WEAPONS ON OR IN PUBLIC RECREATIONAL PROPERTY.

(2) As used in this subsection (c), "prominent locations" about public recreational property includes, but is not limited to, all entrances to such property, any such building or structure located on such property, such as restrooms, picnic areas, sports facilities, welcome centers, gift shops, playgrounds, swimming pools, restaurants and parking lots.

(3) The legislative body of any municipality or committee appointed by such body to regulate public recreational property may exempt public recreational property located within its jurisdiction from the requirements of subdivision (c)(1).

(d) A violation of this section is a Class A misdemeanor.

49.4 Selected Caselaw

State v. Neeley, 2002 TN 1560 (Tenn. Crim. App. 2002) (affirming conviction for possession of weapon with intent to go armed, knife with nine and a half inch blade found on floor of vehicle near defendant's feet).

49.5 Preemption Law

No knife law preemption, firearms law preemption only. *See*, TENN. CODE § 39-17-1314 (2005).

49.6 Places Off-Limits While Carrying

Tennessee prohibits carry of any kind, "with the intent to go armed", of firearms, or any "bowie knife, hawk bill knife, ice pick, dagger, ..., switchblade knife, ... or any other weapon of like kind" on public or private school grounds. The term "weapon of like kind" encompasses "razors and razor blades, except those used solely for personal shaving, and any sharp pointed or edged instrument," with limited exceptions for instructional, food preparation, and maintenance uses. *See*, TENN. CODE § 39-17-1309 (2005).

State law also prohibits possession of weapons, including switchblades, in court facilities. *See*, TENN. CODE § 39-17-1306 (2005).

49.7 School/College Carry

Tennessee prohibits the carry of any kind, "with the intent to go armed", of firearms, or any "bowie knife, hawk bill knife, ice pick, dagger, ..., switchblade knife, ... or any other weapon of like kind" on public or private school grounds. The term "weapon of like kind" encompasses "razors and razor blades, except those used solely for personal shaving, and any sharp pointed or edged instrument," with limited exceptions for instructional, food preparation, and maintenance uses. *See*, Tenn. Code § 39-17-1309 (2005).

49.8 Selected City Ordinances

Memphis – Carry of any kind with intent to go armed of any razor, dirk, bowie knife, or "other knife of like form, shape or size", pocket knife with blade over four inches in length, sword cane, ice pick, or Spanish stiletto prohibited. *See*, MEMPHIS, TENN., CODE OF ORDINANCES § 10-32-2 (2004). Unlawful to engage in "cruising," defined as "driving a motor vehicle past a traffic control point in the area designated as a no cruising zone more than three times in one hour," while also, among other prohibited acts, "[c]arrying in any manner whatever, with the intent to go armed, any razor; dirk; bowie knife or other knife of like form, shape or size; pocket knife with any blade over four inches in length; sword cane; ice pick; ...; Spanish stiletto." *See, id.* at § 11-16-50.

Knoxville – Carry, whether open or concealed, with the intent to go armed, of "any razor, dirk, bowie knife or other knife of like form, shape or size, sword cane, icepick, slingshot, blackjack, brass knuckles, [or] Spanish stiletto" prohibited. *See*, KNOXVILLE, TENN., CODE OF ORDINANCES § 19-104 (2005). Sales of dirks, bowie knives, sword canes, and Spanish stilettos prohibited. *See, id.* at § 19-105. Sale to minor of bowie knives, dirks, hunting knives, or switchblades, except for hunting purposes, prohibited. *See, id.* at § 19-106. Carry of switchblades by minor prohibited. *See, id.* at § 19-107.

49.9 State Resources

Tennessee Department of Safety
1150 Foster Avenue
Nashville, TN 37249
Phone: (615) 251-5216
Fax: (615) 253-2091
Website: http://www.state.tn.us/safety/

Tennessee Attorney General
425 Fifth Avenue North
Nashville, TN 37243
Phone: (615) 741-5860
Website: http://www.attorneygeneral.state.tn.us/

50 Texas – The Lone Star State

Area: 261,797 sq.mi. (Rank: 2nd) Population: 21,779,893 (Rank: 2nd)
Violent Crime Rate (per 100,000 residents): 540.5 (Rank: 39th Safest)
State Motto: *Friendship*

50.1 Knife Carry Law Summary

<u>Note:</u> Blade length limits, if any, in parentheses.

Knife Type	Open Carry	Concealed Carry	Notes
Folding Knives	Yes (< 5½")	Yes (< 5½")	
Fixed Bladed Knives	Yes (< 5½")	Yes (< 5½")	See note[107]
Dirks, Daggers, & Stilettos	No	No	
Automatic Knives	No	No	
Balisongs	No	No	See note[108]

50.2 Discussion

Visitors to the Lone Star State will find a fairly restrictive legal environment for knife carry. Readers may find this perhaps somewhat surprising, given the modern public image and history ("Remember the Alamo!") of Texas, and the grand, rugged scale of the largest of the lower 48 states.

Nevertheless, with respect to knives, Texas law prohibits carry of daggers, dirks, stilettos, automatic knives (switchblades), and large fixed bladed knives such as bowie knives. The state law definition of an "illegal knife" includes any knife with a blade five and a half inches or greater. Granted, this is one of the largest statutory blade length limits in the country, and will no doubt help uphold the public perception that things are big in Texas! Note, however, that the state's appellate courts have held that the five and a half inch limit refers to the entire blade, including any unsharpened portion, and not just to the sharpened edge.[109]

Balisongs, while not specifically listed as a prohibited item, likely fall under the switchblade prohibition, as balisongs do in a number of states. Indeed, a number of appellate court decisions have referred to balisongs in a conclusory fashion as an "illegal knife" type.

State law prohibits carry of switchblades and illegal knives in a wide variety of locations, such as school and educational institution premises, polling places on election day, court facilities, racetracks, and the secured areas of airports. State law also prohibits such carry within 1,000 feet of a place of execution on the day a death sentence is to be carried out, provided the person carrying has received notice of such prohibition.

Finally, readers should be aware that local governments may enact their own ordinances prohibiting or otherwise restricting knife carry in their jurisdictions beyond the restrictions

---

[107] State law specifically prohibits bowie knives, regardless of blade length. *See,* TEX. PENAL CODE § 46.02 (2005).

[108] Balisongs likely fall under the switchblade prohibition, as balisongs do in some states, as a number of appellate decisions have referred to a balisong as an "illegal knife". *See, e.g,* cases cited, Section 50.4, *infra.*

[109] *See, e.g.,* cases cited, Section 50.4, *infra.*

embodied in state law, although most towns and cities, including such large cities as Dallas, do not appear to have done so to any significant extent.

50.3 Selected Statutes

Tex. Penal Code Ann. §§ (2005)

Sec. 46.01. DEFINITIONS. In this chapter:

...

(6) "Illegal knife" means a:

  (A)   knife with a blade over five and one-half inches;

  (B)   hand instrument designed to cut or stab another by being thrown;

  (C)   dagger, including but not limited to a dirk, stilletto, and poniard;

  (D)   bowie knife;

  (E)   sword; or

  (F)   spear.

(7) "Knife" means any bladed hand instrument that is capable of inflicting serious bodily injury or death by cutting or stabbing a person with the instrument.

...

(11) "Switchblade knife" means any knife that has a blade that folds, closes, or retracts into the handle or sheath, and that:

  (A)   opens automatically by pressure applied to a button or other device located on the handle; or

  (B)   opens or releases a blade from the handle or sheath by the force of gravity or by the application of centrifugal force.

Sec. 46.02. UNLAWFUL CARRYING WEAPONS. (a) A person commits an offense if he intentionally, knowingly, or recklessly carries on or about his person a handgun, illegal knife, or club.

(b) Except as provided by Subsection (c), an offense under this section is a Class A misdemeanor.

(c) An offense under this section is a felony of the third degree if the offense is committed on any premises licensed or issued a permit by this state for the sale of alcoholic beverages.

Sec. 46.03. PLACES WEAPONS PROHIBITED. (a) A person commits an offense if the person intentionally, knowingly, or recklessly possesses or goes with a firearm, illegal knife, club, or prohibited weapon listed in Section 46.05(a):

(1) on the physical premises of a school or educational institution, any grounds or building on which an activity sponsored by a school or educational institution is being conducted, or a passenger transportation vehicle of a school or educational institution, whether the school or educational institution is public or private, unless pursuant to written regulations or written authorization of the institution;

(2) on the premises of a polling place on the day of an election or while early voting is in progress;

(3) on the premises of any government court or offices utilized by the court, unless pursuant to written regulations or written authorization of the court;

(4) on the premises of a racetrack;

(5) in or into a secured area of an airport; or

(6) within 1,000 feet of premises the location of which is designated by the Texas Department of Criminal Justice as a place of execution under Article 43.19, Code of Criminal Procedure, on a day that a sentence of death is set to be imposed on the designated premises and the person received notice that:

    (A)   going within 1,000 feet of the premises with a weapon listed under this subsection was prohibited; or

    (B)   possessing a weapon listed under this subsection within 1,000 feet of the premises was prohibited.

...

(c) In this section:

    (1)   "Premises" has the meaning assigned by Section 46.035.

    (2)   "Secured area" means an area of an airport terminal building to which access is controlled by the inspection of persons and property under federal law.

...

(e) It is a defense to prosecution under Subsection (a)(5) that the actor checked all firearms as baggage in accordance with federal or state law or regulations before entering a secured area.

(f) It is not a defense to prosecution under this section that the actor possessed a handgun and was licensed to carry a concealed handgun under Subchapter H, Chapter 411, Government Code.

...

(g) An offense under this section is a third degree felony.

(i) It is an exception to the application of Subsection (a)(6) that the actor possessed a firearm or club:

    (1)   while in a vehicle being driven on a public road; or

    (2)   at the actor's residence or place of employment.

Sec. 46.05. PROHIBITED WEAPONS.

(a) A person commits an offense if he intentionally or knowingly possesses, manufactures, transports, repairs, or sells:

...

(5) a switchblade knife;

...

(d) It is an affirmative defense to prosecution under this section that the actor's conduct:

    (1)   was incidental to dealing with a switchblade knife, springblade knife, or short-barrel firearm solely as an antique or curio; or

    (2)   ...

(e) An offense under this section is a felony of the third degree unless it is committed under Subsection (a)(5) or (a)(6), in which event, it is a Class A misdemeanor.

...

Sec. 46.06. UNLAWFUL TRANSFER OF CERTAIN WEAPONS.

(a) A person commits an offense if the person:

...

(2) intentionally or knowingly sells, rents, leases, or gives or offers to sell, rent, lease, or give to any child younger than 18 years any firearm, club, or illegal knife;

...

(c) It is an affirmative defense to prosecution under Subsection (a)(2) that the transfer was to a minor whose parent or the person having legal custody of the minor had given written permission for the sale or, if the transfer was other than a sale, the parent or person having legal custody had given effective consent.

(d) An offense under this section is a Class A misdemeanor, except that an offense under Subsection (a)(2) is a state jail felony if the weapon that is the subject of the offense is a handgun.

Sec. 46.15. NONAPPLICABILITY. (a) Sections 46.02 and 46.03 do not apply to:

...

(b) Section 46.02 does not apply to a person who:

...

(2) is on the person's own premises or premises under the person's control unless the person is an employee or agent of the owner of the premises and the person's primary responsibility is to act in the capacity of a security guard to protect persons or property, in which event the person must comply with Subdivision (5);

(3) is traveling;

(4) is engaging in lawful hunting, fishing, or other sporting activity on the immediate premises where the activity is conducted, or is directly en route between the premises and the actor's residence, if the weapon is a type commonly used in the activity;

...

(e) The provisions of Section 46.02 prohibiting the carrying of an illegal knife do not apply to an individual carrying a bowie knife or a sword used in a historical demonstration or in a ceremony in which the knife or sword is significant to the performance of the ceremony.

...

(h) For the purpose of Subsection (b)(2), "premises" includes a recreational vehicle that is being used by the person carrying the handgun, illegal knife, or club as living quarters, regardless of whether that use is temporary or permanent. In this subsection, "recreational vehicle" means a motor vehicle primarily designed as temporary living quarters or a vehicle that contains temporary living quarters and is designed to be towed by a motor vehicle. The term includes a travel trailer, camping trailer, truck camper, motor home, and horse trailer with living quarters.

(i) For purposes of Subsection (b)(3), a person is presumed to be traveling if the person is:

(1)   in a private motor vehicle;

(2)   not otherwise engaged in criminal activity, other than a Class C misdemeanor that is a violation of a law or ordinance regulating traffic;

(3)   not otherwise prohibited by law from possessing a firearm;

(4)   not a member of a criminal street gang, as defined by Section 71.01; and

(5)   not carrying a handgun in plain view.

50.4 Selected Caselaw

Ex Parte Turner, No. 08-02-00355-CR, (Tex. Ct. App. 2003) (stating and describing butterfly knife as "illegal weapon")

Jackson v. State, No. 2-03-461-CR (Tex. Ct. App. 2005) (Unpublished opinion) (describing arrest for carry of butterfly knife, and affirming convictions for drug offenses).

Tyler v. State, No. 05-03-01415-CR (Tex. Ct. App. 2004) (Unpublished opinion) (affirming conviction for aggravated assault with deadly weapon, exacto knife with sharp blade).

Walbey v. State, 926 S.W.2d 307, 310 (Tex. Crim. App. 1996) (describing prior arrest for possession of "illegal butterfly knife" and ice pick).

Rainer v. State, 763 S.W.2d 615 (Tex. Ct. App. 1989) (affirming conviction for unlawful carry of illegal knife, hunting knife with sharpened edge less than five and a half inches, but with entire blade exceeding five and a half inches)

McMurrough v. State, 995 S.W.2d 944, 946 (Tex. Ct. App. 1999) (discussing blade length measurement and stating that term "blade" includes both sharpened and unsharpened portion of knife, excluding handle).

50.5 Preemption Law

No knife law preemption, firearms law preemption only. *See*, Tex. Loc. Gov't Ann. § 229.001 (2005).

50.6 Places Off-Limits While Carrying

Texas prohibits the carry of firearms, switchblades, and illegal knives such as daggers, dirks, stilettos, bowie knives and knives with blades exceeding five and a half inches in length, on school and educational institution premises, polling places on election day, court facilities, racetracks, and the secured areas of airports. *See*, Tex. Penal Code § 46.03 (2005). State law also prohibits such carry within 1,000 feet of a place of execution on the day a death sentence is to be carried out, provided the person carrying has received notice of such prohibition. *See, id.*

Note that local governments may enact their own ordinances prohibiting or otherwise restricting knife carry in their jurisdictions beyond the restrictions embodied in state law, although most towns and cities, including such large cities as Dallas, do not appear to have done so to any significant extent.

50.7 School/College Carry

Texas prohibits the carry of firearms, switchblades, and illegal knives such as daggers, dirks, stilettos, bowie knives and knives with blades exceeding five and a half inches in length, on school and educational institution premises. *See*, Tex. Penal Code § 46.03 (2005).

50.8 Selected City Ordinances

Corpus Christi – Carry in public of any straight razor, razor blade, knife having a blade measured from the handle of three inches or longer, any fix blade, switchblade, ice pick, bowie knife, dirk, dagger, spear, machete, hand sickle, or stiletto prohibited. *See*, Corpus Christi, Tex., Code of Ordinances § 33-73 (2006). Certain limited exceptions apply, including an exception for persons "traveling", which under state law means in a private motor vehicle not engaged in criminal activity. *See, id.* at § 33-74, and Tex. Penal Code Ann. § 46.15 (2005). Carry of any knife or dagger manufactured or sold for offensive or defensive purposes prohibited on Corpus Christi International Airport property. *See*, Corpus Christi, Tex., Code of Ordinances § 9-38 (2006).

Laredo – Unlawful to carry illegal knife, such as bowie knife, dagger, dirk, stiletto, poniard, spear, sword, or any knife with blade exceeding five and a half inches, at any public park, public meeting, political rally, parade, or non-weapons-related school, college, or professional athletic event. *See*, Laredo, Tex., Code of Ordinances § 21-152 (2003).

San Antonio – Carry in public of knife with locking blade *less than* five and a half inches prohibited. *See, San Antonio, Tex., Code of Ordinances* § 21-17 (2006). Exceptions exist for hunting, fishing, or "lawful sporting activity", for occupational use, and while traveling, which under state law means in a private motor vehicle not engaged in criminal activity. *See, id.*, and TEX. PENAL CODE ANN. § 46.15 (2005). Carry of weapons, the definition of which includes illegal knives, and knives, prohibited in city-owned buildings. *See, San Antonio, Tex., Code of Ordinances* § 21-157 (2006).

Texarkana – Carry of deadly weapons, including firearms, and "knives, switchblades, swords, or other weapons that could endanger other passengers" prohibited on public transit vehicles, facilities and locations. *See,* TEXARKANA, TEX., CODE OF ORDINANCES § 15-66 (2006).

50.9 State Resources

Texas Department of Public Safety
P O Box 4143
Austin, TX 78765-4143
Phone: (800) 224-5744
Website: http://www.texasonline.state.tx.us/NASApp/txdps/chl/common/jsp/welcome.jsp

Attorney General of Texas
P. O. Box 12548
Austin, TX 78711-2548
Phone: (512) 463-2100
Website: http://www.oag.state.tx.us/

51 Utah – The Beehive State

Area: 82,144 sq.mi. (Rank: 12th)   Population: 2,316,256 (Rank: 34th)
Violent Crime Rate (per 100,000 residents): 236.0 (Rank: 8th Safest)
State Motto: *Industry*

51.1 Knife Carry Law Summary

Note: Blade length limits, if any, in parentheses.

Knife Type	Open Carry	Concealed Carry	Notes
Folding Knives	Yes	Yes	See note[110]
Fixed Bladed Knives	Yes	No	See note[111]
Dirks, Daggers, & Stilettos	Yes	No	
Automatic Knives	Yes	No	
Balisongs	Yes	No	

51.2 Discussion

Visitors to Utah will find a fairly permissive legal environment for knife carry, with a strong legal bias for open, versus concealed, carry. State law permits open carry of a wide range of knives. State law, however, prohibits concealed carry of dangerous weapons without a recognized permit. Fortunately, Utah is a "shall-issue" state and recognizes all other states' concealed weapons permits.

Even without a recognized permit, concealed carry of ordinary folding pocket knives is permitted, although travelers should exercise caution and should probably avoid carrying "tactical" type knives with aggressive weapon-like features or appearances, lest such knives be deemed "dangerous weapons", and thus prohibited items. There is no statutorily defined blade length limit. Concealed carry of dirks, daggers, stilettos, and automatic knives, without a recognized permit, is prohibited. Note that balisongs, while not specifically prohibited, may fall under the switchblade prohibition, as balisongs do in some states. In addition, balisongs are often associated with the martial arts, and perceived as martial arts weapons. Any of these otherwise prohibited knives may be carried concealed with a valid, recognized permit.

State law prohibits carry of dangerous weapons on school premises, and in the secured areas of airports. Utah does not preempt its cities and towns from regulating knife carry, unlike the case for firearms, where the state has prohibited cities and towns from enacting their own firearms carry restrictions, ensuring uniform state-wide firearms laws. As such, local governments may enact their own ordinances prohibiting or otherwise restricting knife carry within their jurisdictions.

---

[110] Readers should note that case law exists where knives with blades as short as four inches were found to be dangerous weapons. *See, e.g.,* cases cited, Section 51.4, *infra.* Travelers would be wise to avoid carry of large folders or "tactical" type folders with overly aggressive appearances or weapon-like features.
[111] Case law exists where courts have found fixed bladed knives with five and a half to six inch blades to be dangerous weapons. *See, e.g.,* cases cited, Section 51.4, *infra.* As such, travelers should avoid concealed carry of large fixed bladed knives without a valid, recognized concealed carry permit.

51.3 Selected Statutes

Utah Code §§ (2006)

76-10-501. Definitions.

As used in this part:

...

(2) (a) "Concealed dangerous weapon" means a dangerous weapon that is covered, hidden, or secreted in a manner that the public would not be aware of its presence and is readily accessible for immediate use.

(b) A dangerous weapon shall not be considered a concealed dangerous weapon if it is a firearm which is unloaded and is securely encased.

...

(5) (a) "Dangerous weapon" means any item that in the manner of its use or intended use is capable of causing death or serious bodily injury. The following factors shall be used in determining whether a knife, or any other item, object, or thing not commonly known as a dangerous weapon is a dangerous weapon:

(i) the character of the instrument, object, or thing;

(ii) the character of the wound produced, if any;

(iii) the manner in which the instrument, object, or thing was used; and

(iv) the other lawful purposes for which the instrument, object, or thing may be used.

(b) "Dangerous weapon" does not include any explosive, chemical, or incendiary device as defined by Section 76-10-306.

...

76-10-504. Carrying concealed dangerous weapon -- Penalties.

(1) Except as provided in Section 76-10-503 and in Subsections (2) and (3):

(a) a person who carries a concealed dangerous weapon, as defined in Section 76-10-501, which is not a firearm on his person or one that is readily accessible for immediate use which is not securely encased, as defined in this part, in a place other than his residence, property, or business under his control is guilty of a class B misdemeanor; and

(b) a person without a valid concealed firearm permit who carries a concealed dangerous weapon which is a firearm and that contains no ammunition is guilty of a class B misdemeanor, but if the firearm contains ammunition the person is guilty of a class A misdemeanor.

(2) A person who carries concealed a sawed-off shotgun or a sawed-off rifle is guilty of a second degree felony.

(3) If the concealed firearm is used in the commission of a violent felony as defined in Section 76-3-203.5, and the person is a party to the offense, the person is guilty of a second degree felony.

(4) Nothing in Subsection (1) shall prohibit a person engaged in the lawful taking of protected or unprotected wildlife as defined in Title 23, Wildlife Resources Code, from carrying a concealed weapon or a concealed firearm with a barrel length of four inches or greater as long as the taking of wildlife does not occur:

(a) within the limits of a municipality in violation of that municipality's ordinances; or

(b) upon the highways of the state as defined in Section 41-6a-102.

76-10-505.5. Possession of a dangerous weapon, firearm, or sawed-off shotgun on or about school premises -- Penalties.

(1) A person may not possess any dangerous weapon, firearm, or sawed-off shotgun, as those terms are defined in Section 76-10-501, at a place that the person knows, or has reasonable cause to believe, is on or about school premises as defined in Subsection 76-3-203.2(1).

(2) (a) Possession of a dangerous weapon on or about school premises is a class B misdemeanor.

(b) Possession of a firearm or sawed-off shotgun on or about school premises is a class A misdemeanor.

(3) This section does not apply if:

(a) the person is authorized to possess a firearm as provided under Section 53-5-704, 53-5-705, 76-10-511, or 76-10-523, or as otherwise authorized by law;

(b) the possession is approved by the responsible school administrator;

(c) the item is present or to be used in connection with a lawful, approved activity and is in the possession or under the control of the person responsible for its possession or use; or

(d) the possession is:

(i) at the person's place of residence or on the person's property;

(ii) in any vehicle lawfully under the person's control, other than a vehicle owned by the school or used by the school to transport students; or

(iii) at the person's place of business which is not located in the areas described in Subsection 76-3-203.2(1)(a)(i), (ii), or (iv).

(4) This section does not prohibit prosecution of a more serious weapons offense that may occur on or about school premises.

76-10-506. Threatening with or using dangerous weapon in fight or quarrel.

Every person, except those persons described in Section 76-10-503, who, not in necessary self defense in the presence of two or more persons, draws or exhibits any dangerous weapon in an angry and threatening manner or unlawfully uses the same in any fight or quarrel is guilty of a class A misdemeanor.

76-10-507. Possession of deadly weapon with intent to assault.

Every person having upon his person any dangerous weapon with intent to unlawfully assault another is guilty of a class A misdemeanor.

76-10-523. Persons exempt from weapons laws.

(1) This part and Title 53, Chapter 5, Part 7, Concealed Weapon Act, do not apply to any of the following:
...
(g) a nonresident traveling in or through the state, provided that any firearm is:

(i) unloaded; and

(ii) securely encased as defined in Section 76-10-501.

(2) The provisions of Subsections 76-10-504(1)(a), (1)(b), and Section 76-10-505 do not apply to any person to whom a permit to carry a concealed firearm has been issued:

(a) pursuant to Section 53-5-704; or

(b) by another state or county.

76-10-528. Carrying a dangerous weapon while under influence of alcohol or drugs unlawful.

(1) Any person who carries a dangerous weapon while under the influence of alcohol or a controlled substance as defined in Section 58-37-2 is guilty of a class B misdemeanor. Under the influence means the same level of influence or blood or breath alcohol concentration as provided in Subsections 41-6a-502(1)(a)(i) through (iii).

(2) It is not a defense to prosecution under this section that the person:

(a) is licensed in the pursuit of wildlife of any kind; or

(b) has a valid permit to carry a concealed firearm.

76-10-529. Possession of dangerous weapons, firearms, or explosives in airport secure areas prohibited -- Penalty.

(1) As used in this section:

(a) "Airport authority" has the same meaning as defined in Section 72-10-102.

(b) "Dangerous weapon" is the same as defined in Section 76-10-501.

(c) "Explosive" is the same as defined for "explosive, chemical, or incendiary device" in Section 76-10-306.

(d) "Firearm" is the same as defined in Section 76-10-501.

(2) (a) Within a secure area of an airport established pursuant to this section, a person, including a person licensed to carry a concealed firearm under Title 53, Chapter 5, Part 7, Concealed Weapon Act, is guilty of:

(i) a class A misdemeanor if the person knowingly or intentionally possesses any dangerous weapon or firearm;

(ii) an infraction if the person recklessly or with criminal negligence possesses any dangerous weapon or firearm; or

(iii) a violation of Section 76-10-306 if the person transports, possesses, distributes, or sells any explosive, chemical, or incendiary device.

(b) Subsection (2)(a) does not apply to:

(i) persons exempted under Section 76-10-523; and

(ii) members of the state or federal military forces while engaged in the performance of their official duties.

(3) An airport authority, county, or municipality regulating the airport may:

(a) establish any secure area located beyond the main area where the public generally buys tickets, checks and retrieves luggage; and

(b) use reasonable means, including mechanical, electronic, x-ray, or any other device, to detect dangerous weapons, firearms, or explosives concealed in baggage or upon the person of any individual attempting to enter the secure area.

(4) At least one notice shall be prominently displayed at each entrance to a secure area in which a dangerous weapon, firearm, or explosive is restricted.

(5) Upon the discovery of any dangerous weapon, firearm, or explosive, the airport authority, county, or municipality, the employees, or other personnel administering the secure area may:

(a) require the individual to deliver the item to the air freight office or airline ticket counter;

(b) require the individual to exit the secure area; or

(c) obtain possession or retain custody of the item until it is transferred to law enforcement officers.

51.4 Selected Caselaw

State v. Archambeau, 820 P.2d 920 (Utah Ct. App. 1991) (affirming conviction, upholding constitutionality of statutory definition of "dangerous weapon" as applied to defendant, and determination of knife with five and a half inch blade, and bowie knife with six inch blade as dangerous weapons).

State v. Pugmire, 898 P.2d 271 (Utah Ct. App. 1995) (affirming conviction for dangerous weapon charge and trial court determination of "buck" knife with four and a half inch blade as dangerous weapon).

State v. Kirkwood, 2002 UT App. 128 (2002) (affirming conviction and upholding jury finding of knife with four inch blade as dangerous weapon).

51.5 Preemption Law

No knife law preemption, firearms law preemption only. *See*, UTAH CODE § 76-10-500 (2006).

51.6 Places Off-Limits While Carrying

Utah prohibits the carry of firearms and dangerous weapons on school premises, and in the secure areas of airports. *See*, UTAH CODE §§ 76-10-505.5, 76-10-529 (2006).

51.7 School/College Carry

Utah prohibits the carry of firearms and dangerous weapons on school premises. *See*, UTAH CODE § 76-10-505.5 (2006).

51.8 Selected City Ordinances

Salt Lake County – Possession or carry of switchblades prohibited. *See*, SALT LAKE COUNTY, UTAH, CODE OF ORDINANCES § 10.64.030 (2006).

Moab – Carry, without written consent of peace officer, of "dagger, stiletto, knife, dirk or other concealed deadly weapon" prohibited. *See*, MOAB, UTAH, CITY CODE § 9.28.020 (2006).

51.9 State Resources

Utah Department of Public Safety
3888 W. 5400 South St.
Salt Lake City, UT 84114-8280
Phone: (801) 965-4445
Website: http://bci.utah.gov/CFP/CFPHome.html

Attorney General of Utah
236 State Capitol
Salt Lake City, UT 84114-0810
Phone: (801)-366-0300
Fax: (801) 538-1121
Website: http://www.attygen.state.ut.us/

52 Vermont – The Green Mountain State

Area: 9,250 sq.mi. (Rank: 43th)   Population: 616,592 (Rank: 49th)
Violent Crime Rate (per 100,000 residents): 112.0 (Rank: 3rd Safest)
State Motto: *Freedom and Unity*

52.1 Knife Carry Law Summary

<u>Note:</u> Blade length limits, if any, in parentheses.

Knife Type	Open Carry	Concealed Carry	Notes
Folding Knives	Yes	Yes	
Fixed Bladed Knives	Yes	Yes	
Dirks, Daggers, & Stilettos	Yes	Yes	
Automatic Knives	Yes (< 3")	Yes (< 3")	
Balisongs	Yes (< 3")	Yes (< 3")	See note[112]

52.2 Discussion

Visitors to the Green Mountain State will find a permissive legal environment for knife carry, a fitting complement to the similarly permissive legal environment for firearms carry. State law allows open or concealed carry of a wide array of knives, from folders to daggers. There is no statutorily defined blade length limit, except for switchblades, which must have blades less than three inches to be legal. Cautious travelers should be aware of the possibility that balisongs may be deemed statutory switchblades, as balisongs are in some states, and thus subject to the less-than-three-inch blade restriction.

Apart from schools and courthouses, no state-wide statutory prohibitions on off-limits locations for otherwise legal knife carry appear to exist, although cities and towns may pass their own ordinances restricting knife carry. Like most states, Vermont does not preempt its cities and towns from regulating knife carry, unlike the case for firearms, where the state has prohibited cities and towns from enacting their own firearms carry restrictions, ensuring uniform state-wide firearms laws. Thus, cities and towns may pass their own restrictions on knife carry, although few appear to have done so.

52.3 Selected Statutes

Vᴛ. Sᴛᴀᴛ. Aɴɴ. tit. 13 §§ (2005)

§ 4003. Carrying dangerous weapons.

A person who carries a dangerous or deadly weapon, openly or concealed, with the intent or avowed purpose of injuring a fellow man, or who carries a dangerous or deadly weapon within any state institution or upon the grounds or lands owned or leased for the use of such institution, without the approval of the warden or superintendent of the institution, shall be imprisoned not more than two years or fined not more than $200.00, or both.

---

[112] Balisongs may be deemed statutory switchblades, as balisongs are in some states, and thus subject to the less-than-three-inch blade restriction.

§ 4004. Possession of dangerous or deadly weapon in a school bus or school building or on school property.

(a) No person shall knowingly possess a firearm or a dangerous or deadly weapon while within a school building or on a school bus. A person who violates this section shall, for the first offense, be imprisoned not more than one year or fined not more than $1,000.00, or both, and for a second or subsequent offense shall be imprisoned not more than three years or fined not more than $5,000.00, or both.

(b) No person shall knowingly possess a firearm or a dangerous or deadly weapon on any school property with the intent to injure another person. A person who violates this section shall, for the first offense, be imprisoned not more than two years or fined not more than $1,000.00, or both, and for a second or subsequent offense shall be imprisoned not more than three years or fined not more than $5,000.00, or both.

(c) This section shall not apply to:

(1)   A law enforcement officer while engaged in law enforcement duties.

(2)   Possession and use of firearms or dangerous or deadly weapons if the board of school directors, or the superintendent or principal if delegated authority to do so by the board, authorizes possession or use for specific occasions or for instructional or other specific purposes.

(d) As used in this section:

(1)   "School property" means any property owned by a school, including motor vehicles.

(2)   "Owned by the school" means owned, leased, controlled or subcontracted by the school.

(3)   "Dangerous or deadly weapon" has the meaning defined in section 4016 of this title.

(4)   "Firearm" has the meaning defined in section 4016 of this title.

(5)   "Law enforcement officer" has the meaning defined in section 4016 of this title.

(e) The provisions of this section shall not limit or restrict any prosecution for any other offense, including simple assault or aggravated assault.

§ 4005. - While committing a crime.

A person who carries a dangerous or deadly weapon, openly or concealed, while committing a felony or while committing an offense under section 667 of Title 7, or while committing the crime of smuggling of an alien as defined by the laws of the United States, shall be imprisoned not more than five years or fined not more than $500.00, or both.

§ 4013. Zip guns; switchblade knives.

A person who possesses, sells or offers for sale a weapon commonly known as a "zip" gun, or a weapon commonly known as a switchblade knife, the blade of which is three inches or more in length, shall be imprisoned not more than ninety days or fined not more than $100.00, or both.

§ 4016. Weapons in court.

(a) As used in this section:

(1)   "Courthouse" means a building or any portion of a building designated by the supreme court of Vermont as a courthouse.

(2)   "Dangerous or deadly weapon" means any firearm, or other weapon, device, instrument, material or substance, whether animate or inanimate, which in the manner it is used or is intended to be used is known to be capable of producing death or serious bodily injury.

(3)   "Firearm" means any weapon, whether loaded or unloaded, which will expel a projectile by the action of an explosive and includes any weapon commonly referred to as a pistol, revolver, rifle, gun, machine gun or shotgun.

(4)   "Law enforcement officer" means a person certified by the Vermont criminal justice training council as having satisfactorily completed the approved training programs required to meet the minimum training standards applicable to that person pursuant to 20 V.S.A. § 2358.

(5)   "Secured building" means a building with controlled points of public access, metal screening devices at each point of public access, and locked compartments, accessible only to security personnel, for storage of checked firearms.

(b) A person who, while within a courthouse and without authorization from the court,

(1)   carries or has in his or her possession a firearm; or

(2)   knowingly carries or has in his or her possession a dangerous or deadly weapon, other than a firearm, shall be imprisoned not more than one year or fined not more than $500.00, or both.

(c) Notice of the provisions of subsection (b) of this section shall be posted conspicuously at each public entrance to each courthouse.

(d) No dangerous or deadly weapon shall be allowed in a courthouse that has been certified by the court administrator to be a secured building.

52.4 Selected Caselaw

State v. Prior, 2002 VT 44 (Vt. 2002) (affirming conviction for, *inter alia*, aggravated domestic assault and upholding fact-finder determination that folding pocket knife was deadly weapon as used).

State v. Turner, 830 A.2d 122 (Vt. 2003) (affirming conviction for aggravated assault with three inch long knife, and jury determination that knife was deadly weapon).

52.5 Preemption Law

No knife law preemption, firearms law preemption only. *See*, Vᴛ. Sᴛᴀᴛ. Aɴɴ. tit 24 § 2295 (2005).

52.6 Places Off-Limits While Carrying

Vermont prohibits the carry of firearms and other dangerous or deadly weapons in schools, school buses, and courthouses. *See*, Vᴛ. Sᴛᴀᴛ. Aɴɴ. tit 13 §§ 4004, 4016 (2005).

52.7 School/College Carry

Vermont prohibits the carry of firearms and other dangerous or deadly weapons in schools and school buses. *See*, Vᴛ. Sᴛᴀᴛ. Aɴɴ. tit 13 § 4004 (2005).

52.8 Selected City Ordinances

No relevant ordinances. An examination of ordinances for a number of municipalities shows no knife-related ordinances with restrictions greater than those embodied in state law.

52.9 State Resources

Vermont State Police
103 South Main Street
Waterbury, VT 05671-2101
Phone: (802) 244-7345
Website: http://www.dps.state.vt.us/vtsp/

Attorney General of Vermont
109 State Street
Montpelier, VT 05609-1001
Phone: (802) 828 3171
Fax: (802) 828 3187
Website: http://www.state.vt.us/atg/

53 Virginia – Old Dominion

Area: 39,594 sq.mi. (Rank: 37th)   Population: 7,293,542 (Rank: 12th)
Violent Crime Rate (per 100,000 residents): 275.6 (Rank: 16th Safest)
State Motto: *Sic Semper Tyrannis (Thus Always to Tyrants)*

53.1 Knife Carry Law Summary

Note: Blade length limits, if any, in parentheses.

Knife Type	Open Carry	Concealed Carry	Notes
Folding Knives	Yes	Yes	See note[113]
Fixed Bladed Knives	Yes	No	See note[114]
Dirks, Daggers, & Stilettos	Yes	No	
Automatic Knives	No	No	
Balisongs	No	No	See note[115]

53.2 Discussion

Visitors to Virginia will encounter a legal environment that strongly favors open, versus concealed, carry of knives. Ordinary folding pocket knives may be carried concealed. State law prohibits concealed carry of a variety of knives, such as dirks, machetes, razors, and such large fixed bladed knives as bowie knives. In addition, as a practical matter, state law bans possession of automatic knives, specifically switchblades and ballistic knives.

There is no statutorily defined blade length limit. While state law technically allows carry of some fixed blades, travelers should be aware that the state's courts have taken a sometimes expansive view of the catch-all provision of the statute that bans "weapon[s] of like kind."[116] Furthermore, recent court decisions have interpreted the catch-all provision to include folding knives with blades as short as three and a half inches, but with "weapon-like" features and appearance. Thus, travelers should exercise caution when carrying any concealed blade, especially folders or fixed blades with overly "tactical," weapon-like appearances or features.

Readers should be aware that balisongs may fall under the switchblade prohibition, as balisongs do in some states. As such, carry of balisongs is not advised.

Virginia prohibits the carry of firearms and other dangerous weapons, including knives other than a folding pocket knife with a blade less than three inches, on elementary, middle, or

---

[113] Case law has sometimes taken an expansive view of the catch-all provision of the concealed carry statute. For example, a folding knife with a three and a half inch locking blade, with certain additional "weapon-like" features, has been held to be a prohibited weapon under the statute. *See*, Ohin v. Comm., 622 S.E.2d 784, 787 (Va. Ct. App. 2005). Travelers would be wise to avoid carry of "tactical" folders with overly aggressive or weapon-like appearances.

[114] State law specifically prohibits concealed carry of such large fixed bladed knives as bowie knives and machetes. *See*, Va. Code § 18.2-308(ii) (2005). Travelers should exercise caution when carrying fixed blades concealed, especially large fixed blades or those with aggressive, weapon-like appearances or features.

[115] Readers should be aware that balisongs may fall under the switchblade prohibition, as balisongs do in some states. As such, travelers should avoid carry of balisongs.

[116] *See*, Va. Code § 18.2-308(v) (2005).

high school property. This prohibition includes school buses, and school-sponsored events. Certain limited exceptions exist, such as for possession in a motor vehicle. State law prohibits carry of firearms, bowie knives, daggers and other dangerous weapons at places of worship while religious meetings or services are underway "without good and sufficient reason," although this phrase is not defined. Carry of firearms and dangerous weapons is also prohibited in courthouses. Finally, state law prohibits carry of firearms and dangerous weapons into air carrier airport terminals, with certain obvious exceptions for passengers traveling and checking or claiming such weapons into, or from, checked luggage.

Note that municipal governments may enact their own ordinances prohibiting or otherwise further restricting knife carry in their jurisdictions, although few cities or towns, with perhaps the notable exception of Richmond[117], appear to have enacted ordinances with restrictions substantially greater than those embodied in state law.

53.3 Selected Statutes

VA. CODE §§ (2005)

§ 18.2-308. Personal protection; carrying concealed weapons; when lawful to carry.

A. If any person carries about his person, hidden from common observation, (i) any pistol, revolver, or other weapon designed or intended to propel a missile of any kind by action of an explosion of any combustible material; (ii) any dirk, bowie knife, switchblade knife, ballistic knife, machete, razor, slingshot, spring stick, metal knucks, or blackjack; (iii) any flailing instrument consisting of two or more rigid parts connected in such a manner as to allow them to swing freely, which may be known as a nun chahka, nun chuck, nunchaku, shuriken, or fighting chain; (iv) any disc, of whatever configuration, having at least two points or pointed blades which is designed to be thrown or propelled and which may be known as a throwing star or oriental dart; or (v) any weapon of like kind as those enumerated in this subsection, he shall be guilty of a Class 1 misdemeanor. A second violation of this section or a conviction under this section subsequent to any conviction under any substantially similar ordinance of any county, city, or town shall be punishable as a Class 6 felony, and a third or subsequent such violation shall be punishable as a Class 5 felony. For the purpose of this section, a weapon shall be deemed to be hidden from common observation when it is observable but is of such deceptive appearance as to disguise the weapon's true nature.

B. This section shall not apply to any person while in his own place of abode or the curtilage thereof.

...

J3. No person shall carry a concealed handgun onto the premises of any restaurant or club as defined in § 4.1-100 for which a license to sell and serve alcoholic beverages for on-premises consumption has been granted by the Virginia Alcoholic Beverage Control Board under Title 4.1 of the Code of Virginia; however, nothing herein shall prohibit any sworn law-enforcement officer from carrying a concealed handgun on the premises of such restaurant or club or any owner or event sponsor or his employees from carrying a concealed handgun while on duty at such restaurant or club if such person has a concealed handgun permit.

...

N. As used in this article:

"Ballistic knife" means any knife with a detachable blade that is propelled by a spring-operated mechanism.

"Spring stick" means a spring-loaded metal stick activated by pushing a button which rapidly and forcefully telescopes the weapon to several times its original length.

O. The granting of a concealed handgun permit shall not thereby authorize the possession of any handgun or other weapon on property or in places where such possession is otherwise prohibited by law or is prohibited by the owner of private property.

---

[117] See, selected city ordinances cited, Section 53.8, *infra*.

P. A valid concealed handgun or concealed weapon permit or license issued by another state shall authorize the holder of such permit or license who is at least 21 years of age to carry a concealed handgun in the Commonwealth, provided (i) the issuing authority provides the means for instantaneous verification of the validity of all such permits or licenses issued within that state, accessible 24 hours a day, and (ii) except for the age of the permit or license holder and the type of weapon authorized to be carried, the requirements and qualifications of that state's law are adequate to prevent possession of a permit or license by persons who would be denied a permit in the Commonwealth under this section. The Superintendent of State Police shall (a) in consultation with the Office of the Attorney General determine whether states meet the requirements and qualifications of this section, (b) maintain a registry of such states on the Virginia Criminal Information Network (VCIN), and (c) make the registry available to law-enforcement officers for investigative purposes. The Superintendent of the State Police, in consultation with the Attorney General, may also enter into agreements for reciprocal recognition with any state qualifying for recognition under this subsection.

...

§ 18.2-308.1. Possession of firearm, stun weapon, or other weapon on school property prohibited.

A. If any person possesses any (i) stun weapon or taser as defined in this section; (ii) knife, except a pocket knife having a folding metal blade of less than three inches; or (iii) weapon, including a weapon of like kind, designated in subsection A of § 18.2-308, other than a firearm; upon (a) the property of any public, private or religious elementary, middle or high school, including buildings and grounds; (b) that portion of any property open to the public and then exclusively used for school-sponsored functions or extracurricular activities while such functions or activities are taking place; or (c) any school bus owned or operated by any such school, he shall be guilty of a Class 1 misdemeanor.

B. If any person possesses any firearm designed or intended to expel a projectile by action of an explosion of a combustible material while such person is upon (i) any public, private or religious elementary, middle or high school, including buildings and grounds; (ii) that portion of any property open to the public and then exclusively used for school-sponsored functions or extracurricular activities while such functions or activities are taking place; or (iii) any school bus owned or operated by any such school, he shall be guilty of a Class 6 felony; however, if the person possesses any firearm within a public, private or religious elementary, middle or high school building and intends to use, or attempts to use, such firearm, or displays such weapon in a threatening manner, such person shall be sentenced to a mandatory minimum term of imprisonment of five years to be served consecutively with any other sentence.

The exemptions set out in § 18.2-308 shall apply, mutatis mutandis, to the provisions of this section. The provisions of this section shall not apply to (i) persons who possess such weapon or weapons as a part of the school's curriculum or activities; (ii) a person possessing a knife customarily used for food preparation or service and using it for such purpose; (iii) persons who possess such weapon or weapons as a part of any program sponsored or facilitated by either the school or any organization authorized by the school to conduct its programs either on or off the school premises; (iv) any law-enforcement officer; (v) any person who possesses a knife or blade which he uses customarily in his trade; (vi) a person who possesses an unloaded firearm that is in a closed container, or a knife having a metal blade, in or upon a motor vehicle, or an unloaded shotgun or rifle in a firearms rack in or upon a motor vehicle; or (vii) a person who has a valid concealed handgun permit and possesses a concealed handgun while in a motor vehicle in a parking lot, traffic circle, or other means of vehicular ingress or egress to the school. For the purposes of this paragraph, "weapon" includes a knife having a metal blade of three inches or longer and "closed container" includes a locked vehicle trunk.

...

§ 18.2-311. Prohibiting the selling or having in possession blackjacks, etc.

If any person sells or barters, or exhibits for sale or for barter, or gives or furnishes, or causes to be sold, bartered, given or furnished, or has in his possession, or under his control, with the intent of selling, bartering, giving or furnishing, any blackjack, brass or metal knucks, any disc of whatever configuration having at least two points or pointed blades which is designed to be thrown or propelled and which may be known as a throwing star or oriental dart, switchblade knife, ballistic knife, or like weapons, such person shall be guilty of a Class 4 misdemeanor. The having in one's possession of any such weapon shall be prima facie evidence, except in the case of a conservator of the peace, of his intent to sell, barter, give or furnish the same.

§ 18.2-283. Carrying dangerous weapon to place of religious worship.

If any person carry any gun, pistol, bowie knife, dagger or other dangerous weapon, without good and sufficient reason, to a place of worship while a meeting for religious purposes is being held at such place he shall be guilty of a Class 4 misdemeanor.

§ 18.2-283.1. Carrying weapon into courthouse.

It shall be unlawful for any person to possess in or transport into any courthouse in this Commonwealth any (i) gun or other weapon designed or intended to propel a missile or projectile of any kind, (ii) frame, receiver, muffler, silencer, missile, projectile or ammunition designed for use with a dangerous weapon and (iii) any other dangerous weapon, including explosives, tasers, stun weapons and those weapons specified in subsection A of § 18.2-308. Any such weapon shall be subject to seizure by a law-enforcement officer. A violation of this section is punishable as a Class 1 misdemeanor.

The provisions of this section shall not apply to any police officer, sheriff, law-enforcement agent or official, game warden, conservator of the peace, magistrate, court officer, or judge while in the conduct of such person's official duties.

§ 18.2-287.01. Carrying weapon in air carrier airport terminal.

It shall be unlawful for any person to possess or transport into any air carrier airport terminal in the Commonwealth any (i) gun or other weapon designed or intended to propel a missile or projectile of any kind, (ii) frame, receiver, muffler, silencer, missile, projectile or ammunition designed for use with a dangerous weapon, and (iii) any other dangerous weapon, including explosives, tasers, stun weapons and those weapons specified in subsection A of § 18.2-308. Any such weapon shall be subject to seizure by a law-enforcement officer. A violation of this section is punishable as a Class 1 misdemeanor. Any weapon possessed or transported in violation of this section shall be forfeited to the Commonwealth and disposed of as provided in subsection A of § 18.2-308.

The provisions of this section shall not apply to any police officer, sheriff, law-enforcement agent or official, or game warden, or conservator of the peace employed by the air carrier airport, nor shall the provisions of this section apply to any passenger of an airline who, to the extent otherwise permitted by law, transports a lawful firearm, weapon, or ammunition into or out of an air carrier airport terminal for the sole purposes, respectively, of (i) presenting such firearm, weapon, or ammunition to U.S. Customs agents in advance of an international flight, in order to comply with federal law, (ii) checking such firearm, weapon, or ammunition with his luggage, or (iii) retrieving such firearm, weapon, or ammunition from the baggage claim area.

Any other statute, rule, regulation, or ordinance specifically addressing the possession or transportation of weapons in any airport in the Commonwealth shall be invalid, and this section shall control.

§ 18.2-309. Furnishing certain weapons to minors; penalty.

A. If any person sells, barters, gives or furnishes, or causes to be sold, bartered, given or furnished, to any minor a dirk, switchblade knife or bowie knife, having good cause to believe him to be a minor, such person shall be guilty of a Class 1 misdemeanor.

B. If any person sells, barters, gives or furnishes, or causes to be sold, bartered, given or furnished, to any minor a handgun, having good cause to believe him to be a minor, such person shall be guilty of a Class 6 felony. This subsection shall not apply to any transfer made between family members or for the purpose of engaging in a sporting event or activity.

53.4 Selected Caselaw

Delcid v. Comm., 526 S.E.2d 273 (Va. Ct. App. 2000) (affirming conviction for concealed carry of butterfly knife, and upholding trial court determination of knife as prohibited weapon).

Farrakhan v. Comm., No. 1804-04-4, slip op. at 5 (Va. Ct. App. Nov 29, 2005) (affirming conviction for concealed carry of kitchen knife with seven and three-quarters inch blade)

Ohin v. Comm., 622 S.E.2d 784, 47 Va. App. 194 (Va. Ct. App. 2005) (affirming conviction for concealed carry of folding knife with three and a half inch locking blade, cross-guard, and "oversized, notched handle" that "enhances the user's grip").

Richards v. Comm., 443 S.E.2d 177 (Va. Ct. App. 1994) (reversing conviction for concealed carry of inoperable switchblade, and holding knife not concealed under meaning of statute).

Wood v. Henry County Public Schools, 495 S.E.2d 255, 255 Va. 85 (Va. 1998) (holding pocketknife not prohibited weapon under statute).

53.5 Preemption Law

No knife law preemption, firearms law preemption only. *See*, VA. CODE § 15.2-915 (2005).

53.6 Places Off-Limits While Carrying

Virginia prohibits the carry of firearms and other dangerous weapons, including knives other than a folding pocket knife with a blade less than three inches, on elementary, middle, or high school property, including school buses, and at school-sponsored events. *See*, VA. CODE § 18.2-308.1 (2005). Certain limited exceptions exist, such as for possession in a motor vehicle. *See, id.* State law prohibits carry of firearms, bowie knives, daggers and other dangerous weapons at places of worship while religious meetings or services are underway "without good and sufficient reason." *See, id.* at § 18.2-283. Carry of firearms and dangerous weapons is also prohibited in courthouses. *See, id.* at § 18.2-283.1. Finally, state law prohibits carry of firearms and dangerous weapons into air carrier airport terminals, with certain exceptions for passengers traveling and checking or claiming such weapons into, or from, checked luggage. *See, id.* at § 18.2-287.01.

53.7 School/College Carry

Virginia prohibits the carry of firearms and other dangerous weapons, including knives other than a folding pocket knife with a blade less than three inches, on elementary, middle, or high school property, including school buses, and at school-sponsored events. *See*, VA. CODE § 18.2-308.1 (2005). Certain limited exceptions exist, such as for possession in a motor vehicle. *See, id.*

53.8 Selected City Ordinances

Richmond – Unlawful to possess any "clasp knife" (generally, folding knife with locking blade) with blade greater than three and a quarter inches. *See*, RICHMOND, VA., CODE OF ORDINANCES § 66-347 (2006). Concealed carry of any "dirk, bowie knife, switchblade knife, ballistic knife, razor," or "any weapon of like kind[,]" prohibited. *See, id.* at § 66-349. Unlawful to furnish dirk, switchblade or bowie knife to any minor, having "good cause to believe" such person is a minor. *See, id.* at § 66-351. Twenty dollar ($20) fee required "for conducting an investigation of the character and qualifications of each person who applies to the chief of police for a permit to purchase any pistol, dirk, bowie knife, sling shot, switchblade knife, any weapon of a like kind or pistol or rifle ammunition." *See, id.* at § 42-119.

53.9 State Resources

Virginia State Police
P.O. Box 27472
Richmond, VA 23261
Phone: (804) 674-2210
Website: http://www.vsp.state.va.us/

Attorney General of Virginia
900 East Main Street
Richmond, VA 23219
Phone: (804) 786-2071
Fax: (804) 786-1991
Website: http://www.oag.state.va.us/

54 Washington – The Evergreen State

Area: 66,544 sq.mi. (Rank: 20th)   Population: 6,068,996 (Rank: 15th)
Violent Crime Rate (per 100,000 residents): 343.8 (Rank: 24th Safest)
State Motto: *Alki (By and By)*

54.1 Knife Carry Law Summary

Note: Blade length limits, if any, in parentheses.

Knife Type	Open Carry	Concealed Carry	Notes
Folding Knives	Yes	Yes	See note[118]
Fixed Bladed Knives	Yes	Yes	See note[118]
Dirks, Daggers, & Stilettos	Yes	No	See note[119]
Automatic Knives	No	No	
Balisongs	No	No	

54.2 Discussion

Visitors to the Evergreen State will find a moderately permissive legal environment for knife carry. State law permits open or concealed carry of ordinary folding pocket knives. Ordinary fixed bladed knives, as well as dirks, daggers, and stilettos may technically be carried openly under state law, although visitors should be aware that many fixed bladed knives, especially large knives such as bowies, and dirks, daggers, and stilettos, will likely be considered *per se* weapons. Given that state law forbids the carrying, exhibition, display, or drawing of any knife or weapon "in a manner, under circumstances, and at a time and place that either manifests an intent to intimidate another or that warrants alarm for the safety of other persons[,]"[120] visitors should exercise considerable caution whenever openly carrying any fixed blade, especially in urban areas, lest they run afoul of this statute.

There is no statutorily defined blade length limit under state law. Automatic knives, to include switchblades and gravity knives, are prohibited. Balisongs may fall under the switchblade prohibition, as balisongs do in some states, and several appellate court decisions have referred to balisongs (butterfly knives) as illegal knives.[121]

State law prohibits carry of dangerous weapons on elementary or secondary school premises, including school-provided transportation (e.g., school buses) and other areas or facilities while being used exclusively by such schools. State law also forbids the possession of weapons in

---

[118] Readers should be aware that local governments may enact their own carry or possession restrictions with regard to knives in their jurisdictions. For example, Seattle prohibits carry of any kind, with certain limited exceptions, of any fixed bladed knives, or folding knives with blades greater than three and a half inches. *See,* SEATTLE, WASH., MUNICIPAL CODE § 12A.14.080 (2006).

[119] State law prohibits the furtive carry "with intent to conceal" any dirk, dagger, or "other dangerous weapon." *See,* WASH. REV. CODE § 9.41.250 (2005). State law also prohibits the carry, exhibition, display, or drawing of any knife with intent to intimidate or that "warrants alarm for the safety of" others. *See, id.* at § 9.41.270. Cautious travelers would do well to avoid carry of dirks, daggers, or stilettos, especially in urban areas.

[120] *See,* WASH. REV. CODE § 9.41.270 (2005). Certain exceptions do exist for persons in their homes, or for lawful self-defense. *See, id.*

[121] *See, e.g.,* cases cited, Section 54.4, *infra.*

the restricted access areas of jails and law enforcement facilities, court facilities, the restricted access areas of mental health facilities for inpatient hospital care and state institutions for the mentally ill, the portions of alcoholic beverage establishments off-limits to persons under twenty-one, and the restricted access areas of airports.

Note that local governments are free to impose their own restrictions or prohibitions on knife carry within their respective jurisdictions, and some, notably Seattle, have done so. Seattle, for example, prohibits the carry, whether open or concealed, of *any* fixed blade, regardless of blade length, or any other knife with a blade greater than three and a half inches, with certain narrow exemptions for bona fide hunting, fishing, or occupational uses.

54.3 Selected Statutes

WASH. REV. CODE §§ (2005)

RCW 9.41.250 – Dangerous weapons — Penalty.

Every person who:

(1) Manufactures, sells, or disposes of or possesses any instrument or weapon of the kind usually known as slung shot, sand club, or metal knuckles, or spring blade knife, or any knife the blade of which is automatically released by a spring mechanism or other mechanical device, or any knife having a blade which opens, or falls, or is ejected into position by the force of gravity, or by an outward, downward, or centrifugal thrust or movement;

(2) Furtively carries with intent to conceal any dagger, dirk, pistol, or other dangerous weapon; or

(3) Uses any contrivance or device for suppressing the noise of any firearm, is guilty of a gross misdemeanor punishable under chapter 9A.20 RCW.

RCW 9.41.270 – Weapons apparently capable of producing bodily harm — Unlawful carrying or handling — Penalty — Exceptions.

(1) It shall be unlawful for any person to carry, exhibit, display, or draw any firearm, dagger, sword, knife or other cutting or stabbing instrument, club, or any other weapon apparently capable of producing bodily harm, in a manner, under circumstances, and at a time and place that either manifests an intent to intimidate another or that warrants alarm for the safety of other persons.

(2) Any person violating the provisions of subsection (1) above shall be guilty of a gross misdemeanor. If any person is convicted of a violation of subsection (1) of this section, the person shall lose his or her concealed pistol license, if any. The court shall send notice of the revocation to the department of licensing, and the city, town, or county which issued the license.

(3) Subsection (1) of this section shall not apply to or affect the following:

(a) Any act committed by a person while in his or her place of abode or fixed place of business;

...

(c) Any person acting for the purpose of protecting himself or herself against the use of presently threatened unlawful force by another, or for the purpose of protecting another against the use of such unlawful force by a third person;

(d) Any person making or assisting in making a lawful arrest for the commission of a felony; or

...

RCW 9.41.280 – Possessing dangerous weapons on school facilities — Penalty — Exceptions.

(1) It is unlawful for a person to carry onto, or to possess on, public or private elementary or secondary school premises, school-provided transportation, or areas of facilities while being used exclusively by public or private schools:

(a) Any firearm;

(b) Any other dangerous weapon as defined in RCW 9.41.250;

(c) Any device commonly known as "nun-chu-ka sticks", consisting of two or more lengths of wood, metal, plastic, or similar substance connected with wire, rope, or other means;

(d) Any device, commonly known as "throwing stars", which are multi-pointed, metal objects designed to embed upon impact from any aspect; or

(e) Any air gun, including any air pistol or air rifle, designed to propel a BB, pellet, or other projectile by the discharge of compressed air, carbon dioxide, or other gas.

(2) Any such person violating subsection (1) of this section is guilty of a gross misdemeanor. If any person is convicted of a violation of subsection (1)(a) of this section, the person shall have his or her concealed pistol license, if any revoked for a period of three years. Anyone convicted under this subsection is prohibited from applying for a concealed pistol license for a period of three years. The court shall send notice of the revocation to the department of licensing, and the city, town, or county which issued the license.

...

(3) Subsection (1) of this section does not apply to:

...

(e) Any person in possession of a pistol who has been issued a license under RCW 9.41.070, or is exempt from the licensing requirement by RCW 9.41.060, while picking up or dropping off a student;

(f) Any nonstudent at least eighteen years of age legally in possession of a firearm or dangerous weapon that is secured within an attended vehicle or concealed from view within a locked unattended vehicle while conducting legitimate business at the school;

...

(4) Subsections (1)(c) and (d) of this section do not apply to any person who possesses nun-chu-ka sticks, throwing stars, or other dangerous weapons to be used in martial arts classes authorized to be conducted on the school premises.

(5) Except as provided in subsection (3)(b), (c), (f), and (h) of this section, firearms are not permitted in a public or private school building.

(6) "GUN-FREE ZONE" signs shall be posted around school facilities giving warning of the prohibition of the possession of firearms on school grounds.

RCW 9.41.300 – Weapons prohibited in certain places — Local laws and ordinances — Exceptions — Penalty.

(1) It is unlawful for any person to enter the following places when he or she knowingly possesses or knowingly has under his or her control a weapon:

(a) The restricted access areas of a jail, or of a law enforcement facility, or any place used for the confinement of a person (i) arrested for, charged with, or convicted of an offense, (ii) held for extradition or as a material witness, or (iii) otherwise confined pursuant to an order of a court, except an order under chapter 13.32A or 13.34 RCW. Restricted access areas do not include common areas of egress or ingress open to the general public;

(b) Those areas in any building which are used in connection with court proceedings, including courtrooms, jury rooms, judge's chambers, offices and areas used to conduct court business, waiting areas, and corridors adjacent to areas used in connection with court proceedings. The restricted areas do not include common areas of ingress and egress to the building that is used in connection with court proceedings, when it is possible to protect court areas without restricting ingress and egress to the building. The restricted areas shall be the minimum necessary to fulfill the objective of this subsection (1)(b).

In addition, the local legislative authority shall provide either a stationary locked box sufficient in size for pistols and key to a weapon owner for weapon storage, or shall designate an official to receive weapons for safekeeping, during the owner's visit to restricted areas of the building. The locked box or designated official shall be located within the same building used in connection with court proceedings. The local legislative authority shall be liable for any negligence causing damage to or loss of a weapon either placed in a locked box or left with an official during the owner's visit to restricted areas of the building.

The local judicial authority shall designate and clearly mark those areas where weapons are prohibited, and shall post notices at each entrance to the building of the prohibition against weapons in the restricted areas;

(c) The restricted access areas of a public mental health facility certified by the department of social and health services for inpatient hospital care and state institutions for the care of the mentally ill, excluding those facilities solely for evaluation and treatment. Restricted access areas do not include common areas of egress and ingress open to the general public;

(d) That portion of an establishment classified by the state liquor control board as off-limits to persons under twenty-one years of age; or

(e) The restricted access areas of a commercial service airport designated in the airport security plan approved by the federal transportation security administration, including passenger screening checkpoints at or beyond the point at which a passenger initiates the screening process. These areas do not include airport drives, general parking areas and walkways, and shops and areas of the terminal that are outside the screening checkpoints and that are normally open to unscreened passengers or visitors to the airport. Any restricted access area shall be clearly indicated by prominent signs indicating that firearms and other weapons are prohibited in the area.

(2) Cities, towns, counties, and other municipalities may enact laws and ordinances:

(a) Restricting the discharge of firearms in any portion of their respective jurisdictions where there is a reasonable likelihood that humans, domestic animals, or property will be jeopardized. Such laws and ordinances shall not abridge the right of the individual guaranteed by Article I, section 24 of the state Constitution to bear arms in defense of self or others; and

(b) Restricting the possession of firearms in any stadium or convention center, operated by a city, town, county, or other municipality, except that such restrictions shall not apply to:

(i) Any pistol in the possession of a person licensed under RCW 9.41.070 or exempt from the licensing requirement by RCW 9.41.060; or

(ii) Any showing, demonstration, or lecture involving the exhibition of firearms.
...
(4) Violations of local ordinances adopted under subsection (2) of this section must have the same penalty as provided for by state law.

(5) The perimeter of the premises of any specific location covered by subsection (1) of this section shall be posted at reasonable intervals to alert the public as to the existence of any law restricting the possession of firearms on the premises.

(6) Subsection (1) of this section does not apply to:
...
(b) Law enforcement personnel, except that subsection (1)(b) of this section does apply to a law enforcement officer who is present at a courthouse building as a party to an action under chapter 10.14, 10.99, or 26.50 RCW, or an action under Title 26 RCW where any party has alleged the existence of domestic violence as defined in RCW 26.50.010; or
...

(7) Subsection (1)(a) of this section does not apply to a person licensed pursuant to RCW 9.41.070 who, upon entering the place or facility, directly and promptly proceeds to the administrator of the facility or the administrator's designee and obtains written permission to possess the firearm while on the premises or checks his or her firearm. The person may reclaim the firearms upon leaving but must immediately and directly depart from the place or facility.

(8) Subsection (1)(c) of this section does not apply to any administrator or employee of the facility or to any person who, upon entering the place or facility, directly and promptly proceeds to the administrator of the facility or the administrator's designee and obtains written permission to possess the firearm while on the premises.

(9) Subsection (1)(d) of this section does not apply to the proprietor of the premises or his or her employees while engaged in their employment.

(10) Any person violating subsection (1) of this section is guilty of a gross misdemeanor.

(11) "Weapon" as used in this section means any firearm, explosive as defined in RCW 70.74.010, or instrument or weapon listed in RCW 9.41.250.

54.4 Selected Caselaw

City of Seattle v. Montana, 129 Wash. 2d 583, 919 P.2d 1218 (Wash. 1996) (Upholding constitutionality of Seattle ordinance prohibiting carry of dangerous weapons).

State v. Myles, 127 Wash. 2d 807, 903 P.2d 979 (Wash. 1995) (affirming conviction for unlawful possession of dangerous weapon, kitchen paring knife with serrated blade).

State v. Winters, No. 30040-1-II (Wash. Ct. App. 2004) (affirming convictions for assault and robbery with deadly weapon enhancements, and upholding jury determination that box-cutter used as deadly weapon).

State v. Parr, 2001 WA 693, slip op. at ¶ 28 (Wash. Ct. App. May 8, 2001) (discussing arrest and referring to knife as "illegal butterfly knife").

State v. Witwicki, 2001 WA 804 (Wash. Ct. App. 2001) (affirming conviction for carrying dangerous weapon on school property, butterfly knife with five inch blade).

54.5 Preemption Law

No knife law preemption, firearms law preemption only. *See*, WASH. REV. CODE § 9.41.290 (2005).

54.6 Places Off-Limits While Carrying

Washington prohibits the carry of dangerous weapons on elementary or secondary school premises, including school-provided transportation (e.g., school buses) and other areas or facilities while being used exclusively by such schools. *See*, WASH. REV. CODE § 9.41.280 (2005).

State law also forbids the possession of weapons in the restricted access areas of jails and law enforcement facilities, court facilities, the restricted access areas of mental health facilities for inpatient hospital care and state institutions for the mentally ill, the portions of alcoholic beverage establishments off-limits to persons under twenty-one, and the restricted access areas of airports. *See, id.* at § 9.41.300.

54.7 School/College Carry

Washington prohibits the carry of dangerous weapons on elementary or secondary school premises, including school-provided transportation (e.g., school buses) and other areas or facilities while being used exclusively by such schools. *See*, WASH. REV. CODE § 9.41.280 (2005).

54.8 Selected City Ordinances

Seattle – "Dangerous knife" includes *any* fixed bladed knife, regardless of blade length, and any other knife with blade greater than three and a half inches long. Carry, whether open or concealed, of dangerous knife prohibited. *See*, SEATTLE, WASH., MUNICIPAL CODE § 12A.14.080 (2006). Exceptions exist for licensed hunters and fishermen while hunting or fishing, and for lawful occupational use if carried openly. *See, id.* at § 12A.14.100.

Cheney – Concealed carry of any dirk, dagger, or other knife, other than ordinary pocket knife, prohibited. *See*, CHENEY, WASH., MUNICIPAL CODE § 9A.07.020 (2006). Exception exists for bona fide hunting, fishing, or camping purposes. *See, id.* at § 9A.07.021.

54.9 State Resources

Washington State Patrol
General Administration Building
P.O. Box 42600
Olympia, WA 98504-2600
Phone: (360) 753-6540
Website: http://www.wa.gov/wsp/wsphome.htm

Attorney General of Washington
1125 Washington St. SE
Olympia, WA 98504-0100
Phone: (360) 753-6200
Fax: (360) 664-0988
Website: http://www.wa.gov/ago/

55 West Virginia – The Mountain State

Area: 24,078 sq.mi. (Rank: 41st)   Population: 1,801,873 (Rank: 37th)
Violent Crime Rate (per 100,000 residents): 271.2 (Rank: 15th Safest)
State Motto: *Montani semper liberi (Mountaineers are Always Free)*

55.1 Knife Carry Law Summary

<u>Note:</u> Blade length limits, if any, in parentheses.

Knife Type	Open Carry	Concealed Carry	Notes
Folding Knives	Yes	Yes (<= 3.5")	
Fixed Bladed Knives	Yes	Yes (<= 3.5")	See note[122]
Dirks, Daggers, & Stilettos	Yes	Yes (<= 3.5")	
Automatic Knives	Yes	No	
Balisongs	Yes	No	

55.2 Discussion

Visitors to West Virginia will find a fairly permissive legal environment for knife carry, with a strong legal bias for open, as opposed to concealed, carry. State law allows open carry of a wide variety of knives, including dirks, daggers, stilettos, and automatic knives. As with most states, readers should exercise caution when carrying large knives openly, especially in urban areas, as such carry is likely to attract law enforcement attention.

State law allows concealed carry of pocket knives with blades three and a half inches or less. Fixed bladed knives, including dirks, daggers, and stilettos with blades three and a half inches or less, may also be carried concealed.

State law prohibits carry of knives, regardless of blade length, in schools and school property, including school buses. In addition, knife carry in courthouses, and in the offices of family law masters, is prohibited.

As is the case in most states, municipalities may enact their own ordinances prohibiting or otherwise restricting knife carry in their jurisdictions.

55.3 Selected Statutes

W. Va. Code §§ (2005)

§61-7-2. Definitions.

As used in this article, unless the context otherwise requires:

...

---

[122] State law allows hunting and fishing knives to be carried for legitimate hunting, fishing, sports or other recreational uses, as well as knives designed as tools or household implements. Such knives are not considered deadly weapons *per se*, unless used or intended to be used as such to inflict serious bodily injury or death. *See*, W. Va. Code § 61-7-2 (2005).

(2) "Gravity knife" means any knife that has a blade released from the handle by the force of gravity or the application of centrifugal force and when so released is locked in place by means of a button, spring, lever or other locking or catching device.

(3) "Knife" means an instrument, intended to be used or readily adaptable to be used as a weapon, consisting of a sharp-edged or sharp-pointed blade, usually made of steel, attached to a handle which is capable of inflicting cutting, stabbing or tearing wounds. The term "knife" shall include, but not be limited to, any dagger, dirk, poniard or stiletto, with a blade over three and one-half inches in length, any switchblade knife or gravity knife and any other instrument capable of inflicting cutting, stabbing or tearing wounds. A pocket knife with a blade three and one-half inches or less in length, a hunting or fishing knife carried for hunting, fishing, sports or other recreational uses, or a knife designed for use as a tool or household implement shall not be included within the term "knife" as defined herein unless such knife is knowingly used or intended to be used to produce serious bodily injury or death.

(4) "Switchblade knife" means any knife having a spring-operated blade which opens automatically upon pressure being applied to a button, catch or other releasing device in its handle.
...

(9) "Deadly weapon" means an instrument which is designed to be used to produce serious bodily injury or death or is readily adaptable to such use. The term "deadly weapon" shall include, but not be limited to, the instruments defined in subdivisions (1) through (8), inclusive, of this section or other deadly weapons of like kind or character which may be easily concealed on or about the person. For the purposes of section one-a, article five, chapter eighteen-a of this code and section eleven-a, article seven of this chapter, in addition to the definition of "knife" set forth in subdivision (3) of this section, the term "deadly weapon" also includes any instrument included within the definition of "knife" with a blade of three and one-half inches or less in length. Additionally, for the purposes of section one-a, article five, chapter eighteen-a of this code and section eleven-a, article seven of this chapter, the term "deadly weapon" includes explosive, chemical, biological and radiological materials. Notwithstanding any other provision of this section, the term "deadly weapon" does not include any item or material owned by the school or county board, intended for curricular use, and used by the student at the time of the alleged offense solely for curricular purposes.

(10) "Concealed" means hidden from ordinary observation so as to prevent disclosure or recognition. A deadly weapon is concealed when it is carried on or about the person in such a manner that another person in the ordinary course of events would not be placed on notice that the deadly weapon was being carried.
...

§61-7-3. Carrying deadly weapon without license or other authorization; penalties.

(a) Any person who carries a concealed deadly weapon, without a state license or other lawful authorization established under the provisions of this code, shall be guilty of a misdemeanor, and, upon conviction thereof, shall be fined not less than one hundred dollars nor more than one thousand dollars and may be imprisoned in the county jail for not more than twelve months for the first offense; but upon conviction of a second or subsequent offense, he or she shall be guilty of a felony, and, upon conviction thereof, shall be imprisoned in the penitentiary not less than one nor more than five years and fined not less than one thousand dollars nor more than five thousand dollars.
...

§61-7-4. License to carry deadly weapons; how obtained.

(a) Except as provided in subsection (h) of this section, any person desiring to obtain a state license to carry a concealed deadly weapon shall apply to the sheriff of his or her county for such license, and shall pay to the sheriff, at the time of application, a fee of seventy-five dollars, of which fifteen dollars of that amount shall be deposited in the courthouse facilities improvement fund created by section six, article twenty-six, chapter twenty-nine of this code. Concealed weapons permits may only be issued for pistols or revolvers. ...

§61-7-6. Exceptions as to prohibitions against carrying concealed deadly weapons.

The licensure provisions set forth in this article do not apply to:

1) Any person carrying a deadly weapon upon his or her own premises; nor shall anything herein prevent a person from carrying any firearm, unloaded, from the place of purchase to his or her home, residence or place of business

or to a place of repair and back to his or her home, residence or place of business, nor shall anything herein prohibit a person from possessing a firearm while hunting in a lawful manner or while traveling from his or her home, residence or place of business to a hunting site and returning to his or her home, residence or place of business;

...

(7) Any resident of another state who has been issued a license to carry a concealed weapon by a state or a political subdivision which has entered into a reciprocity agreement with this state. The governor may execute reciprocity agreements on behalf of the state of West Virginia with states or political subdivisions which have similar gun permitting laws and which recognize and honor West Virginia licenses issued pursuant to section four of this article;

...

§61-7-8. Possession of deadly weapons by minors; prohibitions.

Notwithstanding any other provision of this article to the contrary, a person under the age of eighteen years who is not married or otherwise emancipated shall not possess or carry concealed or openly any deadly weapon: Provided, That a minor may possess a firearm upon premises owned by said minor or his family or on the premises of another with the permission of his or her parent or guardian and in the case of property other than his or her own or that of his family, with the permission of the owner or lessee of such property: Provided, however, That nothing in this section shall prohibit a minor from possessing a firearm while hunting in a lawful manner or while traveling from a place where he or she may lawfully possess a deadly weapon, to a hunting site, and returning to a place where he or she may lawfully possess such weapon.

A violation of this section by a person under the age of eighteen years shall subject the child to the jurisdiction of the circuit court under the provisions of article five, chapter forty-nine of this code, and such minor may be proceeded against in the same manner as if he or she had committed an act which if committed by an adult would be a crime, and may be adjudicated delinquent.

§61-7-11. Brandishing deadly weapons; threatening or causing breach of the peace; criminal penalties.

It shall be unlawful for any person armed with a firearm or other deadly weapon, whether licensed to carry the same or not, to carry, brandish or use such weapon in a way or manner to cause, or threaten, a breach of the peace. Any person violating this section shall be guilty of a misdemeanor, and, upon conviction thereof, shall be fined not less than fifty nor more than one thousand dollars, or shall be confined in the county jail not less than ninety days nor more than one year, or both.

§61-7-11a. Possessing deadly weapons on premises of educational facilities; reports by school principals; suspension of driver license; possessing deadly weapons on premises housing courts of law and in offices of family law master.

(a) The Legislature hereby finds that the safety and welfare of the citizens of this state are inextricably dependent upon assurances of safety for children attending, and the persons employed by, schools in this state and for those persons employed with the judicial department of this state. It is for the purpose of providing such assurances of safety, therefore, that subsections (b), (g) and (h) of this section are enacted as a reasonable regulation of the manner in which citizens may exercise those rights accorded to them pursuant to section twenty-two, article three of the Constitution of the state of West Virginia.

(b) (1) It shall be unlawful for any person to possess any firearm or any other deadly weapon on any school bus as defined in section one, article one, chapter seventeen-a of this code, or in or on any public or private primary or secondary education building, structure, facility or grounds thereof, including any vocational education building, structure, facility or grounds thereof where secondary vocational education programs are conducted or at any school-sponsored function.

(2) This subsection shall not apply to:

...

(C) A person who, as otherwise permitted by the provisions of this article, possesses an unloaded firearm or deadly weapon in a motor vehicle, or leaves an unloaded firearm or deadly weapon in a locked motor vehicle;

...

(3) Any person violating this subsection shall be guilty of a felony, and, upon conviction thereof, shall be imprisoned in the penitentiary of this state for a definite term of years of not less than two years nor more than ten years, or fined not more than five thousand dollars, or both.

...

(g) (1) It shall be unlawful for any person to possess any firearm or any other deadly weapon on any premises which houses a court of law or in the offices of a family law master.

...

(3) Any person violating this subsection shall be guilty of a misdemeanor, and, upon conviction thereof, shall be fined not more than one thousand dollars, or shall be confined in jail not more than one year, or both.

(h) (1) It shall be unlawful for any person to possess any firearm or any other deadly weapon on any premises which houses a court of law or in the offices of a family law master with the intent to commit a crime.

(2) Any person violating this subsection shall be guilty of a felony, and, upon conviction thereof, shall be imprisoned in the penitentiary of this state for a definite term of years of not less than two years nor more than ten years, or fined not more than five thousand dollars, or both.

...

§61-7-14. Right of certain persons to limit possession of firearms on premises.

Notwithstanding the provisions of this article, any owner, lessee or other person charged with the care, custody and control of real property may prohibit the carrying openly or concealed of any firearm or deadly weapon on property under his or her domain: Provided, That for purposes of this section "person" means an individual or any entity which may acquire title to real property.

Any person carrying or possessing a firearm or other deadly weapon on the property of another who refuses to temporarily relinquish possession of such firearm or other deadly weapon, upon being requested to do so, or to leave such premises, while in possession of such firearm or other deadly weapon, shall be guilty of a misdemeanor, and, upon conviction thereof, shall be fined not more than one thousand dollars or confined in the county jail not more than six months, or both: Provided, That the provisions of this section shall not apply to those persons set forth in subsections (3) through (6) of section six of this code while such persons are acting in an official capacity: Provided, however, That under no circumstances may any person possess or carry or cause the possession or carrying of any firearm or other deadly weapon on the premises of any primary or secondary educational facility in this state unless such person is a law-enforcement officer or he or she has the express written permission of the county school superintendent.

55.4 Selected Caselaw

State v. Maisey, No. 31588 (W.Va. 2004) (discussing arrest and conviction for carrying concealed and deadly weapon, and referring to knife as "butterfly knife" or "gravity knife" with four to six inch blade)

55.5 Preemption Law

No knife law preemption, limited firearms law preemption only. *See*, W. Va. Code § 8-12-5a (2005).

55.6 Places Off-Limits While Carrying

State law prohibits the carry of firearms and other deadly weapons, the definition of which includes knives, in schools, school buses, courthouses, and the offices of family law masters. *See*, W. Va. Code § 61-7-11a (2005).

55.7 School/College Carry

State law prohibits the carry of firearms and other deadly weapons, the definition of which includes knives, in schools and on school buses. *See*, W. Va. Code § 61-7-11a (2005).

55.8 Selected City Ordinances

Charleston – Unlawful to carry dirks, bowie knives, razors, "or other dangerous or deadly weapon of like kind or character." *See*, Charleston, W. Va., Code of Ordinances § 78-163 (2005). Unlawful to carry same in designated Sternwheel Regatta area of Kanawha Boulevard during period ten days before Labor Day, and including Labor Day. *See, id.* § 78-164. Carry of such knives prohibited in or upon city hall, municipal auditorium, civic center, all parks and recreation buildings and facilities, and all other buildings or facilities owned or occupied by the City. *See, id.* at § 78-165.

55.9 State Resources

West Virginia State Police
725 Jefferson Road
South Charleston, WV 25309-1698
Phone: (304) 746-2100
Website: http://www.wvstatepolice.com/

Attorney General of West Virginia
1900 Kanawha Blvd.
Charleston, WV 25305-9924
Phone: (304) 558-2021
Website: http://www.wvs.state.wv.us/wvag/

56   Wisconsin – The Badger State

Area: 54,310 sq.mi. (Rank: 25th)   Population: 5,441,196 (Rank: 20th)
Violent Crime Rate (per 100,000 residents): 209.6 (Rank: 6th Safest)
State Motto: *Forward!*

56.1 Knife Carry Law Summary

Note: Blade length limits, if any, in parentheses.

Knife Type	Open Carry	Concealed Carry	Notes
Folding Knives	Yes	Yes	
Fixed Bladed Knives	Yes	No	
Dirks, Daggers, & Stilettos	Yes	No	
Automatic Knives	No	No	
Balisongs	No	No	

56.2 Discussion

Visitors to the Badger State will find a somewhat restrictive legal environment for knife carry. Under state law, ordinary folding pocket knives may be carried openly or concealed. There is no statutorily defined blade length limit under state law, although visitors should be aware that some municipalities do have blade length limits in their jurisdictions.

Wisconsin's broad concealed weapons prohibition strongly cautions against concealed carry of most fixed blades, lest they be deemed a "dangerous weapon" and thus proscribed under state law. Knives such as bowie knives, dirks, daggers, and stilettos are considered *per se* dangerous weapons, and thus may not be carried concealed. State law prohibits mere possession of automatic knives, including switchblades and gravity knives. Balisongs (butterfly knives) fall under the switchblade prohibition, and are thus prohibited as well.

State law prohibits the carry of dangerous weapons on school premises. Local municipal governments may enact their own ordinances prohibiting or otherwise restricting knife carry within their respective municipalities, and a number of municipal governments have done so. For example, Milwaukee has declared that any knife with a blade three inches or longer is *per se* dangerous.

56.3 Selected Statutes

WIS. STAT. ANN. §§ (2005)

939.22 Words and phrases defined. In chs. 939 to 948 and 951, the following words and phrases have the designated meanings unless the context of a specific section manifestly requires a different construction or the word or phrase is defined in s. 948.01 for purposes of ch. 948:

...

(10) "Dangerous weapon" means any firearm, whether loaded or unloaded; any device designed as a weapon and capable of producing death or great bodily harm; any electric weapon, as defined in s. 941.295 (4); or any other device or instrumentality which, in the manner it is used or intended to be used, is calculated or likely to produce death or great bodily harm.

...

941.20 Endangering safety by use of dangerous weapon. (1) Whoever does any of the following is guilty of a Class A misdemeanor:

(a) Endangers another's safety by the negligent operation or handling of a dangerous weapon; or

(b) Operates or goes armed with a firearm while he or she is under the influence of an intoxicant; or

...

941.23 Carrying concealed weapon. Any person except a peace officer who goes armed with a concealed and dangerous weapon is guilty of a Class A misdemeanor.

941.24 Possession of switchblade knife. (1) Whoever manufactures, sells or offers to sell, transports, purchases, possesses or goes armed with any knife having a blade which opens by pressing a button, spring or other device in the handle or by gravity or by a thrust or movement is guilty of a Class A misdemeanor.

(2) Within 30 days after April 16, 1959, such knives shall be surrendered to any peace officer.

948.61 Dangerous weapons other than firearms on school premises. (1) In this section:

(a) "Dangerous weapon" has the meaning specified in s. 939.22 (10), except "dangerous weapon" does not include any firearm and does include any beebee or pellet-firing gun that expels a projectile through the force of air pressure or any starter pistol.

(b) "School" means a public, parochial or private school which provides an educational program for one or more grades between grades 1 and 12 and which is commonly known as an elementary school, middle school, junior high school, senior high school or high school.

(c) "School premises" means any school building, grounds, recreation area or athletic field or any other property owned, used or operated for school administration.

(2) Any person who knowingly possesses or goes armed with a dangerous weapon on school premises is guilty of:

(a) A Class A misdemeanor.

(b) A Class I felony, if the violation is the person's 2nd or subsequent violation of this section within a 5-year period, as measured from the dates the violations occurred.

(3) This section does not apply to any person who:

(a) Uses a weapon solely for school-sanctioned purposes.

...

(d) Participates in a convocation authorized by school authorities in which weapons of collectors or instructors are handled or displayed.

(e) Drives a motor vehicle in which a dangerous weapon is located onto school premises for school-sanctioned purposes or for the purpose of delivering or picking up passengers or property.

The weapon may not be removed from the vehicle or be used in any manner.

(f) Possesses or uses a bow and arrow or knife while legally hunting in a school forest if the school board has decided that hunting may be allowed in the school forest under s. 120.13 (38).

...

56.4 Selected Caselaw

City of Milwaukee v. Hampton, 553 N.W.2d 855, 204 Wis.2d 49 (Wis. Ct. App. 1996) (upholding constitutionality of Milwaukee's concealed weapon ordinance, and affirming conviction for possession in vehicle glove compartment of folding knife with three and three-quarter inch locking blade).

State v. Lemagnes, 438 N.W.2d 597, 148 Wis.2d 953 (Wis. Ct. App. 1989) (unpublished opinion) (discussing seizure of butterfly knife, and affirming conviction for switchblade possession).

State v. Wallis, 439 N.W.2d 590, 149 Wis.2d 534 (Wis. Ct. App. 1989) (describing butterfly knife as "illegal weapon").

State v. Moretto, 144 Wis.2d 171, 423 N.W.2d 841 (Wis. 1988) (upholding validity of search and reinstating conviction for carrying concealed weapon, unsheathed knife found in vehicle with four and a half inch blade).

56.5 Preemption Law

No knife law preemption, firearms law preemption only. *See*, Wis. Stat. Ann. § 66.0409 (2005).

56.6 Places Off-Limits While Carrying

Wisconsin prohibits the carry of dangerous weapons on school premises. *See*, Wis. Stat. Ann. § 948.61 (2005).

56.7 School/College Carry

Wisconsin prohibits the carry of dangerous weapons on school premises. *See*, Wis. Stat. Ann. § 948.61 (2005).

56.8 Selected City Ordinances

Milwaukee County – Unlawful to go armed with concealed and dangerous weapon, with the following knives declared dangerous *per se*: "bowie knife, dirk knife, dagger, switchblade knife, or any knife which has a blade that is automatically opened by slight pressure on the handle or some other part of the knife, or any other knife having a blade three (3) inches or longer[.]" *See*, Milwaukee County, Wis., Code of Gen. Ordinances § 63.015 (2005).

Racine – Possession or carry of any dangerous weapon, whether concealed or in "plain view", prohibited. *See*, Racine, Wis., Municipal Code § 66-58 (2006). Dangerous weapon includes any bowie knife, dirk, dagger, switchblade, straightedge razor, or any knife with blade three inches or longer. *See, id.* at § 66-56.

Sheboygan – Concealed carry of bowie knife, dirk or dagger prohibited. *See*, Sheboygan, Wis., Municipal Code § 70-253 (2005). Unlawful to be armed with switchblade or any knife with blade exceeding three inches in length, or "[a]ny other dangerous or deadly weapon, whether its purpose is offensive or defensive." *See, id.* at § 70-252. Possession of switchblades prohibited. *See, id.* at § 70-258. Unlawful to board bus with dangerous or deadly weapon concealed upon person or effects. *See, id.* at § 70-218.

56.9 State Resources

Wisconsin State Patrol
Division Headquarters
Hill Farms State Transportation Building
4802 Sheboygan Avenue, Room 551
P.O. Box 7912
Madison, WI 53707-7912
Phone: (608) 266-3212
Fax: (608) 267-4495
Website: http://www.dot.state.wi.us/statepatrol/

Attorney General of Wisconsin
123 West Washington Ave.
PO Box 7857
Madison, WI 53707-7857
Phone: (608) 266-1221
Fax: (608) 267-2779
Website: http://www.doj.state.wi.us/

57 Wyoming – The Equality State

Area: 97,100 sq.mi. (Rank: 9th)   Population: 498,703 (Rank: 50th)
Violent Crime Rate (per 100,000 residents): 229.6 (Rank: 7th Safest)
State Motto: *Equal Rights*

57.1 Knife Carry Law Summary

<u>Note:</u> Blade length limits, if any, in parentheses.

Knife Type	Open Carry	Concealed Carry	Notes
Folding Knives	Yes	Yes	
Fixed Bladed Knives	Yes	Yes	
Dirks, Daggers, & Stilettos	Yes	No	
Automatic Knives	Yes	No	
Balisongs	Yes	No	

57.2 Discussion

Visitors to Wyoming will find a permissive legal environment for knife carry, with a strong bias towards open, versus concealed, carry. Most knives may be carried openly under state law. There is no statutorily defined blade length limit under state law, although some cities impose their own blade length limits for certain knives.

Knives such as ordinary folding pocket knives may be carried concealed. Fixed bladed knives that are not designed as, or otherwise considered *per se* weapons, may be carried concealed so long as the circumstances surrounding their carry do not evince an intent to use such knives unlawfully against others. For example, a hunting or fishing knife, while on a bona fide hunting or fishing trip, and used for legitimate hunting or fishing purposes, would likely meet this standard.

Knives such as dirks, daggers, and stilettos that are considered *per se* deadly weapons, however, may not be carried concealed. Automatic knives such as switchblades, while not specifically enumerated as *per se* weapons under state law, are often considered as such, and so the cautious traveler should avoid concealed carry of such knives. Travelers should also be aware that switchblades are enumerated as *per se* weapons under the municipal codes of some of the state's larger cities, and carry is restricted or banned. Balisongs, which are often associated with, and perceived as, martial arts weapons, should not be carried concealed, lest they be deemed weapons, and hence prohibited from being carried concealed.

Wyoming prohibits the possession of deadly weapons in jails, penal institutions, and other correctional facilities, and the state hospital (mental hospital). Towns and cities may pass their own local ordinances prohibiting or restricting knife carry in other areas or locations within their jurisdictions.

57.3 Selected Statutes

WYO. STAT. §§ (2005)

6-1-104. Definitions.

(a) As used in W.S. 6-1-101 through 6-10-203 unless otherwise defined:

...

(iv) "Deadly weapon" means but is not limited to a firearm, explosive or incendiary material, motorized vehicle, an animal or other device, instrument, material or substance, which in the manner it is used or is intended to be used is reasonably capable of producing death or serious bodily injury;

...

6-8-103. Possession, manufacture or disposition of deadly weapon with unlawful intent; penalties.

A person who knowingly possesses, manufactures, transports, repairs or sells a deadly weapon with intent to unlawfully threaten the life or physical well-being of another or to commit assault or inflict bodily injury on another is guilty of a felony punishable by imprisonment for not more than five (5) years, a fine of not more than one thousand dollars ($1,000.00), or both.

6-8-104. Wearing or carrying concealed weapons; penalties; exceptions; permits.

(a) A person who wears or carries a concealed deadly weapon is guilty of a misdemeanor punishable by a fine of not more than seven hundred fifty dollars ($750.00), imprisonment in the county jail for not more than six (6) months, or both, unless:

(i) The person is a peace officer;

(ii) The person possesses a permit under this section; or

(iii) The person holds a valid permit authorizing him to carry a concealed firearm authorized and issued by a governmental agency or entity in another state that recognizes Wyoming permits, is a valid statewide permit, and the state has laws similar to the provisions of this section, as determined by the attorney general, including a proper background check of the permit holder.

...

57.4 Selected Caselaw

State v. McAdams, 714 P.2d 1236 (Wyo. 1986) (upholding constitutionality of concealed weapons statute).

Johnston v. State, 747 P.2d 1132 (Wyo. 1987) (affirming conviction for aggravated assault and battery with butterfly knife).

57.5 Preemption Law

No knife law preemption, firearms law preemption only. *See,* WYO. STAT. § 6-8-401 (2005).

57.6 Places Off-Limits While Carrying

Wyoming prohibits the possession of deadly weapons in jails, penal institutions, and other correctional facilities, and the state hospital (mental hospital). *See,* WYO. STAT. § 6-5-209 (2005).

57.7 School/College Carry

No apparent state law limitation for non-students. Students who carry or possess deadly weapons on school grounds or school buses may, however, be suspended or expelled. *See,* WYO. STAT. § 21-4-306 (2005).

Towns and cities may pass their own local ordinances prohibiting or restricting carry on school grounds.

57.8 Selected City Ordinances

Cheyenne – Unlawful to carry concealed any knife with blade exceeding four inches in length, any dirk, dagger, sword-in-cane, or any other dangerous or deadly weapon. Unlawful to carry openly any such item "with the intent or avowed purpose for injuring any person." *See*, CHEYENNE, WYO., CITY CODE § 9.24.040 (2006). Possession of switchblades prohibited. *See, id.* at § 9.24.050. Carry or possession of deadly weapons on school grounds or school buses prohibited. *See, id.* at § 9.24.090.

Casper – Concealed carry of switchblades, fixed bladed knives of any length, folding knives with blades greater than four inches in length, swords-in-canes, or any other dangerous or deadly weapon, prohibited. *See*, CASPER, WYO., MUNICIPAL CODE § 9.44.020 (2006). Prohibition does not apply to those with appropriate concealed weapons permits. *See, id.*

Laramie – Concealed carry of knives with blades over five inches long, or other deadly weapons, prohibited. *See*, LARAMIE, WYO., MUNICIPAL CODE § 9.28.010 (2005).

57.9 State Resources

Wyoming Highway Patrol
State Headquarters
5300 Bishop Blvd.
Cheyenne, WY 82009-3340
Phone: (307) 777-4301
Website: http://whp.state.wy.us/

Wyoming Attorney General
123 Capitol Building
Cheyenne, WY 82002
Phone: (307) 777-7841
Fax: (307) 777-6869
Website: http://attorneygeneral.state.wy.us/

About the Author

David Wong is an attorney in private practice in Massachusetts. He has been teaching and training in a variety of self-defense disciplines for a number of years, from firearms to knives to defensive tactics for high-risk situations, and holds instructor certifications from several nationally recognized training academies. David is an NRA Life Member and NRA-certified firearms instructor, and has taught both lawfully-armed civilians and sworn law enforcement officers as an adjunct instructor at the SigArms Academy in Epping, NH. He is a member of the International Association of Law Enforcement Firearms Instructors (IALEFI), and is a charter member of the International Law Enforcement Educators and Trainers Association (ILEETA). The author has been collecting knives for many years, and regularly carries a pocket knife as part of his daily attire. This book was inspired by the author's extensive cross-country travels, and the need to have an easy, accurate summary of the knife-related carry laws of each state.

Printed in the United States
82264LV00002B/169-262